The Cubs
and the A's of 1910

The Cubs and the A's of 1910

One Dynasty Ends, Another Begins

RICHARD BRESSLER

McFarland & Company, Inc., Publishers
Jefferson, North Carolina

All photographs by the *Chicago Daily News*,
Chicago History Museum.

Library of Congress Cataloguing-in-Publication Data

Names: Bressler, Richard, author.
Title: The Cubs and the A's of 1910 : one dynasty ends,
another begins / Richard Bressler.
Description: Jefferson, North Carolina : McFarland & Company, Inc.,
Publishers, 2016. | Includes bibliographical references and index.
Identifiers: LCCN 2016039858 | ISBN 9781476664361
(softcover : acid free paper) ∞
Subjects: LCSH: Chicago Cubs (Baseball team)—History. | Philadelphia
Athletics (Baseball team)—History. | Baseball—United States—History. |
Baseball teams—United States—History. | Baseball players—United States.
Classification: LCC GV875.C6 B68 2016 | DDC 796.357/64097309041—dc23
LC record available at https://lccn.loc.gov/2016039858
British Library cataloguing data are available

**ISBN (print) 978-1-4766-6436-1
ISBN (ebook) 978-1-4766-2455-6**

© 2016 Richard Bressler. All rights reserved

*No part of this book may be reproduced or transmitted in any form
or by any means, electronic or mechanical, including photocopying
or recording, or by any information storage and retrieval system,
without permission in writing from the publisher.*

Front cover: Frank Chance (left), player/manager
for the Chicago Cubs, and Connie Mack, manager
of the Philadelphia Athletics; photographs
by Paul Thompson, circa 1910 (Library of Congress)

Printed in the United States of America

*McFarland & Company, Inc., Publishers
Box 611, Jefferson, North Carolina 28640
www.mcfarlandpub.com*

To all baseball fans:
don't ever give up hope

Acknowledgments

As a fan of baseball and a lover of old baseball stories, this project has been lots of fun. However, I could not do it alone. I spent a week in Cooperstown at the Baseball Hall of Fame Library. Thanks to the staff there for their help. It's a great place to immerse yourself in baseball of the past. Thanks to the Champaign Public Library and the Urbana Free Library. Thanks also to the University of Illinois Library, and its Newspaper Library, for digital and microfilm access to the 1910 editions of various newspapers. It is nice when one's local public libraries can supply most of the materials needed for a project. Thanks to Jerry Goodbody for the loan of his *Baseball Encyclopedia*, in memory of time we spent in the past going over a prior edition, discovering obscure facts about the game and its players. The photographs in this book were secured at the Chicago History Museum. Thanks to the library staff there for their help. Thanks to Dick Goodbody for assistance on the photographs. Thanks to Bob Der Avedisian for reviewing material related to this project. Thanks to Burks Oakley and Mike Kulas for the computer help, the only way a digitally challenged person such as myself could get something like this in by a deadline.

Table of Contents

Acknowledgments	vi
Preface	1
Introduction	2
1. The A's	7
2. The Cubs	27
3. Spring Training	40
4. April–May	53
5. June	66
6. July	84
7. August	113
8. September–October	132
9. The World Series	147
Epilogue	163
Appendix 1: Hitting and Pitching Statistics	177
Appendix 2: World Series Statistics	182
Chapter Notes	185
Bibliography	191
Index	193

Preface

As things stand at the time this is written, the Chicago Cubs have the longest championship drought in American professional sports. As a person who grew up in Chicago, I am very familiar with this fact. For most of my life, the two longest championship droughts in American sports were the two Chicago baseball teams. The team I root for, the White Sox, broke an 87-year championship drought in 2005. The Cubs are at 107 years and counting. Since their dominant run from 1906 to 1910, which will be discussed in this book, the Cubs have made the World Series six more times. As far as I can determine, they were not favored going into the World Series of 1918, 1929, 1932, 1935, 1938, or 1945. The last time the Cubs entered the World Series as a favorite was in 1910. There was a dominant team, the Cubs, which was in the midst of the best ten-year run of regular season baseball, based on winning percentage, of any team since the creation of the American League in 1901. There was a young team, the A's, taking the next step of winning the American League pennant after coming close the year before. Both teams spread-eagled their closest competitors, winning the pennant by more than ten games. Their meeting in the World Series was clear by the end of August. This confrontation would either continue the Cubs' dominance or be a changing of the guard.

As a baseball fan who likes to read about the game, I knew which books and sources I wanted to use in researching this book. I focused on the two teams that played in the 1910 World Series, telling their history and how these teams came together. There is some comment on other teams in each league, but I tried to focus on the Cubs and the A's. Here is the story. I hope you like it.

Introduction

One of the constants in the sports world is the changing of the guard. There is usually some person or team at the apex of their sport. Some champions are one-time winners who do not require unseating, as they have just warmed the seat. A changing of the guard takes place when an upcoming person or team defeats a multiple title holder. In our 21st century sports world, this is taking place all the time, in various individual and team sports around the globe. This book addresses the first time it happened in the most popular sport in the USA in the 20th century.

Speaking as a baseball fan, I understand that baseball does not hold the primary spot in the affections of American sports fans in the 21st century. It has been overtaken by football and crowded by basketball, with many other sports competing for our attention. In the early 20th century, there were three sports that had nationwide popularity. They were baseball, boxing, and horse racing, in that order. In 1910, there was an attempt to unseat the dominant champion in boxing. The heavyweight champion of the world, Jack Johnson, participated in a fight in July 1910 that was important enough to cause riots, and eventually led to a Broadway play and movie. It was the single most popular sporting event of that year, with a long buildup that led to a boxing match that took place on one day. The baseball season led to a World Series featuring the team that had dominated the sport since 1906, against a team of mostly young players looking to take their spot as a dominant team. This story started as soon as the 1909 baseball season ended, and this changing of the guard is the focus of this book.

Boxing and horse racing had their moments of massive public interest, but no other sport captured the American public in the early 20th century like baseball. (I will be using the modern spelling of the sport. Most of the 1909–1910 sources said base ball). The sport had been growing in popularity since the Civil War, and professional leagues had operated since 1871. The first presently recognized major league started in 1876, the National League. Baseball then was surprisingly similar to sports today. Income and expenses of the teams are grossly different, but there is the constant fight between owners and players, efforts to organize players, efforts to organize owners, complaints of fans regarding the length of games, complaints of fans about overpaid players and plutocratic owners, and so on. Any blog one might see today covering complaints about any team sport will have its parallel in the newspapers and books written about baseball in the period from 1876–1914.

During this period, baseball was the most popular team sport throughout the U.S. There were teams all over the country. These were town teams, college teams, sandlot teams, and area teams in big cities. The players on these teams played because they wanted to, not for pay. The lower level professional teams, referred to even then as the minor leagues, often played against these amateur teams, both for financial reasons and to discover good players. Minor league teams signed many of these amateur players. The stories told by these players stressed that the salaries they signed for were considered a large step up the economic ladder. That was true, even though the monthly salaries seem minuscule to us today. As is true with most sports, the hungriest players were the best. A salary of $50 a month in 1880 was much more than an uneducated young man could make in the labor market. Baseball had been codified and popularized by amateur gentlemen before the Civil War, but its growth during and after the Civil War spread the sport beyond the control of these upper class gentlemen. Teams from mill towns, steel towns, mining towns, and immigrant communities in big cities became more prominent. By 1900, a shrewd baseball executive could see the possibility a second major league.

This shrewd executive stepped forward after the 1899 season. Ban Johnson was the president of the Western League, a high-level minor league based in the Midwest. Before the start of the 1900 season, Johnson changed the name of his league to the American League. After the National League shed four franchises on March 8, 1900, Johnson made a big move in upgrading his league in fact as well as name. He moved franchises into Chicago, Detroit and Cleveland, bigger cities than the others in his league. He negotiated with the National League owner in

Chicago and secured his permission, for $1,000, to approve the Chicago team in the American League. The American League now had eight teams in medium to large cities in the Midwest (Chicago, Milwaukee, Minneapolis, Kansas City, Indianapolis, Cleveland, Detroit, and Buffalo). This league respected the contracts signed by players in the National League, and operated in 1900 at the highest minor league level.[1]

By the end of the 1900 season, Ban Johnson was ready to turn the American League into a second major league. Over the winter of 1900–1901, Johnson enlisted allies to make the jump to major league status. He was the main driver in this process, but he needed lots of help. Some of the baseball men operating the teams in the 1900 American League were ready to help put together teams that were competitive. That was one part of the equation. Dealing with the press was another part. Ban Johnson had been a sportswriter in Cincinnati and had contacts with newspapermen all over the northeast quarter of the country. The third part of the equation was money. Johnson was constantly on the lookout for rich baseball fans who were interested in owning a team. Charles Somers, a Cleveland coal magnate, came on board with the deepest pockets. All this activity led to a pronouncement by *The Sporting News* that was summarized by this headline:

IMMINENT DANGER
PROFESSIONAL BASE BALL IN A BAD WAY[2]

By 1900, *The Sporting News* had become the leading national publication in terms of reach and coverage regarding baseball. This doomsaying would continue for the next couple of years.

After lots of maneuvering, the American League started operation as a self-proclaimed major league in April 1901. There were eight franchises: Baltimore, Boston, Chicago, Cleveland, Detroit, Milwaukee, Philadelphia and Washington. The owners of these teams had accomplished a lot over the winter. They had signed enough players to stock eight teams with 14–16 players each. They had secured playing grounds and built wooden stands around these diamonds. They agreed on a 140-game schedule. As would be expected in such a quick startup, some teams were better off than others. The Chicago team had won the AL pennant in 1900 and kept most of their players. Where were the other teams going to get players to compete with such a powerhouse? The answer was to raid the National League. This led to what historian Bill James calls the Sixth Baseball War, which lasted from 1901 to 1903.[3] The reserve clause in baseball contracts had existed since 1879 and had been challenged often since then. The reserve clause bound the player to the team he signed with in perpetuity, even though the contract was usually for one year. The American League did not sign any National Leaguers who were under contract for the 1901 season, but anyone who had not signed for that season was considered fair game. This led to the sort of shenanigans a sports fan of my age (born 1953) became familiar with during the NFL-AFL war of the sixties, and the NBA-ABA war of the seventies. Players jumped teams, player salaries rose significantly, lawsuits were filed, and lawyers made out like bandits.[4] However, this war formed Major League Baseball as we would know it for the 20th and 21st centuries (so far).

The American League survived this conflict by being aggressive. Many players were signed before the 1901 season. Enough were of major league quality that the American League outdrew the National League in the cities where they competed directly (Boston, Chicago, Philadelphia) in 1901.[5] The American League continued this strategy in 1902, signing more National League players, and losing some to the NL. By the end of the 1902 season, many NL owners were ready to negotiate for peace. This was accomplished over the winter of 1902–1903.

The settlement of this war left the big leagues in a configuration that would stand for the next 50 years. The American League cities were: Boston, Chicago, Cleveland, Detroit, New York, Philadelphia, St. Louis, and Washington. The National League cities were: Boston, Brooklyn, Chicago, Cincinnati, New York, Philadelphia, Pittsburgh, and St. Louis. All of these franchises exist today, several in different cities. But this settlement set up the leagues as we know them. Now a champion could be determined, which happened in the first World Series, arranged informally between AL champ Boston and NL champ Pittsburgh after the 1903 season. After Boston won, there were still no rules or requirement that another World Series would take place after the next season.[6] NL champion New York refused to meet the AL champ, Boston, after the 1904 season, due to ill feelings between New York manager John McGraw, New York owner John T. Brush and Ban Johnson. They were happy to leave the AL for the NL in 1902. The outcry from fans, press and players caused the new ruling body of baseball, the National Commission, to write and ratify rules for World Series in the future.[7] The 1905 World Series between the New York Giants and Philadelphia A's was the first official World Series, played under the auspices of the National Commission. This capsule history of major league baseball brings us to the teams that will be the subject of this book.

1

The A's

The public face of the Philadelphia Athletics (usually called the A's) since their inception in 1901 was Connie Mack. He was born Cornelius McGillicuddy, third child of Irish immigrant parents, on December 22, 1862, in East Brookfield, Massachusetts. His father Michael was in the Union army at the time, serving in the 51st Massachusetts Regiment after securing a $150 bounty. This bounty looked good, considering Michael McGillicuddy had been earning $2 a day as a wheelwright. In January 1863, Michael went on the sick list while serving in North Carolina. Other soldiers called his ailment "southern malaria." While it is not clear exactly what ailed him, Michael McGillicuddy was broke in terms of money and broken in health when he was discharged from the army in July 1863. Cornelius grew up in a household with an ill father, a strong mother named Mary, and several siblings.[1]

As his father was not physically able to work full-time, all the children had to pitch in. Cornelius started working in the summer of 1872. His first job was at the local cotton mill, running errands and carrying material around the mill, for $6 a month. He had been playing ball since he could run around in the field across from his home. The game he played at first was called four-o-cat, which resembled cricket more than baseball, using a flat bat and putting out a batter by catching a batted ball on the fly (no gloves) or by hitting the runner with a thrown ball. The McGillicuddys were able to buy the cottage where they lived for $625 in October 1875, with a $400 mortgage. The cottage was deeded to Mary McGillicuddy, quite unusual for this time.[2]

Cornelius went to school through the eighth grade, quitting in June 1877. He had an early growth spurt, and was over six feet by the age of 14. He went to work full-time, after four years of working during the summer at Stoddard's farm and market across from the ball field.

In his later years, Connie Mack would always acknowledge the influence of his mother, and ignore his father except to say he "had a drinking problem." By this time, Michael could only work about one day a week, and spent most of his time and all of his money in the local tavern, located 300 yards from their home. Michael and Mary had five sons who lived to adulthood. Two followed Michael's path and became alcoholics, while three followed Mary's path and became productive, responsible adults. The whole family was called Mack by their neighbors, and by this time Cornelius was being called Connie, which stuck. Their name was never legally changed, and Connie Mack was Cornelius McGillicuddy on legal documents until his death.

At the age of 15, Connie started working in local shoe factories, continuing his employment at Stoddard's during the summer. Connie played for the factory ball team until 1879. By this time, baseball was being played as the main ball game, replacing cricket-type games. Baseball in 1877–1879 was not like it is today. Most players did not wear gloves. Pitchers threw underarm or sidearm from 45 feet (changed to 50 feet in 1881), and were supposed to pitch the ball where the batter requested it (low or high). Catchers stood 10–15 feet behind the batter and often caught the ball on the bounce. Catchers wore no equipment. Connie Mack had been playing catcher and pitcher on the factory team. He made the town team at the age of 16 in 1879. He was the primary catcher and wore a glove for the first time that year. He demonstrated his serious approach to the game that summer. Connie and pitcher John Williams made a trip to the nearby town of Ware to talk to major league pitcher Candy Cummings to learn how to throw a curve ball, supposedly invented by Cummings. This lesson cost $10, a major investment in 1879. The team played in the Central Massachusetts Amateur Base Ball Association. There are no records of how they did until 1883. The East Brookfield team played exhibition games against two National League teams in 1882. In 1883, Mack was elected captain, even though he was the youngest regular on the team. Their season, played only on weekends, ended up with East Brookfield and North Brookfield tied for the league lead. Each team had lost one game during the year, to the other. This led to a one-game playoff on Wednesday, September 19. Both towns turned out en masse for the game, and as was common during this time, lots of money was wagered on the outcome. Both teams featured mostly Irish lineups. The game was a nail-biter, with East Brookfield ahead, 2–1, with two out in the ninth inning.

East Brookfield's pitcher struck out the next batter, but Mack dropped the third strike. He picked it up and threw out the runner, causing a celebration for the East Brookfield players and fans.[3] Many years later, he told sportswriter Fred Lieb that he felt "as much of a thrill recalling the details of this game as I ever did out of any World Series game. I have enjoyed many victories—games which meant much to me and my Athletic club. But I don't think any other brought me greater joy than when East Brookfield won. At the time, it seemed to be the most important baseball game that was ever played."[4] Soon after the game, the umpire asked Mack if he intended to become a professional ballplayer, and said he would recommend Mack if he wished. Mack decided right then that he would try.

Mack's battery mate in East Brookfield, Will Hogan, signed with the Meriden team in the Connecticut State League for the 1884 season. When the 1884 season started, Hogan was having problems with the catcher on the Meriden team. Hogan persuaded his team to give Mack a tryout, resulting in a telegram (the first telegram the family ever received) sent to Mack on Thursday, April 17. On Friday, Mack gave notice at the shoe factory that Saturday would be his last day. Monday he went to Meriden. On Wednesday he played in an exhibition game against Yale, getting a good write-up in the Meriden newspaper. On Wednesday he received two telegrams with offers from other teams in the same league. Mack asked for $90 a month from the Meriden team and got it. This started a professional career in baseball that would last 66 years.[5]

Mack played three seasons of minor league ball in Connecticut. The 1884 season was 50 games long. The Meriden team made it through the season, but barely. At the end of the season, the team showed a $500 deficit, including some unpaid wages. Mack decided to sign with another team for 1885, as it was not clear the Meriden team would operate. After receiving his back pay, Mack was able to spend the off-season not working, his first extended leisure time in his life. He signed with Hartford in the Southern New England League for 1885 at a salary of $125 a month. Part of his time and money was spent escorting Margaret Hogan, the sister of Will, to dances and shows. His season in Hartford in 1885 was similar to 1884. The league the team was in collapsed, one team moving up to a higher level, others disbanding. Mack made it through the season, playing three different positions (catcher, outfield, second base). He was the regular catcher for Frank Gilmore, the best pitcher on the Hartford team. Both Gilmore and Mack were thin and were nicknamed the "Bones Battery." He was exposed to major league play, as Hartford was a regular exhibition stop for major league teams traveling between Boston and New York. After the 1885 season was shortened due to financial problems, Gilmore and Mack joined other teams for barnstorming games. One of those games was against the New York Giants of the National League. Mack performed so well that the Giants manager offered him a contract for 1886. Mack had to turn him down, as he had already signed with Hartford (even though the Hartford team was not yet sure what league they would be playing in) for the 1886 season for $165 a month. Mack played for Hartford in 1886. The Hartford team experienced their usual financial problems, which were solved after the September 7 game, when the son of the owner of the Washington team in the National League bought the contracts of the Bones Battery (Gilmore and Mack) for $3,500. Gilmore was their main target, but Gilmore insisted on having Mack catch him in the majors. Mack played his last game for Hartford on September 9, 1886.[6]

During the rest of the 1886 season, Mack and Gilmore were a battery for the team. The season ended October 8, and the team played exhibition games for another ten days. After the end of the exhibition games, the manager gave Mack $800 and signed him to an 1887 contract for $2,250. Mack was now a major leaguer. Mack would see parts of the country he had never seen before, as his travels up to now had been limited to the area between Boston and Washington. There were no locker rooms for visiting teams in major league ballparks. Road teams changed at their hotels. Any injuries were treated by the athletes themselves, as there were no trainers. Mack had to make the team, even though he was signed for the 1887 season. Mack's strength was not his batting. According to his recollection much later, Mack said he was an adequate hitter when the batter was allowed to request pitches high or low. However, that rule changed for the 1887 season, and batters would now have to deal with whatever pitches the pitcher threw. For this season only, it would take four strikes to strike out a batter, and a walk would count as a hit. Mack had to make the team based on his catching prowess and baseball brain. He was successful, becoming the regular catcher for Washington in 1887. He hit .201, but his defense kept him in the lineup. He was known as a pepperpot, always talking to the batters. He bent the rules whenever he could, becoming known for tipping bats to cause batters to miss pitches. According to some accounts, he invented the play of throwing out the trailing runner on a double steal, throwing to second instead of third.[7]

Mack played for Washington through the 1889 season. He signed for $2,500 for the 1888 season right after the 1887 season, which gave him the security to marry his hometown love, Margaret Hogan, on November 2, 1887. The newlyweds lived in Washington the next two summers, dealing with the warmest weather in the major leagues (with the possible exception of St. Louis). Mack caught 79 games in 1888, hitting .187 for a last-place team. He signed for $2,750 for 1889, which shows his value was not at the bat. Rules about balls and strikes were finally settled in 1889, four balls for a walk, three strikes and you're out. This caused a rise in the league's batting average of 25 points. Mack had his best offensive year by far, hitting .293 with 26 stolen bases. Washington remained a last-place team. Now the larger forces of management and labor forced a change for the 1890 season. Owners had unsuccessfully tried to enforce salary caps on players since the start of the major leagues. The owners had been taking deductions from players for various reasons, such as taking a day off to get married or showing up drunk at a game. The players countered by forming the Brotherhood of Professional Base Ball Players, led by John Montgomery Ward, a leading pitcher who was a lawyer. By the end of the 1889 season, the dispute between the owners and the Brotherhood led to the formation of the Players' League for the 1890 season. Mack was involved to the point of becoming a 2½ percent owner of the Buffalo team, and persuading most of the Washington NL team to jump to the Buffalo Players' League team for 1890. He did this even though he now had a wife and two children. The upside of the new league was that Mack signed a three-year contract, with no reserve clause, for $2,750 a year.[8]

The Players' League was a failed experiment in the workers running a business. As the *New York Sun* pointed out in an editorial:

> The Brotherhood of Ball Players have one great difficulty to contend with: the trust or combination against them which they are seeking to overthrow is composed of eight or ten members. The one they would like to form is composed of nearly 150 members. That is much more difficult to handle than the other. They will need not only loyalty but enthusiasm all along the line.[9]

There were three major leagues in 1890: the National League, the American Association, and the Players' League. The Players' League tried a gimmick to increase scoring. The balls were supplied by an ex-player, Tim Keefe. The scores and statistics indicated that the ball was juiced. As the Buffalo team was mostly the last-place Washington team of 1889, the Buffalo team took up residence in the Players' League cellar. On September 14, the team fired their manager and named Connie Mack captain. This meant he was the manager for the rest of the year, but the Bisons went 5–14 to solidify their last-place standing. The team was in dire financial straits and defaulted on wage payments after August. The Players' League stopped operation after the 1890 season. The National League and American Association agreed that the rights to the players from the Players' League would revert to the teams that had them under contract for the 1889 season. As the Washington club in the National League had gone out of business, Mack would be a free agent. He signed with Pittsburgh of the National League for $2,400 for the 1891 season.

Mack spent the next six years in Pittsburgh. For the first three years, he was strictly a player, but encountered people who would figure in his life in baseball. The Pittsburgh manager in 1891 was Ned Hanlon, the center fielder, who took Mack under his wing. Hanlon, soon to become famous as the manager of the Baltimore Orioles, is in the Baseball Hall of Fame. A business that printed and sold scorecards for Pittsburgh games was run by Harry Stevens and Ed Barrow. Both of these men befriended Mack and stayed friends for life. Stevens was the man who popularized the hot dog and became the leading supplier of concessions at major league ballparks. Barrow became a rival manager and competed with Mack until Barrow's death. Mack's first three years as a player in Pittsburgh were fairly normal for him. He was known as a good fielder, a very smart player, and not a very good hitter. The Pirates (who got this name in 1891) finished last in 1891. The other major league, the American Association, folded after the 1891 season. The National League grew to 12 teams in 1892 and split their season to produce champions of the separate halves. Mack signed for $2,400 for 1892. He had a decent year, hitting .243. The Pirates finished sixth and fourth in the two half-seasons. All the Pittsburgh players were confronted with a choice just after the season: sign for $2,400 now or $2,100 in the spring. All signed for $2,400 for 1893. Even though this figure was about four times what the average American earned, it was the same amount Mack made in 1891. It was also a significant year in his personal life. His father died on September 11, 1892. Mack was present, having been called home from Brooklyn. His wife was pregnant with their third child, gave birth on November 27, and never recovered from that ordeal. Margaret Mack died on December 15. Mack was living in Spencer, Massachusetts, near East Brookfield. Mack took over the deed to the family home in East Brookfield, and during the season would leave his children with his mother, who mostly raised them.[10]

Baseball underwent a big change in 1893. The distance from the pitching rubber to home plate changed to the present distance, 60 feet, six inches.[11] This led to a rise in batting average from .245 to .280.[12] The Pittsburgh team improved to a second-place finish, and Mack batted .286. However, this was his last good year, due to an injury. On June 13, facing the defending champion Boston Beaneaters, Mack tried to block the plate on a double steal of second and home. Herman Long slid into Mack, causing a broken ankle. He would miss the rest of the season and said later: "I was never the same player after that. I was slower on the bases and couldn't stoop as well behind the plate."[13] Mack signed again for $2,400 for the 1894 season, a good salary as the country was still reeling from the "Panic of 1893." The 1894 season would get Mack started on the career that made his name. The Pirates got off to a fair start before slumping in June. The owner, Captain Kerr, called Mack in and offered him the manager's job. Mack stuck up for the current manager, Al Buckenberger, which convinced the owner to keep him. When things got worse, Captain Kerr fired Buckenberger on September 1, and again offered Mack the job. Mack took it, starting off as a player-manager on September 2, 1894, and signing a contract for 1895 at the same $2,400 salary. His career as a manager didn't end until 1950.[14]

Mack was player-manager of the Pirates until September 21, 1896. Managers in those days were not limited in their job, like current baseball managers, to on-the-field issues. They were like soccer managers are now. They were in charge of on-field performance, making substitutions during games and deciding lineups, and most off-the-field actions, such as signing players, trading players, and dealing with the press. There was an owner above them, but most managers handled all baseball-related business for the club. Mack knew he had a meddling owner in Captain Kerr, but went about his job as best he could until he was fired. Mack would say later that he was not really ready and learned on the job as manager. Mack's home in Pittsburgh was where the current PNC Park now stands. He learned that it was tougher to manage the roughnecks on his team than to be their teammate. Mack's Pittsburgh teams played ball like the Baltimore Orioles, bending the rules as much as they could. As Bill James states in the Historical Baseball Abstract, there was one word for the style of play in the 1890s: dirty.[15] Mack encouraged his team to play that way, and he rode opposing players with the best of them. He was not an umpire baiter like his contemporary John McGraw. Much later in his life, Mack put these times in perspective.

> Baseball historians dwell considerably on the "days of violence." These days make exciting reading, but it should be considered in proper perspective, that during these same times there was violence everywhere; it was an age of violence. There was violence in the Wild West when it was being settled. There was violence in the upbuilding of the country. Political campaigns had riots. Three Presidents were assassinated. Labor had its uprisings. Early baseball was characteristic of its times.[16]

After dropping from first place on August 9, 1895, to sixth on September 6, he boiled over. After a call on the bases by umpire Hank O'Day (an old teammate of Mack's in Washington), Mack argued enough to be thrown out of the game. That was the only ejection of Mack's entire career. It didn't help the team much, as they finished seventh in a 12-team league, with a record of 71–61. Mack signed a contract for $2,400 for 1896 just after the 1895 season. He was very optimistic, but the team got off to a bad start that continued. On Saturday, July 25, Captain Kerr traded the best player on the Pirates, Jake Beckley, to the New York Giants for Harry Davis. Mack was not informed until the trade was finalized. Mack lasted until September 17, 1896, when he was fired by Captain Kerr. He knew this was coming and had been negotiating with the Milwaukee club of the Western League. Milwaukee signed him to manage their team for the 1897 season. Mack said later that he was happy to go to the minors, so he could learn how to lead men.[17]

In Milwaukee, Mack had an ideal ownership situation. The Brewers were owned by three men, brothers Henry and Matthew Killilea and Fred C. Gross. Henry Killilea was the operating partner. Henry assured Mack, "You're in charge. Handle the club as if it belonged to you. Engage the players you think will strengthen the team without consulting me or any directors of the club."[18] Mack was skeptical about this after his Pittsburgh experience. It turned out that Henry Killilea was speaking the truth. Mack had to operate a team in a city he had never visited before the start of the 1897 season, and basically do it alone. He was the field manager, contract negotiator, scout, public relations director, purchasing agent, and traveling secretary. He continued as a player until his final appearance on Labor Day, September 4, 1899. His pay for all this was $3,000 plus 25 percent of the profits. The team finished third after staying around the middle of the pack of an eight-team league. His performance in 1897 helped the team to make an $8,000 profit, making his total compensation $5,000. It was not unusual at this time for a player or manager to make more money in the minors than in the majors. The financial performance of the club convinced the owners to leave Connie Mack alone in his operation of the club.

Mack continued to be a fiery manager, getting on his players and opponents. By the end of 1897, he had concluded that this behavior was hurting his team. His solution to this problem was told to Fred Lieb much later:

> I then dressed with the players [he was still a player-manager], and there were the usual arguments after we lost a tough game. And in trying to fix blame, hot words often were spoken on both sides. Then one day something came up that made me real sore. I was so mad I knew I couldn't talk calmly. So I waited around until all the players had dressed and gone home. Then I changed my clothes in the solitude of the clubhouse and was alone with my thoughts. I was still hot as I went home, but when I awoke the next morning it was just another ball game we had lost. It was a bonehead play, yes, but the ballplayers are human, and it was all part of baseball.[19]

This maturing led Mack to one of his most famous procedures. Former players on the A's agree that Mack would never upbraid a player after a mistake on the bench or in the clubhouse the same day. Often, Mack would meet the player in private the next day, go over the play, and suggest another way to handle it. Thus Mack had learned to handle the inevitable losing that comes in a baseball season.

Mack worked hard to improve the Brewers. In 1898, the Spanish-American War interfered with spring training, and the Brewers got off to a slow start. Mack heard and read about his inadequacies, but ignored the noise. A 23–8 record in August led to a rise in the standings, and the team finished third, six games out. Mack was developing a preference for younger players and made his first discovery of a top-notch prospect. In early August, the team played an exhibition in Waupun, Wisconsin. The center fielder for the Waupun team impressed

Mack enough to sign him. The center fielder, Clarence "Ginger" Beaumont, played for Mack until he was traded to Pittsburgh before the 1899 season. Beaumont played in the major leagues until 1910, when we will meet him again. Mack earned $3,000 in 1898, as the problems caused by the war eliminated any profit for the Brewers. The club was happy with his performance, signing Mack to another $3,000 contract for 1899. By this time, Mack had come to the attention of the president of the Western League, Ban Johnson.[20]

By 1899, Mack decided that young players were the way to go. His team was older and prone to drinking too much. Another baseball war loomed, as some rich folk talked about restarting the American Association. After the 1899 season, Ban Johnson decided to change the name of the Western League to the American League and improve their chance to succeed by moving into larger cities in the Midwest. When the National League decided to drop four teams in March 1900, Johnson was ready. The St. Paul team (owned by Charles Comiskey, a Chicago native) moved to the south side of Chicago. Johnson found a Cleveland coal dealer with deep pockets, Charles Somers. After the Cleveland franchise in the National League was dropped on March 8, 1900, Somers bought the Grand Rapids franchise for $2,500 and promptly moved it to Cleveland. Johnson assigned Mack to help Somers put together a ball club. Mack spent March putting together two teams in the league, Milwaukee and Cleveland. By the time he was done, only three players remained from the 1899 Milwaukee club. The 1900 team had a better mixture of younger and older players.

The 1900 Brewers started fast, winning 11 of their first 15 games. Then things fell apart, mostly due to injuries. By early July, Mack was looking around for more pitching. He heard that Pittsburgh had suspended their best left-hander, Rube Waddell, who had caused problems for Pirates manager Fred Clarke during the past three years. In the Western League, Mack had seen him pitch several times and knew both how good Waddell was as a pitcher, and how unreliable he was as a person. Mack had enough need for pitching to go to Pittsburgh and ask owner Barney Dreyfuss if he could borrow Waddell. Dreyfuss said, "go ahead, we're not using him." Mack found Waddell in Punxsutawney, Pennsylvania, where he had been playing while under suspension by the Pirates. After much persuasion, both verbal and monetary, Mack got Waddell to come with him to Milwaukee on July 25. Waddell worked nine games in three weeks, winning five and losing two with two ties. He was a great drawing card and a willing pitcher. The Pirates noticed and asked for Waddell to be returned. Mack knew he had to comply and told Waddell to report to Pittsburgh. Waddell was happy in Milwaukee and refused. He was able to stay in Milwaukee until August 31, when Pittsburgh catcher Chief Zimmer arrived to take him back to Pittsburgh. Mack told Zimmer to take Waddell shopping, which did the trick. Waddell's presence in Milwaukee had lifted the Brewers into contention, and his absence guaranteed they would not win the pennant. The Brewers finished second, four games behind Chicago.[21]

Soon after the 1900 season, Mack was named to a committee along with Ban Johnson and Charles Somers. It soon became obvious that these men were looking for possible ballpark sites in cities such as Boston, New York, Philadelphia and Washington. The rumors that the American League was going to try to become a second major league were true. National League players had formed a new association, the Players' Protective Association, in June 1900. The Players' Protective Association wooed Johnson, who was sympathetic with their concerns. The Association backed the American League in a statement after the end of the 1900 season. It soon became clear that Somers was financing teams in several cities. One was Philadelphia, where an entity formed with a handshake issued 500 shares jointly to Charles Somers and Cornelius McGillicuddy. Ban Johnson offered 25 percent of this entity to two sportswriters in Philadelphia, Frank Hough of the *Philadelphia Inquirer* and Samuel Jones of the *AP*. None of this was official, and Somers eventually owned the Cleveland team and a major portion of the Boston team. No one was concerned about any conflict of interest. On November 20, the American League owners met in Chicago. There were six clubs—Cleveland, Baltimore, Washington, Milwaukee, Chicago and Detroit. They named Ban Johnson president, secretary and treasurer at a salary of $5,000, and agreed to operate for ten years. These teams established a procedure for admitting new franchises.[22] After the meeting, Henry Killilea told a Milwaukee reporter, "I guess Connie Mack will be going to Philadelphia."[23]

Mack returned to Milwaukee on December 2, 1900. He sidestepped questions as to whether he would return to Milwaukee the next season. He was present at a meeting of the board of directors of the Milwaukee club on December 3 when they bought all his stock in the club. After a short visit to East Brookfield, Mack spent the rest of the winter on American League business. He and Somers had already agreed to put $10,000 into the Philadelphia franchise, Somers supplying $7,500, Mack $2,500. Somers owned the Cleveland club but let someone else run it. Somers bought the Boston club and ran it until selling it in July 1902, when he returned to Cleveland. During this winter, Mack found ballpark sites for both Philadelphia and Boston. After signing a lease, he left the business end of the ballpark in Boston to Somers, but handled the entire deal in Philadelphia. He found two possible sites in Philadelphia. His sportswriter partners recommended the Columbia Street site. Mack preferred the other site, but went along with his partners. He signed a ten-year lease for this ground on January 21, 1901. The league was meeting again on January 28. On January 26, Mack typed a letter to Ban Johnson that had one sentence: "I herewith make application for the franchise for membership in your league for the city of Phil. Pa. and agree to comply with all conditions and requirements of the American League if granted such franchise."[24] The six members of the league approved Mack's application unanimously on January 28. After this approval, the now seven members took up Charles Somers' application for the Boston franchise, which was also approved unanimously. This was done even though Somers owned half of the Cleveland franchise, and three fourths of the Philadelphia franchise. The National League had refused to talk to the Players' Protective Association, so the stage was now set for a battle between the National and American Leagues for ball players.[25]

    Ban Johnson told Mack that he needed a prominent local backer. Johnson had in mind Ben Shibe, who had been in the business of manufacturing sporting goods since 1865. By 1900, Shibe was 65 and still active in the business. His partner, Al Reach, was the president of the Philadelphia Phillies of the National League. Shibe had been an investor in the Philadelphia Athletics of the American Association and had not enjoyed the experience. Mack met with Shibe in early January 1901, and at some point in January persuaded Shibe to be his partner. Shibe consulted with Reach about how to proceed. Reach (who was 49 percent owner of the Phillies) told Shibe to take 50 percent, so he would have an equal voice in any major actions. Shibe took this advice, and his involvement was announced on February 20. This helped Mack, as Shibe had a spotless reputation for integrity in Philadelphia. Shibe supplied the money to build their ballpark and to acquire players. The $7,500 invested by Charles Somers was used as well. The official books of the entity that owned the Philadelphia Athletics show numerous stockholders and officers. None of those meant anything. After paying Charles Somers back his $7,500 on October 20, 1902, Mack and Shibe were equal partners until Ben Shibe's death.[26]

This Philadelphia team had two and a half months to build a ballpark and stock a team. Mack was in charge of all of this, using money supplied by Shibe. Ground was broken on the Columbia Street Grounds on January 28, 1901. By the time spring practice began on April 1, the stands were complete and the field was laid out. There was not much grass on the field, but it was usable. After much encouragement by the newspapers, Mack named the team the Athletics after the club in the American Association, the Philadelphia Athletics, which last operated in 1891. He was trying to get as many players as possible from the Phillies and secured half their pitching staff, three pitchers. He made his biggest splash by signing the Phillies' best player, second baseman Napoleon Lajoie, to a two year contract at $4,000 a year. He pursued others, ending up with enough players to field a competitive team by the middle of April. Mack was also a member of the league's rules committee, along with Charles Comiskey (owner of the Chicago team) and John McGraw (manager of the Baltimore team). The rules controversy this year was the "foul strike rule." Before 1901, foul balls did not count as strikes, unless the tip hit the catcher. The NL changed to the rule in effect now, that the first two strikes could be accomplished by foul balls. The National League also changed the hit batsman rule in 1901, so that a hit batsman was not awarded first base, but the pitch was a ball. The AL let that rule stand. The National League also changed the rule requiring the catcher to take up a position right behind the batter for all pitches. The American League did not change this until 1903. Hence, before there were two strikes on the batter, American League catchers would continue to line up ten feet or so behind the batter, catching the ball on the bounce without a mask. These catchers would move up and put on the mask when two strikes were on the hitter, or if there was a fast base runner on base. The American League met on March 20, 1901, and approved 25-cent general admission as against 50 cents in the National League. Ban Johnson made clear that he expected clean play and vowed to back his umpires in disputes with teams. Before the season started, the owner of the Phillies filed suit in Pennsylvania state court asking that the players the A's signed be returned to him under the reserve clause. Most of the other owners in both leagues held off on legal action, with the intention of this being the test case. The American League felt this was important enough to reimburse the A's for half of their legal costs in this case.[27]

The complete 15-man roster of the A's was published on April 1. Two players on this list were future Hall of Famers Christy Mathewson and Vic Willis. Mack lost both of them in ways that showed how each league was putting pressure on its players. Mathewson was still in college, and his NL rights were held by the New York Giants. He had not played in the NL in 1900, so had not signed any contract with the Giants. Mack (who was not bound by the NL agreement) signed him to a $1,200 contract in January, with the understanding that Mathewson would remain in school at Bucknell until he graduated in June. The Giants' owner heard of this and threatened Mathewson with legal action. Even though there was no true legal recourse against the existing contract with Mack, Mathewson caved and signed with the Giants. Mack held this against Mathewson the rest of his career. Vic Willis had been a good pitcher for the Boston NL club for three years, reaching the NL salary limit of $2,400 in 1900. Mack offered him $3,500. Willis verbally agreed and took a $450 advance, but did not sign a contract. The Beaneaters eventually matched the A's offer, and Willis reported to their club in April. Mack thought he had legal recourse against both players, but the American League had decided to stay out of the courts unless approved by AL attorneys. The AL advised Mack to let these players go. Now he could finally get to business on the field.[28]

Mack put together a representative team in 1901. The best player by far was Napoleon Lajoie, who led the league in batting average (.426, still the American League record), runs (145), hits (229), doubles (48), home runs (14), runs batted in (125, though not yet an official statistic of the time), and slugging percentage (.635). Mack always maintained that this season was the best he ever saw a player have. Two players on this team played a big part in this season and would remain on the A's through 1910, Harry Davis and Eddie Plank. The A's finished fourth behind Chicago, Boston, and Detroit with a record of 74–62. The A's drew 206,329 spectators as opposed to the second-place Phillies of the National League, who drew 234,937. It is thought the A's made a small profit. Mack's 1901 salary of $3,500 was raised to $5,000 for 1902. Most importantly, the court case regarding the contracts of Lajoie and the other Phillies who had jumped to the A's had been decided in the favor of the A's. The Phillies appealed that decision in November.[29]

Mack signed another NL player before the 1902 season, outfielder Topsy Hartsel of the Cubs, would remain with Mack through 1911. He signed three more Phillies and got the team to spring training in April, before the start of the season on April 23. On April 21, the Pennsylvania Supreme Court handed down its decision on the Lajoie case. The decision stated that the reserve clause held, and Lajoie was the property of the Phillies. This decision was not yet enforceable, but would be as soon as a lower court issued an injunction, which happened on April 28. This injunction meant that the players involved must play for the Phillies and no one else, in Pennsylvania. As this was a state court decision, it had no validity outside Pennsylvania. Other decisions in other courts did not honor this precedent. The players affected by this decision could remain with the A's, but could play only road games. There were five players involved in the decision: Lajoie, outfielder Elmer Flick, and pitchers Bill Bernhard, Chick Fraser, and Bill Duggleby. They were free agents outside of Pennsylvania. Flick signed with Cleveland of the AL. Fraser and Duggleby returned to the Phillies. After waiting a while, Lajoie and Bernhard signed with Cleveland. The three players on the Cleveland team could not play in Philadelphia because of the injunction, but they played the rest of the season with Cleveland. Mack pulled off one of the best managing jobs in baseball history after his team was gutted in April. He got Rube Waddell, even though his contract status was unclear. Waddell, whom Mack always called Eddie, joined the team on June 26 and went 24–7 the rest of the year, leading the league in strikeouts. Mack found an ideal battery mate for Waddell in Ossee Schrecongost. Mack found a second baseman in Danny Murphy, who remained with the A's through 1913. All these moves and others led to Mack's first pennant. The A's had an 83–53 record and won the league by five games. As the AL and NL were still battling, there was no championship series between the league winners that season. The A's drew 100,000 more fans than the Phillies.[30] Earlier in the season, John McGraw left the Baltimore team and blasted the American League. One of his comments was that the Philadelphia team made no money and was a "white elephant." This was embraced by the Philadelphia press and by the A's. They added a white elephant emblem to their uniforms, and this symbol is still used by the Oakland A's franchise.[31]

After the 1902 season, both leagues took stock and started the peace process. Negotiations lasted two days in January 1903, resulting in a signed agreement. The teams promised to respect each other's contracts and closed out all legal cases regarding the reserve clause. The playing rules for each league were made identical, even though Mack still opposed the foul strike rule. The lineup of teams in the American League for the 1903 season was: Boston, Chicago, Cleveland, Detroit, New York (moved from Baltimore), Philadelphia, St. Louis (moved from Milwaukee), and Washington. This lineup would last until 1954. The American League owners passed a resolution just before the 1903 season setting a $2,400 salary limit. Even though two American League owners (Comiskey and Mack) had joined the Players' League as players, all the owners wanted to maximize their profits now that the reserve clause was back in place.[32]

The next two years were good ones for the A's, but did not result in winning pennants. Mack added one player who would remain on the 1910 team, pitcher Charles "Chief" Bender. The team had similar records in each year: 75–60 in 1903 and 81–70 in 1904 (when the American League adopted a 154-game schedule). The best pitchers remained Waddell and Plank, while Murphy, Davis and Hartsel led the offense. The team was still a little mature and rowdy for Mack's taste, as he had not yet acquired the younger, better educated players he craved. In 1905, with a 16-man roster, the A's had a 92–56 record and won the pennant by two games. Two young players joined the team who were on the 1910 team, outfielder Bris Lord, aged 21, and pitcher Jimmy Dygert, aged 20. Neither made a big impression in 1905, when the team was led by veterans. Waddell behaved himself throughout the year, posting a 27–10 record. The rest of the pitching staff performed well, with Plank posting a 24–12 mark, Andy Coakley 18–8, and Chief Bender 18–11. This pitching staff, minus Waddell who missed the World Series with a sore arm, continued to perform well against the New York Giants, posting a 1.67 ERA for the Series. But the Giants won in five games, posting a record 0.00 ERA, losing one game on three unearned runs. Mack was satisfied that this team had reached its potential. The club was satisfied with Mack, whose salary was raised to $10,000.[33]

Mack knew it was time to start looking for younger position players. His pitchers were all in their 20s and pitching well. He had five regular players in their 30s, including 39-year-old Lave Cross, his third baseman. All sports teams are in a constant state of replenishment, which Mack knew he needed to continue. In 1906, he brought three youngsters to the A's. Rube Oldring was an outfielder, Jack Coombs a pitcher, and Eddie Collins a shortstop. The A's finished fourth in 1906 with a 78–67 record, due to hitting problems. Their pitching was still good, but not good enough that year. The White Sox won the pennant with a .230 batting average, still the lowest batting average of any pennant winner. The A's were better in 1907, with an 88–57 record. Mack was signing young players, but still playing veterans. Eddie Collins was on the team most of the year, but played in just 14 games as Mack kept him close on the bench and imparted wisdom. The A's had six regular position players in their 30s. The pennant race included a three-game series between the A's and Detroit in Philadelphia starting September 27. The A's lost the first game on Friday, giving the Tigers a 1½-game lead. It rained Saturday, and there was no Sunday ball in Philadelphia. A doubleheader was scheduled for Monday, drawing a then-record crowd for the major leagues of 24,127. The young Tigers center fielder, Ty Cobb, called the only game completed that day the greatest game he ever played in. The A's led, 7–1, after five innings. The Tigers fought back and were down 8–6 in the ninth. Cobb hit a two-run homer off Waddell in the ninth and each team scored one run in the 11th. In the bottom of the 14th, Harry Davis hit a fly into the crowd, which was behind ropes on the field, a double under the ground rules. After some delay, the umpire called Davis out due to crowd interference. Mack said later that this was the most upset he ever was due to an umpire's call. The next batter hit a single that would have scored a runner at second. The game ended in a 17-inning tie, and the second game of the doubleheader was not played. Under the rules, neither game was made up. This helped the Tigers to hold a 1½-game lead and win the pennant. Mack knew this was the best this team could do and determined to step up his replenishment of talent.[34]

In 1908, Mack ran 37 players through the A's, 19 of them making their major league debuts. The A's finished with a 68–85 record, well out of one of the greatest pennant races in AL history. The Tigers won by ½ game, leading to a rule change that any team in the race had to make up all their games, as the Tigers played one less game than the second-place Cleveland Naps. Meanwhile, Mack implemented his long-term vision. Players signed this year included Jack Barry, Frank Baker, John McInnis, Amos Strunk, Harry Krause, and Joe Jackson. Mack now had potential replacements for all his older players except at catcher. He played these youngsters occasionally, mainly keeping them near on the bench, and working them out hard in the mornings before games.

Mack and his field captain, Harry Davis, were constantly teaching these youngsters the finer points of the game and letting them make suggestions themselves. In 1908, five of Mack's regular position players were in their 30s. That would change the next year.[35]

When the 1909 season started, the A's had a new home. Starting in 1906, Ben Shibe had been secretly buying up land bounded by 20th and 21st Streets and Lehigh and Somerset Streets. The land cost $128,000. The politics of the new park fell into place on February 24, 1908, when the city council approved use of the land in one piece. The kind of use was not specified. The A's announced the building a new ballpark, which caused land values in the area to rise. Ben Shibe was in charge of building the park, with input from Mack. This was an era of building new, concrete and steel ballparks. Shibe was the innovator, as Shibe Park was the first of these stadiums to be completed. It had a seating capacity of around 30,000 and many new features. Both clubhouses had showers, three for the A's, two for the visitors. There was an umpires' dressing room. The outfield was banked, which allowed spectators on the field to have a decent view. Building started on April 16, 1908, and the cornerstone was laid on October 3. Total cost of the building project was $315,000. Other major league owners were impressed that the A's would spend nearly $500,000 on their own ballpark. The A's had issued bonds for $200,000 and secured a mortgage of $150,000. The economics of the ballpark were favorable enough that other owners followed.[36] Existing stadiums were rebuilt in New York (NL), Cleveland (AL) and St. Louis (both franchises in the same park). New stadiums were built within the next five years in Pittsburgh (NL), Chicago (AL), Brooklyn (NL), Detroit (AL), and Boston (both leagues in separate parks).[37] The new park in Philadelphia would see a new team in 1909.

In 1908, the average age of the eight regular position players listed for the A's in the *Baseball Encyclopedia* was 30.5.[38] This included Jack Coombs (25 years old) as one of the outfielders, even though he pitched in 25 games with a record of 7–5. Coombs played 47 games in the outfield, which was fourth most on the A's. The man he replaced, Socks Seybold, was 37 years old. The average age of the A's regular infield (Harry Davis, 1B, Danny Murphy, 2B, Simon Nicholls, SS, Jimmy Collins, 3B) was 32. In 1909, the average age of the eight regular position players was 27.63. The infield average (Harry Davis, 1B, Eddie Collins, 2B, Jack Barry, SS, Frank Baker, 3B) was 25.5, skewed by Harry

Davis, who was 35. Mack's investment in young position players paid off this year, as Collins, Barry, Baker and outfielder Rube Oldring established themselves as solid big leaguers. Young pitchers Harry Krause (21) and Jimmy Dygert (24) joined veterans Plank, Bender, Coombs and 30-year-old newcomer Cy Morgan, acquired on June 5, 1909, from the Red Sox.[39]

The 1909 season was the debut of what became a great A's team. Barry and Baker were hurt at the beginning of the year, requiring McInnis to play shortstop. Mack had not yet decided on a position for the 18-year-old McInnis, who performed adequately while Barry was out. When Barry and Baker returned by the end of April, McInnis took up his place next to Mack on the bench, playing 19 games that year. Collins, Barry, Baker, Oldring, Krause and Dygert proved themselves solid contributors in a close pennant race. Mack's only failure with the young players was Joe Jackson. Jackson had hit well in spring training, while

Connie Mack in 1910 at Comiskey Park, Chicago.

being continually homesick. Mack noticed and sent him to Savannah, where he remained until September. Jackson returned in September, playing five games hitting .294. Mack was still not sure about the 19-year-old Jackson. In late June, the A's started playing good ball, but they were 4½ games behind Detroit when they left on a road trip to every other town in the league and made up 20 percent of their schedule. The trip started great, the A's winning 12 of 14 games on the first three stops in Boston, New York and Detroit, leaving Detroit one-half game off the league lead. They then slumped, going 3–10 in Cleveland, St. Louis and Chicago. A four-game sweep of Washington got the A's back home with a 19–12 record on the trip, 6½ games out. Then they took on the Tigers in Detroit, and by the end of that trip the A's had a half-game lead. The games between the A's and Tigers were fiercely competitive. On August 24, Cobb slid into third, causing a ten-stitch cut on Baker's right arm. Mack called Cobb a few names, and Cobb returned the favor. The newspapers in each town turned up the rhetoric. By September 16, when the Tigers came to Philadelphia for a four-game series with a four-game lead, Cobb had to be escorted to and from the ballpark. The A's won three out of four to close the gap to two games. In the last game of the series, Barry tried to block second when Cobb was trying to steal. This resulted in a ten-inch cut on Barry's leg, and Barry missed the rest of the season. The A's faded without Barry, ending the year three games out of first. Even so, the year was a ringing success for the A's and Mack. They won 95 games, the most in their young history. Attendance of 674,915 was second in the majors, and more than double the Phillies'. Mack had the team he wanted.[40]

2

The Cubs

By the end of the 1909 season, the Chicago National League team had enough history, and nicknames, that the team was not identified with just one man, like the A's and Mack. The National League started in 1876. Only two franchises from that League still exist as original, continually operating franchises. One is the Braves, who have gone through three homes (Boston, Milwaukee, and Atlanta) and many more nicknames. The other is the Cubs, who have been in Chicago since 1876.

The first professional baseball league in the U.S. was the National Association of Professional Baseball Players, founded in 1871. This league was very loosely organized, and both the Boston Red Stockings (who became the Braves) and the Chicago White Stockings (who became the Cubs) were members. This league operated as the only professional league until 1875, and operated as a minor league for a couple more years. In 1875 the new owner of the Chicago team, William Hulbert, persuaded four of the best players on the Boston team to jump to his team. These players, led by Albert Spalding, led the Chicago team to the pennant in the National Association. The other owners in the National Association were angry enough to kick the Chicago team out of the Association.[1] Hulbert thought enough of the business prospects of baseball to form a new league. He recruited franchises in New York, Cincinnati, Hartford, Louisville, Philadelphia, St. Louis, and the Boston club to join his Chicago club in the National League. The league operated under the leadership of Morgan Bulkeley for one year. After 1876, William Hulbert took over the presidency of the league, while continuing to operate the Chicago White Stockings. Hulbert ran both the league and the team until his death just before the 1882 season began.[2]

The minority owner of the Chicago team was Albert Spalding. Spalding later became majority owner, having the financial muscle to do this based on the sporting goods business he had founded while still a player (he retired as a player in 1877).[3] This team, still known as the White Stockings, was in the midst of the most successful stretch in team history. From 1880 through 1886, the White Stockings won five pennants. They were led by Adrian "Cap" Anson, the first player in major league history to produce more than 3,000 hits. Anson was with the White Stockings from 1876 until 1897, becoming captain in 1879. This role morphed at some point into being named manager, with no real change in duties. Anson was one of the towering figures of 19th century baseball, for both good and bad. He led the White Stockings into participation in two series with winners of the rival American Association in 1885–1886, splitting the two series with the St. Louis Browns, led by Charles Comiskey. He was credited with many innovations, such as hit and run plays, signals between players, platooning, and pitching rotations (when Anson started out many teams used only one pitcher a year). He was a disciplinarian, often enforcing rules with his fists, as he was bigger than most of his players at 6 feet, 230 pounds. He and another manager, Harry Wright, took their respective teams south in March 1886, the first spring training camps for baseball teams.

Anson also shared in the common prejudices of his time. He disliked Irishmen intensely, making the lives of his many Irish players uncomfortable. But this was mild treatment compared to how he felt about blacks. Anson is often blamed for instituting the "color line" in major league baseball, which dates back to at least 1867. Anson certainly shared the common prejudice against blacks held by most white Americans in the post–Civil War era. Two instances are told of his taking action on this prejudice. In 1884, the Toledo team of the Northwestern League had an African American catcher, Moses Fleetwood Walker. When the Chicago team played an exhibition game in Toledo, Anson threatened to boycott the game if Walker played. The Toledo team said they would withhold Chicago's share of the gate receipts unless they played, and Chicago played the game. On July 14, 1887, the Chicago team was to play the Newark Little Giants in a mid-season exhibition. The Newark battery consisted of two African Americans, pitcher George Washington Stovey and catcher Fleetwood Walker. Anson refused to play against the two, and the Giants backed down.

This might be described as turning down the chance to break the existing color line.[4]

Another innovation in Anson's career was the long-term contract. In 1888, after he had led the White Stockings both on and off the field to five pennants, the club signed Anson to a 10-year contract. As sometimes happens today, this contract became a burden for the team. Spalding sold his interest in the team to his minority owner, James Hart, in 1891 so Spalding could concentrate on his sporting goods business. Anson thought he was supposed to have an opportunity to buy the team, and as a result had a poor relationship with Hart.[5] The performance of the team slipped in the 1890s partly because Anson did not like having Irishmen on his team, and Irish-American players were dominant in the 1890s.[6] Anson and the Colts (the Chicago team's nickname starting in 1890) honored the 10-year contract. After the 1897 season, the club did not re-sign Anson. Local newspapers started calling the team the Orphans. The Orphans had two managers from 1898 through 1901 and continued to perform poorly. The Orphans lost some players to the new American League in the war, but kept the player who turned out to be most important to their future, a young catcher from California signed in 1898, Frank Chance. The Orphans signed another catcher in 1901, John Kling, who beat out Chance to be the starting catcher. A new manager, hired for the 1902 season, would start the franchise on the way back to the top.

In the 1890s, the two best teams in the National League were the Boston Beaneaters (now the Braves) and the Baltimore Orioles (who were resurrected in the American League in 1901). The Orioles were known for their dirty play, taking advantage of the fact that the sole umpire on the field could not see very much while the ball was in play. The Orioles were known for riding the opposition and the umpire, and cheating as much as they could get away with.[7] Boston did not play that way. They used the rules to their advantage as much as they could, but were known for their gentlemanly and fair play. The manager of the Boston team was Frank Selee, one of the few managers in history who never played pro baseball. He started as a manager in local amateur leagues in Massachusetts in 1885. He moved to the minors the next year, managing there until 1889. Boston hired him in 1890. Selee signed six future Hall of Famers during his tenure in Boston and won five pennants in the 1890s. He was known for teaching clean play and respecting his players. His credo was: "If I make this pleasant for the players, they reciprocate."[8] Due to disagreements with the Boston owner in 1901 (when he lost most of his roster to the Boston AL club), Selee was fired after the season. Hart hired Selee to manage the Orphans.

The hiring of Selee was the start of the rise of the Chicago NL team in the new century. Selee held a tryout camp before the start of the 1902 season, discovering one player. That player thought he was a third baseman, but Selee moved Joe Tinker to shortstop. He looked at his two catchers, Chance and Kling, and decided on Kling. He could tell that Chance was a fine player and persuaded Chance, much against his desire, to move to first base. Selee had started the process of getting Jimmy Slagle while they were both in Boston. The Boston owner did not like Slagle and released him near the end of the 1901 season. Selee got Baltimore of the AL to sign Slagle, and then bought Slagle before the 1902 season for Chicago, securing a fine centerfielder. Selee brought his second baseman, Bobby Lowe, with him from Boston. Lowe played 117 games for Chicago in 1902 before getting injured in late August. Selee put out an appeal for another second baseman. A scout he knew recommended someone from Troy, NY, and Selee accepted the recommendation. When John Evers arrived, no one thought he could really play, as he was so small and slight. Having no alternative, Selee put him in for 26 games and was impressed enough to sign Evers for the 1903 season. The Chicago NL team finished 1902 with a 68–69 record, but with these moves, the now renamed Cubs had the start of a good team.

Bobby Lowe was the captain of the Cubs in 1902, but after spring training in 1903 it was clear that Evers would be the starting second baseman. The captain was normally a starter and normally named by the manager. Selee tried something new, letting the players select their own captain. Selee made it known he favored Doc Casey, a 32-year-old third baseman acquired over the winter from Detroit. But he let the players decide. The result of the election, per Evers' account, was Chance 11, Casey 4, Kling 2. Chance would be the leader of the Cubs on the field. This appointment became more important as it became clear that Selee was ill with tuberculosis. Selee remained with the team until the middle of 1905, when he had to quit due to his condition. Selee solicited Chance's input on further player moves after Chance assumed the captaincy. Chance wanted to get a pitcher from the Omaha team, Mordecai Brown. The Omaha team told Selee that Brown had a bad arm, and Selee passed. Brown was sold to the St. Louis NL team and went 9–18 in 1903. After the 1903 season, due to the peace agreement signed between the leagues before the season, there were local series between teams in opposing leagues. These series started between the two St. Louis teams, the two Philadelphia teams, Cleveland and Cincinnati in Ohio, and the two Chicago teams. The Chicago teams were more ambitious than the others, scheduling a 15-game series. The players were not too thrilled, as they would receive minimal extra pay. Both teams played their regular players. The best pitcher on the Cubs for the past two years was Jack Taylor, who had gone 23–11 and 21–14. Taylor won the first game of the City Series but was drilled the next three times he started. The series ended in a 7–7 tie, both in games and in the 15th game. Taylor was under suspicion after the series that he was paid to pitch poorly by gamblers, stating a year later: "Why should I have won? I got $100 from Hart for winning, and I got $500 for losing."[9] Hart and Selee both believed this story and made Taylor available to be traded. The St. Louis Cardinals were the trade partners, getting Taylor and catcher Larry McLean for catcher Jack O'Neill and pitcher Mordecai Brown. This was a good end to a season that resulted in an 82–56, third-place finish for the Cubs.

Selee knew the athletic director of the University of Illinois, George Huff, and hired him as a scout in 1902. Huff sent a pitcher from his university, Carl Lundgren, who made the staff in 1902, remaining an effective starter through 1907. In 1903, Huff found three players who became regulars for Selee. Ed Reulbach was a pitcher for Notre Dame who had impressed Huff. Huff heard of a pitcher named Lawson playing in Sedalia, Montana, and made a trip to see him. Lawson disappeared before Huff got there. Huff later heard of a pitcher named Sheldon in the Green Mountain League in Vermont who was winning big. Huff visited Vermont and determined that Lawson, Sheldon and Reulbach were the same person pitching under different names. Huff signed Reulbach to a contract for the 1904 season, which Reulbach spent in the minors under control of the Cubs. Huff also heard of a good player at the Des Moines team and made a trip there. He was not impressed with the player he had gone to scout, but with another player, Artie Hofman. The Cubs purchased Hofman, who had played a little for Pittsburgh in 1903 before being sold to Des Moines. Cubs outfielders other than Slagle were getting old, so Selee told Huff to be on the lookout for good young outfielders. Huff heard of some good ones playing in Syracuse and made a trip there. He came back with two, Frank

Schulte and Mike Mitchell. The Cubs tried out Mitchell and traded him to Cincinnati, where he started an eight-year major league career. Schulte made the Cubs in 1904, moving into the everyday lineup in 1905. Huff's year as a scout in 1903 is one of the better ones in major league history.[10]

The Cubs improved to 93–60 in 1904, finishing 13 games behind the Giants. Selee's illness got worse. He left the running of the team on the field to his captain, Chance. According to Evers, Selee was not sold on Hofman and Slagle. Chance had to talk Selee out of getting rid of both of them. Chance was tough and hard-headed. He literally proved that in 1904. He crowded the plate as a right-handed batter. Pitchers would try to move him off the plate. On May 30 in the first game of a doubleheader in Cincinnati, Reds pitcher Jack Harper had hit Chance twice already before Chance stepped in during the ninth inning. This time, the inside pitch froze Chance and hit him flush in the side of the head. Chance was knocked out cold for several minutes, then got up and went to first base. He played the second game, getting hit twice more in that game. Chance would end up getting hit more than a hundred times in his career. Even limited to 124 games, Chance led the Cubs in batting average, stolen bases, and home runs in 1904.[11]

Change was coming to the team in 1905. Chicago was established as a fine baseball market by 1904. Both teams were profitable, and attendance had increased since the settlement of 1903. Both teams were part of the elite in their league. Competitive balance was a problem in the early 20th century in each league. From 1901–1913, only three teams won the NL pennant: Chicago, New York, and Pittsburgh. From 1901–1919, four teams won the AL pennant: Boston, Chicago, Detroit, and Philadelphia. Owning a Chicago team was attractive. Charles Comiskey was established as the owner of the White Sox, and that was his only business. The owner of the Cubs, James Hart, owned and ran the Chicago Gravel Company, his main business interest. Hart let it be known in National League circles that he was ready to sell out. One of the first to learn this fact was a press agent in Cincinnati, Charles Murphy. He had started out as a pharmacist, later becoming a sportswriter. He was a friend of fellow Cincinnati sportswriter Ban Johnson, who helped him become the press agent for the Indianapolis team in the Western League, owned by John T. Brush. By 1905, Brush owned the 1904 NL pennant winner, the New York

Giants. Brush passed along the news about the possibility of Hart selling the Cubs. Murphy was the first potential buyer to talk to Hart, securing an option to buy the club by throwing in a finder's fee to Hart. Now Murphy had to find the money. He had $15,000 in savings, so he needed about $90,000 to pay the entire $105,000 price. He wanted to run the club himself, so he was looking for a silent partner. He knew such a person in Cincinnati. Charles Phelps Taft was the son of one former member of the Cabinet (Alonso Taft, Attorney General under President Grant), and the older half-brother of another (William Howard Taft, in 1905 Secretary of War under President Theodore Roosevelt). Charles Taft had been a one-term Congressman from Cincinnati in the 1890s and was now in the newspaper business, where he met Murphy. Murphy persuaded Charles Taft to loan him $90,000, to be paid back out of the profits of operating the Cubs. The deal was announced on July 15, 1905, but not closed until November. Hart continued to run the Cubs, with input from Murphy. In November, the ownership structure was Murphy 45 percent, Charles Taft 45 percent, and John Schmalstig (Taft's agent in this matter) 10 percent. After the 1906 season, Taft and Murphy offered Chance the opportunity to buy 10 percent of the team for $10,000. Chance accepted and became a part-owner.[12]

Murphy's input would be needed before the end of the year. By August 1905, Frank Selee determined he could not continue, resigning after 90 games had been played. There are two versions of why this happened. One is that Selee left voluntarily due to tuberculosis. The other is that Murphy forced Selee out to secure Chance as his manager.[13] With Murphy's approval, Hart named Chance interim player-manager. The Cubs had a record of 52–38 at the time. Their record under Chance was 40–23, resulting in a 92–61 record, in third place, 13 games behind the Giants. As soon as the deal to buy the team was finalized, Murphy took the interim tag off Chance's title, naming him manager.

Chance told Murphy what he needed. Chance requested some catching help, and Murphy secured Pat Moran from Boston. Chance was satisfied with Tinker and Evers in the middle of the infield, himself at first, and Hofman as the all-around sub. He needed a third baseman, even though he had a rookie named Hans Lobert. Chance knew who he wanted from playing in California over the winters with and against Harry Steinfeldt, now with Cincinnati. Steinfeldt had been injured for some of 1905, but still had a decent year while note getting along with manager Joe Kelley. The Cubs offered 18-game winner Jake Weimer to the Reds, and secured Steinfeldt and another player in a trade completed on October 24, 1905. At the winter meetings in December, the Cubs were one of three teams pursuing Brooklyn outfielder Jimmy Sheckard. The offer of two 1905 regulars (third baseman Doc Casey and left fielder Billy Maloney) and two subs turned the trick. This trade was finalized on December 15, 1905. Having purchased Jack Pfiester from Omaha, Chance felt he had four solid pitchers, and good catching with Kling and Moran. The infield was now set as Chance, Evers, Tinker and Steinfeldt. The trade in December set the outfield as Sheckard, Slagle and Schulte. Hans Lobert, now expendable, was sold to Cincinnati in January 1906. After these deals were complete, Murphy was quoted as saying, "Unless we are crippled by accidents, I certainly think we will make a bid for the flag."[14]

Even though their main competition, the New York Giants, started the 1906 season with a uniform reading "World Champions" across their chest, Murphy was right. The 1906 Cubs compiled the best regular season since 1900 based on winning percentage. The Cubs were good, not great, at the start of the season, having a 29–15 record on June 1. After that, they swept all before them, going 87–21 the rest of the regular season for a 116–36 final record, still the record for winning percentage for a season after 1901 (the 2001 Seattle Mariners tied the 116-win total, but in a longer season with a lower winning percentage). Through the regular season, everything went right for the Cubs. Chance played 136 games, the most in his career, leading the team in walks, runs, and stolen bases. Evers played every game. Tinker was steady at short. Steinfeldt had his best year in the majors, leading the team in batting average and RBI and leading the league in hits. The outfield was solid. Kling recovered from a .218 batting average in 1905 to hit .312 in 1906. And he handled the best pitching staff in the National League.

The Cubs led the league with a 1.76 team ERA, with Brown producing a league-leading 1.04 mark. Two new pitchers, Jack Pfiester and Orval Overall, had fine seasons. The Cubs even got Jack Taylor back from St. Louis, now that Hart was no longer in control. Taylor had one of the more notable feats as a major league pitcher come to an end in 1906. From June 21, 1901, through August 9, 1906, Taylor started 187 games (97 with the Cubs, 90 with the Cardinals), and finished them all.[15] On the pitching staff was an example of Frank Chance's competitiveness and vengeance as well. Early in the season, Chance traded with Cincinnati to secure Jack Harper, the pitcher who had knocked him out cold in 1904. Harper was used in one game in 1906 and buried on the bench, ending his career. One did not mess with Frank Chance.

The Cubs won the pennant by 20 games and did not play any meaningful games after September 1.[16] Their crosstown rivals, the White Sox, had to scratch and claw to win the pennant by three games. The White Sox had the lowest batting average ever for a pennant winner, earning their nickname as the "Hitless Wonders." The World Series, the first one-city World Series (admittedly, only the third World Series ever), was the biggest thing up to then in Chicago sports history, with the Cubs as big favorites. As has been demonstrated many times in all sports, anything can happen in a short series. The overconfident Cubs were beaten, 4–2, by the White Sox, even though the White Sox hit .198 as a team. The Cubs hit .196, but did not have as many timely hits. The unlikely hero was George Rohe, a third baseman who subbed for Lee Tannehill and hit .333.[17] While Murphy was disappointed in the World Series result, he was not disappointed in the bottom line. The Cubs had their best attendance so far in 1906, 654,300. With both Chicago teams winning pennants, total baseball attendance in Chicago was 1,239,523. Total New York attendance, with three teams, was 1,114,950.[18] The operating profit from the Cubs was enough that Murphy could fully pay off his loan from Taft, which he did.

A final note is needed about Frank Selee, who died of tuberculosis in Denver in 1909 without getting back into baseball. Many people consider the 1927 Yankees as the best team of all time. Bill James makes the point in his guide to baseball managers that Frank Selee built the two greatest teams before 1927. Due to the influence of John McGraw, Wilbert Robinson and Hughie Jennings, many people think the 1894 Baltimore Orioles were the best 19th century team. James says that the 1897 Boston Beaneaters, built by Selee, were the best. And the 1906 Cubs, mostly built by Selee, were the best team in the 20th century before 1927.[19]

Most followers of baseball thought the Cubs' loss in the World Series of 1906 was a fluke. The Cubs proved this was true over the next two years. After the 1907 season, Chance said, "Had we lost I would

36   The Cubs and the A's of 1910

Frank Chance at bat in 1910. Notice the catcher is stooping, not crouching, and lack of shin guards.

have had to retire to the Sierra Madre mountains to escape hearing from the anvil chorus."[20] The Cubs saved Chance from this fate with another dominating performance. They won 107 games, making their win total in two consecutive seasons 223, a record. Their hitting diminished, with no .300 hitters. Injuries were a problem, with Chance and Schulte each missing more than 40 games, while Tinker missed 38. Artie "Circus Solly" Hofman was the utility man who came to the rescue. Hofman played in 134 games, playing every position except pitcher and catcher. Pitching was the Cubs' strength again in 1907. Their five main starters (Brown, Overall, Lundgren, Pfiester and Reulbach) had a record of 92–33 and completed 96 of 126 starts. The Cubs finished 17 games ahead of Pittsburgh, which had the best record against the Cubs this year, 10–12. This time the Cubs completed the job, winning the World Series against the Tigers in five games, one of which ended in a tie.[21]

The second consecutive championship in 1908 would be much

more difficult. The 1908 season featured outstanding pennant races in each league, all-time great players, heated rivalries, and one of the most infamous plays in baseball history setting up a classic regular season finale. In the National League, the race from the beginning was between three teams, the Cubs, Giants and Pirates. In 1908, Cubs pitching was not quite so balanced. Brown and Reulbach had great years, 29–9 and 24–7 respectively. Brown pitched 13 times in relief, being credited long afterward with leading the NL in saves, a statistic not created until 1969. Reulbach helped the Cubs' cause soon after the Merkle game (see below) by pitching a shutout in both ends of a doubleheader on September 27, in the heat of a tight pennant race.[22]

The Cubs' season turned on two similar plays which were called differently. On September 4 in Pittsburgh, the game was tied in the bottom of the ninth, two out and the bases loaded. The Pittsburgh batter singled to the outfield, the runner on third scored, and the fans came onto the field, which was common in 1908. Johnny Evers called for outfielder Artie Hofman to get him the ball, as the runner from first, Pirates rookie Warren Gill, had gone to the clubhouse without touching second. The lone umpire of that game, Hank O'Day, had been watching the runner score and did not see whether Gill touched second. Hence, O'Day would not call Gill out. Both Evers and O'Day filed this situation away in their memory.[23]

What became known as the "Merkle game" was played in New York on September 23. The Giants had a half-game lead before the game, after losing four games in a row, including a doubleheader to the Cubs on September 22. The pitchers were Jack Pfiester for the Cubs and Christy Mathewson for the Giants. Pfiester pitched well in 1908, with a 2.00 ERA, and earned the nickname "Giant Killer" with his success against New York. Mathewson was in the midst of the best year of his Hall of Fame career, posting a 1.43 ERA and a record of 37–11, leading the league in games, starts, complete games, innings pitched, strikeouts, ERA, and hits allowed. Through 8½ innings, it was a classic pitchers' duel, tied 1–1. With two outs in the bottom of the ninth, the Giants had Moose McCormick on third, rookie Fred Merkle on first, and Al Bridwell at bat. Bridwell singled to center, McCormick scored, and Merkle lit out for the clubhouse in deep center field after he saw McCormick score, as the entire crowd was now flooding the field. Evers remembered the play in Pittsburgh and called for Hofman to get him the ball. After some problems, which are different in each telling of the story, Evers got a ball and stood on second, claiming a force-out. There were two umpires at this game, Hank O'Day at home plate and Bob Emslie on the bases. Emslie had been watching the ball and could not make a call. Emslie asked O'Day for help. O'Day had seen that Merkle had not touched second and called Merkle out for the third out of the inning, creating a tie game. By this time the field was full of fans, and it was dark anyway. The game was declared a 1–1 tie and would have to be replayed in its entirety, if necessary.[24] There were two weeks left in the season, and the league hoped it would not have to rule on the Giants' protest of this decision. However, the teams ended up with identical 98–55 records, so league president Harry Pulliam ruled that the tie game stood and had to be replayed on October 8.

That game, often incorrectly called a playoff game, was simply the last game of the year, a make-up for the Merkle game. The National League had instituted a rule before the 1908 season requiring that teams in contention had to play all 154 games if necessary to resolve the pennant. The American League did not have that rule in 1908, allowing Detroit to win the pennant with a record of 90–63 against Cleveland's record of 90–64. The American League adopted this rule in 1909. The make-up game was played in New York on October 8, with the same starting pitchers as on September 23. Mathewson, understandably, had told his wife the morning of this game that he was worn out and not sure if he could pitch. He did the best he could, going seven innings and leaving behind, 4–1. After Pfiester allowed a first-inning run, Chance called on Brown, who finished the game as a 4–2 winner.[25]

The World Series started on October 10 in Detroit. The teams were the same as in 1907, Cubs and Tigers, and the result was the same, the Cubs winning in five games. This time the Tigers won one game, but their fans were so discouraged that only 6,210 showed up for the final game in Detroit. The Cubs became the first team to win two straight World Series titles under the modern league structure.[26]

Entering the 1909 season, the Cubs' reputation was at its height. A Washington sportswriter wrote: "They were grizzlies, these Cubs. Ursine Colossi who towered high and frowningly and refused to reckon on anything but victory."[27] While the Cubs were on the train from Chicago to New York for their final game with the Giants in 1908, Chance said, "Whoever heard of the Cubs losing a game they had to have?"[28] Their performance in 1909 did not change anything. Kling asked Murphy for a leave of absence, which was granted, spending 1909 in his hometown of Kansas City. Chance played only 92 games due to injuries, and Evers missed a month due to a nervous breakdown. Even with these problems, the Cubs won 104 games. They still hold the record for games won in three consecutive years (1906–1908) with 322, and in four consecutive years (1906–1909) with 426. The Cubs finished 12 games ahead of the Giants, but six games behind the Pirates. Hence, even though the Cubs had another great year in 1909, they were eager to reclaim their place atop the National League when the 1910 season rolled around.[29]

3

Spring Training

After the 1909 regular season, many big leaguers continued playing for a while. Unlike today, the average pay for major leaguers was somewhat in line with the average pay for a worker. The average salary for a full-time worker in the U.S. in 1908 was about $800, which was considered sufficient to support a family. Major leaguers had no minimum salary, but you would be hard-pressed to find someone making less than $1,000 for a full major league season. The best-paid players made between $8,000 and $10,000.[1] So, after a season making an average of about $3,000, players were willing to play in exhibition games. It was common for teams to play their natural rivals in the other league, as there was no official interleague play except the World Series. Playing at the same time of the World Series was common, as there were no radio or television broadcasts, and the normal way for a baseball fan to keep up on the World Series was reading newspaper accounts the next day. In 1909, there were only two of these series played opposite the World Series. One was between the Boston Red Sox and the Brooklyn Superbas. The other was in Chicago. There had been no exhibition series in Chicago since 1905, as at least one of the Chicago teams was in the World Series in 1906, 1907, and 1908. The series in Chicago started on October 8, 1909, the same date the World Series started in Pittsburgh. The format was the same, and as in the World Series, the players got a share of the proceeds from the first four games. The Cubs beat the White Sox four games to one, getting a small share of revenge for the 1906 World Series. The teams played their regulars, and the starting pitchers participated in all the games (Brown, Reulbach, and Overall for the Cubs; Ed Walsh, Doc White and Frank Smith for the White Sox). Total attendance at these five games was about 90,000, and the players' share of the proceeds was $23,910, according to the *Chicago Tribune*. Figuring rosters of 16 players for each team meant a player's share of $747, good pay for one week's work in 1909.[2]

Even though the color line still held in organized baseball, teams in organized baseball would play exhibition games against African American teams. The leading Negro (as these teams were referred to in 1909) team in the Midwest was the Chicago Leland Giants. "Giants" was a code word for a black team in this era and long afterwards. Unless it was the New York Giants, it was a black team. The Chicago Leland Giants barnstormed around the Midwest playing all comers for part of their income in 1908 and 1909. They also competed in the Chicago City League against semi-pro teams like the Spaldings, the Logan Squares, the West Ends, Riverview Park, and others familiar to Chicagoans. Another team that participated in this league, and played against the Chicago Leland Giants, was the Anson Colts, led by Cap Anson as their player-manager. The Chicago Leland Giants won the Chicago City League in both 1908 and 1909. Their reward was to play a series against the Cubs after the Cubs-White Sox series concluded in 1909. This was a three-game series, swept by the Cubs. The Cubs played their regulars and used three of their front-line pitchers. Brown started the first and last games, Ruelbach started the second game, and Overall relieved in the second game.[3] After this series, Frank Chance remained in Chicago until October 27, announcing on his last night that the Cubs needed one right-handed pitcher for next year, which he expected to find among the players who were coming to training camp. He assured fans that the Cubs would win the National League pennant in 1910.[4]

The A's did not play the Phillies after the 1909 season, instead scheduling a series just before 1910 Opening Day. Connie Mack attended the World Series, rooting for the Tigers of his current league against his old team, the Pirates. After the series ended in a seven-game Pirates victory, Mack was ready for more baseball. He led an American League squad, mostly made up of his players, against a National League all-star squad. These teams started in Chicago on October 17 and played each other for a month on their way west to Denver. Then the teams split up and barnstormed separately throughout the West and Southwest. The tour broke even, but Mack was happy his team was mostly together and staying in shape. Frank Baker stayed on the tour until November 13, when he got married in

San Francisco and went on a honeymoon to Mexico. The tour ended in New Orleans.[5]

Other parties were noticing that baseball appeared to be a profitable business. There was a proposal floating around this off-season to start a new 12-team league. This proposal turned out to be hot air. The National League wanted to extend to a 168-game schedule, and Brooklyn owner Charles Ebbets wanted to extend the end of the season to include another holiday, Columbus Day. The American League wanted to cut the schedule to 140 games and start later. The leagues settled on the same 154-game schedule, but the National League season would end on October 15 in 1910.[6]

Relations between major league clubs and minor league clubs were different in those days. If the player showed well in the minors, and a major league scout happened to see him on a good day, he could be given a chance on a major league club. There was no official farm system. Relations between major and minor league teams were more nuanced. Connie Mack kept a book on all minor league clubs he dealt with. He had a network of friends around the country who would tip him off if they saw a good player. This was how he learned about many of the young players he was constantly trying out. Another example of the way Mack worked with a minor league club took place in November 1909. The Baltimore Orioles, a top minor league club, were sold for $35,000. The buyer, Jack Dunn, did not have that kind of money. It was thought that he borrowed it from Mack and Shibe. During the 1910 season, Mack would send six players under contract with the A's to play for the Orioles. For most of his time as owner of the independent Orioles, Dunn would give Mack first crack at his players when he was ready to sell them.[7]

The Cubs went to training camp first. The team gathered in Chicago on February 26 and left that evening for West Baden, Indiana, for a five day stay. The intention was to work out indoors there before heading to the main training camp site, New Orleans. Everybody from the 1909 team was signed for 1910 except Jimmy Sheckard, and all were on the train except six players: Harry Steinfeldt, Joe Tinker, Jimmy Archer, Floyd Kroh, Sheckard, and Heinie Zimmerman. Steinfeldt's and Tinker's absences were expected, and they had been given dates in March to report to the team. The others were not excused, but Chance and Murphy expected no problems with these players. The only question hanging over the Cubs' roster in 1910 was John Kling.

3. Spring Training 43

Kling had been the Cubs regular catcher from 1901 (when he beat out Chance) through 1908. Kling had asked President Murphy for a leave of absence for the 1909 season, which Murphy granted. It is still not clear if this was a holdout, as Kling made no attempt to return during the 1909 season. He spent the 1909 season running his billiard parlor in Kansas City and competing in billiards tournaments. He won tournaments in 1908 and 1909 and made noises that he would not continue his baseball career. However, in February 1910, Kling applied to the National Commission for reinstatement. As he had been under contract for 1909 at a salary of $4,500, the Cubs and the National Commission had to agree to Kling coming back under the same salary for 1910. The decision process on Kling's reinstatement started February 5, when he applied to the National Commission. The decision of the National Commission was not finalized for a couple of months. When asked, Chance and Murphy said they would welcome Kling if he was allowed to play, but that they were not counting on it.[8]

On March 3, the Cubs left West Baden for New Orleans. They had their first full outdoor workout in New Orleans on March 5. By this time all players were in camp except Steinfeldt and Tinker, who had permission to report later. The first injury of the camp occurred that first day, when right fielder Frank Schulte suffered a split finger when making his first catch of a fly ball. This kind of injury was common with the tiny gloves used by players in the field, not much bigger than a glove used for cold weather.[9] Schulte had one of the better nicknames in baseball, "Wildfire." This name came from his friendship with Lillian Russell, a leading actress of this era. During spring training a couple of years prior, both the Cubs and Russell found themselves in Vicksburg, Mississippi. Russell hosted the Cubs team for a dinner, after her show called "Wildfire" ended that evening. In honor of this event, Schulte named one of his horses "Wildfire." Remember, ownership of multiple horses by a well-off person was normal in the early 1900s, particularly someone like Schulte, who lived near his birthplace in rural upstate New York in the off-season. When his teammates learned of this, they started kidding him and nicknamed him "Wildfire," which stuck.[10] At this point of his career, Schulte was known as a steady outfielder and hitter with good power. He was one of the few players in this era who held the bat at the end and swung for power. His career average through 1909 was .269. He had driven in the go-ahead run in the decisive game of the 1908 pennant race, and had been a regular since 1905, first in left field and now in right field. Schulte was popular with his teammates and a close friend of one of the beat writers from the *Chicago Tribune*, Ring Lardner. They were close enough that if Chance wanted to tell Schulte something regarding off-the-field issues, he told Lardner, who would pass it on to Schulte. Lardner and Schulte were constant companions.[11] In many of Lardner's articles, there is a poem supposedly written by Schulte. Here is one example, from March 5, 1910:

> A good left fielder, bear in mind,
> He must be absolutely blind,
> For if he had two open eyes
> The sun would shine into those eyes
> And spoil his chance of catching flies.
> He must be crazy as a rat,
> I'll tell you why I say that:
> A good left fielder, friend, is Sheck,
>   [Jimmy Sheckard, the Cubs' regular left fielder]
> And heaven knows, his mind's a wreck.[12]

It is safe to say that Lardner was ghosting these poems for Schulte. Schulte had been a member of the outfield of Sheckard, Slagle and Schulte from 1906 to 1908. An interesting fact about this outfield, and about the ethnic makeup of baseball at this time, is that these three often communicated in German on the field.[13]

The A's arrived at their training camps on March 1, 1910. That word "camps" is correct. Rookies and prospects went with Connie Mack to Atlanta. Mack was confident enough in his regulars, most of whom were quite young, to send them to Hot Springs, Arkansas, with Harry Davis in charge. Mack did not prescribe any regimen for this crew, trusting them to get ready at their own pace and method. Under Davis' direction, the regulars, both position players and pitchers, never touched a baseball during their ten days in Hot Springs. They hiked, ran, and played golf.[14] One of the larger differences between the way teams were run in 1910 and how they are run today is the leeway allowed by the manager, both in training and during a game. Harry Davis had been with the A's since 1901, signing on May 21 of that year. Mack and Davis had been thrown together in 1896, when the owner of the Pittsburgh club acquired first baseman Davis in a trade without Mack's knowledge. Davis played for Mack for two months in Pittsburgh before Mack was fired as manager. Mack was impressed with Davis' smarts and professionalism. Davis played for four teams in the National League from 1896 to 1899. He quit the game in 1900, moving back to his

3. Spring Training

Frank "Wildfire" Schulte in 1910.

hometown of Philadelphia and working as an accountant for the Lehigh Valley Railroad. Mack admired Davis for his timely hitting and clean living and named him captain in 1905. Here is Davis' description of the duties of a captain:

Placing players in the field correctly according to the batter and the pitcher. The captain calls the player who is to take a fly ball. Must watch his pitcher closely to see when the time is ripe for a change, or when the twirler needs a moment or two to collect himself. He should create opportunities for the men to pull themselves together when they have become confused. He must be able to anticipate the wishes of the manager in order that valuable time not be lost and valuable points given to the opposition by his running to the bench to receive information. The captain must also watch the play of his opponents in the field in order to impart to his players any weakness he may discover or to the umpire any infringement of the rules by opposing players. The captain should be on the coaching lines as much as possible to give his player the benefit of his knowledge and observation.[15]

If this sounds mostly like what a manager does today, it is. Player-managers were still common in baseball, with four full-time players managing in 1910 (all in the National League), and four other managers who played more than once this season. Mack had been captain of his teams in Washington and Pittsburgh, and expected Davis to operate as he had. Davis was the oldest player on the team along with Topsy

Hartsel, both 36 in 1910. Mack knew Davis would be the leader and let him get on with it.

Mack worked with his rookies and prospects in Atlanta while the veterans were in Hot Springs. He gave his full attention to these youngsters, hoping to find a diamond in the rough. He was unsuccessful, finding no one who would help his team this year. The only one who went north with the team, first baseman Ben Houser, would hit .188 in 26 games. Eddie Collins contributed a couple of articles to the *Philadelphia Bulletin* in March, about staying in shape over the winter and training while in Hot Springs. The team united in Atlanta on March 12, and Mack took over. Mack sent the youngsters, a complete team called the Colts or Yannigans, on a long tour in the South and Midwest, playing games until April 13. He entrusted this group to Stuffy McInnis, who was only 19 himself. Mack was not afraid of giving responsibility to his players.[16]

The Cubs started playing exhibition games on March 6, beating the New Orleans Pelicans, 6–1. The only regular was Hofman, playing third base. The veterans were more interested in a bantamweight world championship fight in New Orleans that night.[17] The veteran pitchers threw for the first time on March 7. Big Jeff Pfeffer started on March 9, winning a complete game, 6–1. Pfeffer had come up with the Cubs in 1905, then spent 1906–1908 with Boston (NL) and 1909 in the minors. He was trying to get back in the majors. On March 9, President Murphy was visited in New Orleans by Fred Clarke, the player-manager of the Pirates. Clarke was trying to sell Murphy a tarpaulin to be used in rain delays in Chicago. The first tarpaulin had been used in Pittsburgh in 1908, and Clarke had an interest in the company that manufactured them. The weather gods must have been listening to their conversation, as the Cubs were rained out on March 10.[18] The Cubs played two more games against New Orleans, winning both. The only regulars who played were pitchers Ed Reulbach and Rube Kroh, and Jimmy Archer, the regular catcher in 1909. On March 13, Chance got into uniform for the first time this year. Ring Lardner reported, "Manager Chance came out in uniform and practiced around 1st base before the game. He is a likely looking 1st sacker and ought to win a regular place on the team if he doesn't drop dead."[19]

Still an effective player, Frank Chance in 1910 was as identified with the Cubs just as Connie Mack was with the A's. Chance had been with the Cubs since 1898, longer than Mack had been with the A's.

Both Chance and Mack subverted the normal stereotype of ballplayers in this time. Ballplayers were expected to be rude, crude, uneducated, and prone to drink. Many major leaguers fit this description, but neither Mack nor Chance did. Chance was born in 1876 in Fresno, California, son of a man who had come to California in a covered wagon and become a banker. By 1897, Chance had graduated from Washington College in Irvington, California, and was a licensed dentist. He was known there as a great athlete, played on the college baseball team, and was nicknamed "Husk." He was discovered by William Lange, a California native and the center fielder for the Chicago National League team from 1892–1899. Chance started with the Orphans in 1898 as a catcher, catching future Hall of Famer Clark Griffith in his first game. Chance was stubborn about wanting to be a catcher. Even though he was not a regular until 1902, he filled in by playing catcher, outfield, and occasionally first base. Frank Selee wanted Chance to move to first base full-time in 1902, but Chance played just 39 games there that year. Chance finally capitulated in 1903, playing 121 games at first, and immediately becoming the best first baseman in the National League. Chance was a great player from 1903 to 1906, averaging .318 with 51 stolen bases, 66 walks, and fine numbers in other offensive categories. He was an excellent defensive first baseman whose one weakness is shown by another number.[20] The average number of games he played in these four years was 125, in an era when regular players were expected to play all games when healthy. Of course injuries occurred, but Chance seemed to invite injury. This was noted by Christy Mathewson in *Pitching in a Pinch*: "Chance is the sort of athlete who is likely to get injured.... If he has to choose between accepting a pair of spikes in a vital part of his anatomy and getting a put-out, or dodging the spikes and losing the put-out, he always takes the put-out."[21] He stood close to the plate as a right-handed hitter and often was hit by a pitch. This caused headaches, and he often could not play because of these pains. Chance was known as a very nice man off the field and a good businessman. But on the field and as manager, he was a fierce competitor. The sports world acknowledged his reputation with a nickname, "The Peerless Leader." He was often called the P. L. or the whole nickname in contemporary newspaper articles. Through 1909, his winning percentage was .688, by far the best of any active major league manager.

Chance had played a full season for him in 1908, 126 games, while leading the Cubs to victory in one of the great pennant races in major league history. But his performance had diminished, and that continued in 1909. Chance was able to play only 92 games in 1909, hitting .272 with 29 stolen bases.[22] He turned 33 in September 1909, and continued to have problems with injuries. One of the unspoken needs of the Cubs in this spring training was someone to fill in for Chance when the inevitable injuries occurred. Chance himself knew this and tried out several players at first base during spring training. The one who made the team was Fred Luderus. He was from Milwaukee and had been in the minors since 1906. The Cubs bought his contract before 1910 training camp, and Luderus beat out the competition to be the back-up first baseman.[23]

The A's veterans remained in Atlanta until March 27. They played intrasquad games and games against the Atlanta minor league team. Mack left the running of the team during games to Davis, only determining when to change pitchers. Baker hurt his knee and had to miss about a week of activity. Mack had determined the last two springs that Baker could show up and start hitting immediately, so he was not worried about him. During a March 26 game against Atlanta, Eddie Collins, a left-handed hitter, hit two long triples to right field. There was a sign on the right field wall that promised to lay 10,000 bricks for any player who hit this sign. The *Philadelphia Bulletin* reported that Collins was trying to hit this sign, as he had gotten engaged over the winter and was thinking about building a new home. Collins was showing good form, as well as contributing three articles in February and March to the *Bulletin* about various baseball topics. It is not clear if Collins wrote these articles himself or if they were ghosted. As Collins was one of Mack's college men, he could have written them himself. Mack had shown he preferred college men, but would keep anyone who had talent and enthusiasm for major league play.[24] Mack had acquired an 18-year-old outfielder from South Carolina in 1908. He let Joe Jackson stay with the Greenville, South Carolina, team until their season ended, then called him up. Jackson reported on August 17, 1908. He did not play that day, and that night went back to the railroad station and caught a train back to Greenville. This happened each time Jackson came north in 1908. He played in five games for the A's, batting .130. Jackson came to spring training in 1909 and performed well enough to make the team. However, he continued to make his homesickness known. Mack sent Jackson to Savannah, Georgia, for the 1909 season, calling him up at the end of the season again. Jackson hit .294 in five games. Mack brought Jackson to camp again in 1910. Jackson performed well on the field but did not get along with his teammates and did not show the enthusiasm for baseball Mack preferred. Jackson was still with the A's when they reached Baltimore on March 30, after playing against his old Greenville team on March 28.[25]

On March 14, the Cubs played their first game against major league competition as the Cleveland Naps came to New Orleans for five games. The Naps played some of their regulars, eventually starting their regular lineup on March 17–18. The Cubs used young pitchers trying to make the team, like King Cole and Eddie Stack. The only regular who played was Hofman, who got his first hit of the spring on March 17, in a game described in the *Tribune* as "too awful to describe." On March 16, two positive events occurred for the Cubs. Joe Tinker reported, stating that he was ready to go and that John Kling (whom he had seen in Kansas City) was proceeding with his reinstatement process and would report as soon as that was completed. Once Jimmy Sheckard signed his contract,[26] all members of the Cubs were under contract for 1910.

The National Commission would make the decision on Kling. The National Commission, the ruling body of baseball, consisted of three members: the President of the American League (Ban Johnson), the President of the National League (Thomas Lynch, in his first year) and August Herrmann, President of the Cincinnati Reds. This commission was a result of the peace settlement in 1903. The American League owners had been impressed enough with Herrmann's peacemaking efforts to agree to his appointment as head of the Commission. The status of Kling's reinstatement was a constant story during this spring. The Cubs played their last game in New Orleans against the Pelicans on March 20, the day Kling threatened the National Commission with a lawsuit, a threat the Commission shrugged off. The Cubs went on the road until Opening Day. Most of the regulars (except Evers and Steinfeldt) played in Mobile on March 22. Three players who would not make the team missed curfew the previous evening. Chance cut one and fined the other two.

The Cubs played in Alabama through March 25, in Montgomery and Birmingham. One regular who had not reported yet was Harry Steinfeldt. This was okay with Chance, as a dispute in a spring game in 1908 in Birmingham had resulted in a $3,000 judgment against

Steinfeldt. Chance had been tipped off that he would be served this judgment if he appeared in Birmingham. He took the regulars, except Hofman, to Memphis. Charley Williams, the traveling secretary, was also told that he would be served in Birmingham. Williams went to Birmingham with the club, settled the hotel bill on arrival for the entire stay, and left town for Memphis right away. The story on the March 24 game makes it clear that the Cubs were trying to get out of the state as soon as possible. On March 26, the 1909 lineup appeared in a game for the first time this spring, and Brown and Overall pitched.[27]

This day the Cubs acquired Ginger Beaumont as an extra outfielder. Clarence (known as "Ginger" due to his red hair) Beaumont had been signed to his first professional contract by Connie Mack in Milwaukee in 1898. Mack sold Beaumont to Pittsburgh later that year, and Beaumont was an excellent lead-off man in the majors from 1899 through 1907, averaging over .300 and 25 stolen bases each year as a center fielder. He was with the Pirates until 1907 and was the first batter ever in a World Series in 1903. During his last two years with Boston in the National League, he had shown a decline in skills, but

Ginger Beaumont in 1910, his last year.

3. Spring Training   51

Chance thought that Beaumont would be an improvement over the backup outfielders he had in 1909.[28]

The Cubs remained in Tennessee until March 30, playing in Memphis and Nashville. The Cubs won all these games, playing their regulars against the resident minor league teams. On March 28 in Nashville, the Cubs were told before they left for the game to walk through the hotel lobby in their socks. The reason for this was that the Yannigans from the A's had been in this same hotel a few days before and had walked through the lobby with their spikes on.[29] This is one example of how different things were in those days. When on the road, teams normally changed into their uniforms at their hotel and took a horse-drawn vehicle to the ballpark. This was changing in major league ballparks, which now required a visitors' locker room, but not in the minors. Another development on March 28 was the decision of the National Commission to reinstate Kling, subject to a $700 fine and Kling accepting his $4,500 salary already agreed to for 1909. The Cubs were banned from trading or selling Kling during the 1910 season. There would be further noise about this decision. The article in the *Chicago Tribune* showed an action picture of Kling in full catcher's gear. Anyone would notice some equipment missing. He never wore shin guards throughout his career.[30] Shin guards for catchers had been invented by Roger Bresnahan around 1906. The guards he used were similar to cricket pads and were a bit clunky. The other Cubs catchers had tried these pads during 1910 training camp and decided not to use them. So during the 1910 season, Cubs catchers would not use shin guards.

After some games around Baltimore, the A's returned to Philadelphia to play a pre-season series against the Phillies. The regulars played, and their regular pitchers pitched the entire five-game series. Mack left Davis to run the team, while Mack went off and traveled with the Yannigans for their last few games. Jackson was playing with the Yannigans, and Mack noticed he was still not getting along with his mates. Mack asked waivers on Jackson. Brooklyn claimed him, but withdrew their claim a week later. Mack was able to send Jackson to New Orleans with a right to get him back. After the Yannigans returned to Philadelphia, Mack selected his team. The regulars were set: Davis 1B, Collins 2B, Baker 3B, Barry SS, Hartsel LF, Oldring CF, Murphy RF, Thomas C. The substitute position players were: McInnis, Morrie Rath and Ben Houser, IF; Amos Strunk and Heinie Heitmuller, OF; Joe Lapp and

Paddy Livingston, C. The pitchers were Bender, Coombs, Dygert, Krause, Morgan and Plank. This 22-man roster was the largest had Mack carried up to this time. The Tigers were the three-time defending AL champs, but Mack stated before the season that he felt he had the team to win the pennant. Their quest would start in Washington on April 14.[31]

The Cubs continued to play against minor league teams until Opening Day. The first half of April took them to Louisville, Indianapolis, Dayton, Columbus and Toledo. The regulars did not lose a game, but they played only against minor leaguers. The Cubs split their team a couple of times, the subs playing different minor league teams. The Kling drama continued to play out. Kling paid the $700 fine to the National Commission but tried to hold out for more money than the $4,500 he had signed for in 1909. Kling made threats that he would become a professional billiards player or try to form a new barnstorming team. The Cubs ignored these goings-on and prepared to play the season without him. President Murphy made a deal on April 10, trading three prospects for veteran Brooklyn pitcher Harry McIntire. McIntire was a 32-year-old right-hander with a record of 46–98 from 1905 to 1909. The Cubs were pleased with this deal, as they thought McIntire was a good pitcher stuck on a bad team. Ed Reulbach had been diagnosed with diphtheria on April 9, catching it from his son. Chance selected his team after this trade. The regular position players were: Chance 1B, Evers 2B, Steinfeldt 3B, Tinker SS, Sheckard LF, Hofman CF, Schulte RF, Archer C. The substitutes were Zimmerman, Luderus and John Kane, IF; Beaumont, OF; and Tom Needham; C. The team expected Kling to join sometime soon, but had no definite date yet. The pitchers were: Brown, Cole, Kroh, McIntire, Overall, and Pfiester. Lew Richie would be added to the pitching roster in May. Reulbach was to join the team as soon as he recovered, not a sure thing with diphtheria in 1910. President Murphy wrote an article for the *Chicago Tribune* saying that he thought the Cubs had a good chance to regain the pennant in 1910. Their journey would start in Cincinnati on April 14.[32]

4

April–May

Baseball fans (also called bugs or cranks in newspaper articles of this time) always have a rooting interest in the pennant race. Another high-profile contest was initiated before the 1910 season. This was a prize for the highest overall batting average, one prize to cover all major leaguers. The prize was offered by the Chalmers Motor Company of Detroit. The automobile was the glamor technology of the day, still in the process of taking over from horse-powered transportation. Most car companies in 1910 were making expensive cars, like the Chalmers car offered that retailed for $1,500. The future of car-making had already made its appearance on October 1, 1908, when the first Model T rolled off the assembly line at Ford in Detroit. Some ballplayers owned cars, but they were a minority. Automobiles were still considered a luxury in 1910.[1] One player who figured to be in the hunt for this prize was in the automobile business in 1909. Ty Cobb was the authorized dealer for Hupmobile in Augusta, Georgia. Cobb had not shown up at the Tigers' 1910 training camp in San Antonio. His excuse was that he needed to sell four more automobiles. He finally sold these cars, then sold his dealership and reported to the Tigers on April 9 in Evansville, Indiana. Cobb expressed his interest in winning the Chalmers car, but said owning an automobile dealership was not for a ballplayer.[2] He did not lose interest in the automobile business, however. It was thought he made his first purchase of United Motors (which became General Motors) stock around this time. Looking at the last three years, the two best hitters in baseball would be the favorites for this award. In 1909, Cobb had the best batting average by 30 points (over Eddie Collins). In 1908, Honus Wagner had the highest average. And in 1907, Wagner and Cobb tied for the highest average. A close race for the batting crown would add extra interest in baseball, so the National Commission approved this prize on March 25, 1910.[3]

The 1910 season started on April 14. The A's opened in Washington, where a tradition started when the umpire gave the game ball to President William Howard Taft before the game, and Taft threw it to Walter Johnson, the starting pitcher. This was the first of 14 consecutive Washington openers for Johnson, who shut out the A's on one hit. That hit was a fly ball by Baker into the crowd on the field, a ground rule double under the rules used when fans were allowed to stand in the deep outfield. Johnson sent the game ball to the White House, asking for a signature, which Taft supplied.[4] The A's lost two out of three games in Washington, but that was the end of their bad news for April. They won their home opener against the New York Highlanders, Bender getting his second win and complete game before a crowd of 15,000. Their next game featured two pitchers who threw altered deliveries: Cy Morgan of the A's and Russell Ford of the Highlanders. Ford won, the Highlanders getting one run off the spitballs of Morgan. The A's got no runs off Ford and were not sure what his out pitch was. (It would be two years before his secret—scuffing the ball—was revealed.) The league would see a lot of that mystery pitch this year. These two games against the Highlanders were the only home games for the A's in April, due to rain. The A's took three games in Boston, with one rainout. Krause pitched a shutout on April 22.

More rain problems waited for them in New York. After a rainout on the 26th, the A's were up 4–0 in the top of the fifth on April 27 when rain washed out the rest of the game. There were no suspensions of play back then, and the entire game had to be replayed, with the statistics not counting. The A's were scheduled for four games in New York over five days and could only get two games in. Ford beat the A's again on April 28, and the A's won on the 30th.[5] Why no game on April 29? Because it was a Sunday. There was no Sunday baseball in most major league cities in 1910: Boston, Brooklyn, Cleveland, New York, Philadelphia, Pittsburgh, and Washington. This was due to "blue laws," Puritan leftovers banning certain activities on Sunday. Sunday ball was allowed in Chicago, Cincinnati, Detroit, and St. Louis.[6] So the A's finished April with a record of 6–4 before returning to Philadelphia for a long home stand.

The Cubs started their season in Cincinnati, the hometown of President Taft and residence of their silent partner owner, Charles Taft.

4. April–May

The Reds' home stadium had not yet been upgraded to a concrete and steel facility, so some of the crowd of 21,221 had to stand in the outfield behind ropes. The ground rule in Cincinnati called a ball hit into this crowd a triple. The Cubs had two of those, hit by Schulte, but scored no runs. The Reds scored one run in the ninth inning for the win. Both starting pitchers pitched complete games, with a time of game of 1:50. According to the *Tribune* account, three bad calls by the umpires hurt the Cubs. The article noted there were two umpires, per a new rule this year[7] in both leagues. It is humanly impossible for one umpire to see everything going on in a baseball game, so players took advantage whenever they could. It was hoped that having two umpires would help clean up the game. The Cubs started the season by splitting four games in Cincinnati. The third game of the series was played thanks to a tarpaulin sold to the Reds by Pittsburgh manager Fred Clarke. To help the pitcher grip the ball on a wet day, there was a pile of sawdust on the back of the mound, as this was before rosin bags.[8] The next stop was St. Louis for two games. The first was snowed out, the Cubs winning the only game played there.

The Cubs' home opener was on April 21 against Cincinnati. The Cubs had an old-style ballpark, not the new concrete and steel kind. West Side Grounds had been the Cubs' home since 1893. The ballpark had double-decked wooden bleachers seating about 16,000, and a vast outfield. If the crowd was large enough, fans stood in the outfield behind ropes. The Cubs won, with Brown pitching and Needham catching.[9] It was reported that Kling was going to perform in vaudeville to earn his $700 fine, then report to the Cubs around May 2. Chance continued to say he would welcome Kling if he settled his dispute with the National Commission, but meanwhile the Cubs could win with the catchers they had.[10] The rest of the Reds series was rained out. The Cubs played four more games in April, ending the month with a record of 6–4. The April 30 game was in Pittsburgh, starting a nine-day stretch of games against the Pirates, in both cities. After the April 30 games showed that status was quo in the National League. The Giants were in first, the Pirates a half-game behind, and the Cubs two games behind the Giants.[11]

Remember that in 1910, fans not attending the game had one way to learn the result—newspapers. There was no radio or television. During tight pennant race games, or World Series games, there could be a re-creation of the ongoing game on a large board. This could be done with telegraph or telephone lines to a bar or auditorium, and then the results of an at-bat and inning would be put on a background of a baseball diamond.[12] But fans learned about their teams mainly from newspapers. There were weekly magazines such as *The Sporting News* and *Sporting Life* for more information, but the daily newspaper was the quickest technology of the day. As is still true, the quality and presentation of the information was dependent on the reporter covering the team. Newspapers did not pay very well, but they could boost the reporter's ego by giving him a byline. The *Philadelphia Bulletin* did not give bylines in the sports page in 1910. The *Chicago Tribune* did. In 1910, the *Tribune* followed the same procedure it followed until a few years ago. The reporters covering each Chicago team switched teams mid-season. When I was growing up, this meant the All-Star break. In 1910, this meant July 4. Hence the reporter covering the second half of the Cubs' season in 1910 was I. E. Sanborn, whose nickname was either Izzy or Sy. Sanborn covered the games competently but was a step down from the writer who covered the Cubs before July 4 and later wrote special stories just before and during the World Series. This journalist became one of the more famous writer-journalists in America in the 1920s. However, in 1910, R. W. (Ringgold Wilmer) Lardner was a 25-year-old sportswriter, in his third year of covering major league baseball.[13]

Ring Lardner was born in Niles, Michigan, in 1885. He grew up as the youngest of six children in a wealthy family. He was schooled at home until age 13 and was not allowed out of the family compound unless in the company of an adult. He went to Niles High School, and that was the end of his formal education. During his time in high school, his father lost most of the family fortune. By the time Ring finished high school, it was clear he would have to earn a living. His father sent Ring to the Armour Institute of Technology in Chicago for one term, which established that Ring had no future in the technical vocations. He returned to Niles and worked for the local gas company until he was hired as a sports reporter by the *South Bend Times* in January 1906. He was at the *Times* until November 1907. He served his apprenticeship by covering all local sports in South Bend, including the South Bend team in the Central League, Class B minor league baseball, and Notre Dame football in their pre–Knute Rockne days. While on vacation during the 1907 World Series, he visited the press box at West Side Park. He was hired by the *Chicago Inter-Ocean* to start in

November 1907. In July 1907, Ring had met Ellis Abbott, a 20-year-old junior at Smith College, at a party in Niles. He decided that Ellis was the woman he wanted to marry and pursued her throughout the summer. Ellis was from Goshen, Indiana, and was a member of the same social class as Lardner, small-town elite. They carried on their long-distance courtship over the next four years.

Lardner started out with the *Chicago Inter-Ocean* as a general assignment sports reporter, covering anything and everything his first winter in Chicago. On February 1, 1908, he was hired by the *Chicago Examiner*, the Hearst morning paper. His salary was $25 a week, a $6.50 raise over the *Inter-Ocean*. He would cover any sports event assigned outside the baseball season, but he was the reporter (identified as James Clarkson, an existing byline) covering the White Sox when spring training started. Lardner was on the White Sox beat all of 1908, which was a great year to break into the majors as a writer. The 1908 pennant race was as exciting in the American League as in the National that year. The White Sox finished third, 1½ games out, and were in the race until the last day. Lardner's work was good enough for him to be hired away from the *Examiner* by the *Chicago Tribune* right after the 1908 season concluded. He was now a sportswriter on the leading morning newspaper in Chicago, with weekly pay of $35. During the next two baseball seasons, he covered both Chicago teams, alternating with Sanborn. During the off-seasons, he covered whatever the editors assigned him. At the age of 23, with only three years of experience under his belt, Lardner was a leading sportswriter in the second biggest city in the U.S.[14]

By the 1910 season, Lardner was established with both Chicago baseball teams as a baseball writer. In those days, the teams paid the traveling expenses of the reporters covering the team. The newspaper was liable for telegraph expenses and the writer's salary. Hence, most writers were members of the "gee whiz" school of sports writing, staying on the good side of the teams that were paying their expenses on the road.[15] Athletes were portrayed as larger than life, and very few warts were exposed. The results of this kind of writing can be seen from an anecdote about the White Sox. After the 1906 World Series, the champion White Sox went on a tour of Wisconsin, playing exhibition games in late October. When they got off a train in a small Wisconsin town, there was a small crowd to greet them. One small boy looked at the players, turned to his parents and said, "Why, they are only men, aren't they!"[16] Lardner was one of the first writers to stress the humanity of ballplayers. He was often called the founder of the "aw nuts" school of sports writing, but this would come later in his career. In 1910, Lardner was in a great position to observe the full spectrum of this world. He loved baseball throughout his youth, played the game in Niles, and at this point thought he had one of the great jobs in the world. He was 25, in the same age range as the players. He was knowledgeable about the game and could judge good and poor play. He was going through the same things the players were going through at the same age: traveling, working, getting along in the world. And Lardner had the greatest gift any reporter or observational writer could have; he was a good listener, even though not much of a talker when sober. Lardner liked to drink, no bad thing when traveling with a ball club in this era. However, when sober, he was very hard-working and reticent.[17] Another thing he was going through at the same time as some of the players he covered was wooing and winning a wife. He and Ellis were still conducting a long-distance courtship mostly by letter, which would end in formal engagement in November 1910, and marriage in June 1911, which lasted until his death in 1933. Many members of the Cubs would also wait for letters at the various hotels on the road. Lardner detailed this to Ellis in a letter written in 1910:

> Speaking of letters, I have a new job. I don't know what to call it. It consists of standing perfectly still and listening while one or the other of two ball players reads me his latest letter from his girls—from one of his girls, rather. It seems these two—who are Mordecai Brown and Frank Schulte—must confide in some one. The only reason I know of that I am the victim is that they can trust me to keep still. We all came into the hotel together tonight and there was mail for everybody. I took my letter from you and started for my room when Mr. Brown stopped me. He said he wanted to talk to me awhile and I told him I had a letter to read. He said: "You read yours and I'll read mine and then we'll swap." I didn't want to make it look like a one-sided deal, so I told him mine was from my sister and wouldn't interest him. So I had to read his and, as soon as I was through, Schulte gave me a sign that he wanted to see me and there was another one to read. And all the time they were detaining me, I wanted to get away and read your letter again.[18]

Some of the married players had other things on their mind:

> You ought to hear the athletes discuss the relative merits of their babies. There was an argument in my room last night that was the funniest I ever heard. Mr. Hofman's Mary Jane has two teeth and two others are just breaking through. She weighs twenty-five pounds. Mr. Reulbach's Edward has four whole teeth and weights twenty-six pounds. But Mary Jane can pound her fist on the arms of a

chair and laugh at the noise. Yes, but Edward is a boy. Whereupon I told them my four month old nephew—there isn't any such—could dive from a tower ninety feet high into a dishpan full of salt water without making a splash. I wanted to get them out of my room so I could go to sleep. One of them left a five o'clock call for my room by way of revenge. Whenever they start their debates in Schulte's presence, he quiets them by saying, "Wait till you hear what my dog can do."[19]

Anyone who has read Lardner's short stories about baseball can see where he got the raw material. As Davy Jones said in *The Glory of Their Times*, "We had stupid guys, smart guys, tough guys, mild guys, crazy guys, college men, slickers from the city, and hicks from the country. And back then a country kid was likely to really be a country kid."[20] Lardner met them all on the Cubs and White Sox from 1908–1910. It is likely that anyone traveling with a baseball team since the founding of the game could have come up with the same raw material. And while Lardner would not go too far in the direction of debunking the players and the game, he would start the tearing down some of the myths. Players in Lardner's stories come through as human beings, warts and all.

The A's took control of the American League race in May. Because of the geographic split in the league, four American League teams were considered eastern (Boston, New York, Philadelphia and Washington) and four western (Chicago, Cleveland, Detroit and St. Louis). It was common for teams to make long eastern and western road swings, and also to be home for long stretches while other teams traveled. The A's had played only eastern teams in April, and all but two games had been on the road. This was more than balanced off in May. The A's were home from May 2–27, playing everyone except the New York Highlanders. The A's took advantage of this home stand, starting it off with a 12-game win streak against Boston, Washington, Cleveland and Chicago. They got this streak off to a rousing start on May 2 against Boston. Plank pitched a complete game, but was down 6–2 in the middle of the ninth. Against a good pitcher, Eddie Cicotte, the A's rallied. The first two batters reached and Eddie Collins performed his good luck ritual, throwing all the bats into a random order just outside the dugout, as there was no bat rack in those days. This led to: Barry's single, Lapp's RBI single, a Hartsel strikeout, and Oldring's two-run single. Oldring took second on throw home, Smokey Joe Wood came in to pitch, and Collins hit a game-winning two-run single.[21]

Quite a win, and the A's followed up. In wins on May 3, 5, 6, 7, and 9, each pitcher threw a complete game. In order: Krause, Morgan, Krause, Bender, Plank. Connie Mack did not believe in a regular rotation. He would rather match pitchers up against teams he thought the pitcher could succeed against. On May 10, the 12–4 A's faced the 12–6 Cleveland Naps, Cy Morgan versus Addie Joss. The A's scored on a Joss error in the bottom of the eighth inning. The Naps tied it in the ninth after Mack ordered an intentional walk to Lajoie with a runner on second. The next hitter, first baseman George Stovall, doubled in the tying run. Neither pitcher gave up any more runs, and darkness stopped the game after 13 innings as a 1–1 tie. This was the only game the A's did not win from May 2–18. The weekday games in Philadelphia started at 4 pm, to allow fans to come to games right after work and before dinner.[22] There were no lights and no daylight savings time. Hence, in early season weekday games, the games had to move along quickly. One of the current arguments against speeding up play in baseball is that there is no clock in baseball. However, that was not true in 1910. As Bill James states in his *Historical Baseball Abstract*:

> Baseball's poetic and lyrical celebrants are fond of pointing out that baseball is the only major team sport without a clock. What these people don't understand is that until around 1945, baseball did have a clock. It was called the sun. Baseball games, until the advent of night ball, had to be crisply played because they often didn't start until late afternoon, and they had to be finished by sundown, and sundown then was an hour sooner than it is now. Umpires, until World War II, were very much in the habit of enforcing a certain degree of attention to time.[23]

When the Tigers ended the A's winning streak on May 19, they did it in emphatic fashion, winning 14–2. As this was the first meeting between the two top teams from 1909, this was an important series. It ended evenly, the teams splitting four games from May 19 to 23. The A's ended the home stand sweeping four games from the St. Louis Browns. Their record after the May 27 home game was 23–7. They went to Boston for five games in four days, winning three. Their record at the end of May was 26–9, and they were ahead of the second-place New York Highlanders (23–10) by two games.[24]

One of the key pitchers during this streak was Cy Morgan, who threw complete games on May 5, 10, 13, 18, 26, and 31, winning four and losing one with one tie. He was also knocked out in the fifth inning on May 24, the hottest day of the year so far. Morgan was off to a good start, backing up his 16–11 record and 1.65 ERA with the A's in 1909. Morgan, whose given name was Harry Richard, started in the minors at the age of 23 in 1901. He had trials with the St. Louis Browns in parts of the 1903, 1904, 1905, and 1907 seasons, never quite making the team there. He was traded to the Red Sox in 1907, sticking the rest of the year and 6–6 there after starting 2–5 in St. Louis. Morgan had a decent year in 1908, ending up 14–13 on a sub–.500 team in Boston. He started the 1909 season with a 2–6 record, but both of his wins were against the A's. Mack figured it would be better to have Morgan than have Morgan beating him. On June 5, 1909, the A's acquired Morgan from Boston for pitcher Biff Schlitzer and $3,500. Morgan was known as a good curveball pitcher who would often experience control problems. He was working on a spitball to increase his effectiveness. By 1910, the spitball was a good pitch for Morgan. He was known as a bad fielder in Boston, often watching from the mound on ground balls hit to the right side. He liked to sing and dance and drink, eventually going on the vaudeville stage in 1911. During his four-year run with the A's from 1909–1912, Morgan was a reliable pitcher for Mack.[25]

On May 1, the Cubs were in the midst of an unusual series with the champion Pirates. The Cubs had played St. Louis in Chicago on April 29, then played Pittsburgh in Pittsburgh on the 30th. May 1 was a Sunday, and there was no Sunday ball in Pittsburgh. So the teams traveled back to Chicago, played one game on Sunday (won by the Cubs, 2–1, in an hour and 20 minutes), and returned to Pittsburgh for three more games. President Taft attended the May 2 game, won by the Pirates 5–2 in one hour 26 minutes. After two more games, the teams both returned to Chicago for a three-game series. One game was rained out, and the teams split the other two. So the Cubs and Pirates played seven consecutive games against each other (the Pirates winning five), involving four trips between Chicago and Pittsburgh. This was the low point in the Cubs' record this year. They were 8–8, in fourth place, four games behind the Giants. The Giants came to Chicago, and the Cubs won three of four games. Jack Pfiester, known as the "Giant Killer," pitched a three-hit shutout against the Giants on May 9. The next day's game was described by Lardner as "so awful it was good." Chance was sick, so Evers managed the game. McGraw and one of his players were ejected, Mathewson started but was pinch-hit for in the sixth inning, and the Cubs scored five runs against the reliever to win, 9–5. On May 11, Kroh pitched a complete game, beating the Giants, 4–3. Kling started this game, his second of the season. Prior to this, the catching had been done by Jimmy Archer and Tom

Needham. The Cubs had another catcher, Pat Moran, on the roster until May 11, when he was sold to the Phillies. The Cubs had not yet used what they hoped would be their regular lineup, as Sheckard, Chance, and Tinker had been hurt. In the last game of the Giants series, a new rule came into play, to the detriment of the Cubs. Chance was still out, but sat in the stands for the game. Before the game, acting manager Evers turned in a starting lineup with McIntire as starting pitcher. Between the time of turning this lineup in and the start of the game, Chance told Evers to change starting pitchers. Brown warmed up and wanted to start the game. McGraw complained to the umpires, who ruled that McIntire must pitch to one batter. This was due to a new rule taking effect for the 1910 season. McIntire started the game, which the Giants won 9–1. After this stretch of games against their main rivals, the Cubs were third behind the Pirates and Giants.[26]

Now came a two-week period when the Cubs played lesser teams (Boston, Brooklyn and Philadelphia) at home. They made hay, losing on May 13 and 14 to Boston before running off an 11-game winning streak. There were some rainouts, and the Cubs played makeup games on May 28–29 against Pittsburgh and a doubleheader on May 30 against St. Louis. It shows how the business of baseball worked back then that on May 27, in the midst of this home stand, the Cubs played an exhibition game in Macomb, Illinois. Reulbach started that game, his first start since his illness. Three other regulars played in that game. The Cubs were still not at full strength. Fred Luderus had played more games than Chance at first base. Reulbach had not started an official game. Brown had spent a good amount of time away from the team due to his father's illness and death. Then on May 19, Evers was involved in an automobile accident. Evers was driving on Van Buren Street, near the ballpark, when his car was hit by a trolley car. A passenger in Evers' car, Charles McDonald, was killed. An inquest was held on May 21, attended by Evers, who was accompanied by Steinfeldt and club secretary Williams. Evers expressed his remorse to McDonald's father and stated he would stop automobiling. Evers sat out the rest of this month, playing next on June 1. Even with these problems, the Cubs played well in May. They took over first place on May 26, swept two games from the Pirates, and split a doubleheader with the Cardinals on May 30, stopping the win streak. The Cubs were in first place by a game over the Giants, heading east for their first long road trip of the year.[27]

This was accomplished even with all the injuries and problems the Cubs had experienced so far this year. It is a testimony to the total team built by Selee, then Chance and Murphy. A couple of the youngsters had performed well so far. Leonard Leslie "King" Cole was drafted by the Cubs in the fall of 1909. He came to spring training in 1910 as a 23-year-old with a small shot at making the team. He impressed Chance with his stuff on the mound and his inability off the field. Lardner made several references to Cole's lack of mental acuity. One specific action Chance took was to ban Cole from team poker games, as he lost most of his meal money to his teammates. Cole was known to sleepwalk on Pullman cars, a dangerous activity.[28] Cole pitched his first game in Cincinnati the third game of the year, winning 10–5. He pitched and won again on April 28. His next game was on May 8, mostly due to several rainouts. He started and left in the eighth inning with a lead, but the Cubs lost. Cole went to his hometown of Bay City, Michigan, the next day to get married. He pitched three more times in May, winning each time. Cole's record of 5–0 established him as a regular option when Chance was selecting pitchers.

Another young player who made a big impact for the Cubs in 1910 was Henry "Heinie" Zimmerman. Zimmerman was from the Bronx and quit school at age 15, first becoming a caddy at a local golf course, then apprenticing to a plumber. His forte was baseball, and he signed a minor league contract at age 18 in 1906. The Cubs called him up at the end of 1907, and he was on the team for all of 1908 and 1909.[29] Zimmerman was another player who impressed with his lack of brains. In 1908, Zimmerman and Sheckard got into one of those silly disputes that happen when people are together over the course of a long season. Zimmerman charged Sheckard, Sheckard threw something, Zimmerman picked up the first thing he could reach and threw it at Sheckard. Zimmerman had picked up a bottle of ammonia, which shattered on Sheckard's forehead, with the ammonia running into Sheckard's eyes. Sheckard's sight was saved by the fact that this dispute took place in West Side Park, across the street from Cook County Hospital. But Sheckard missed the next 39 games and had a poor year. Zimmerman also ended up in the hospital, because Chance and the other Cubs beat the crap out of him.[30] Even with these problems, Zimmerman's talent at baseball led the Cubs to keep him. Zimmerman played 48 games in 1908 and 65 games in 1909, playing second base, third base, shortstop and the outfield. So far in 1910, he had played second base when Evers was out, and shortstop when Tinker was injured. His pinch-hitting

Heinie Zimmerman, 1910. Note fielder's glove in his back pocket.

average as of the end of May was .500 (3-for-6). On May 11, Zimmerman had four hits and four errors in one game. Zimmerman, whatever his mental deficiencies, was the main utility man on a team where most of the regulars were veterans who had played a lot of games in the last five years and were subject to injuries. Zimmerman would play an important part in the Cubs' story this year.

One excuse for problems was gone by the end of May. On May 18, Jimmy Sheckard and Artie Hofman claimed that "the comet" gave them problems trying to catch fly balls.[31] In April, the *Philadelphia Bulletin* published a cartoon showing a leaping catch by a Phillie as an imitation of a comet. And on May 19, when the A's were beaten by the Tigers, 14–2, the *Bulletin* headline read, "Athletics Struck by Detroit Comet."[32] Fortunately for all concerned, Halley's Comet's passage by Earth was completed by the end of May. Maybe that was why there were so many rainouts in April and May, but now the baseball season could go on full steam ahead.

5

June

Both the A's and Cubs ended May in first place. Both had been helped by a long home stand taking up most of May. Both teams would be tested by making a long road trip around the rest of the league. The A's, one of the eastern teams, continued a road trip started in Boston on May 28 and went to Detroit, Cleveland, St. Louis, Chicago, and New York before getting home on June 25. The Cubs spent May 31 traveling to Boston, their first visit to the East Coast this year. Their trip took them from Boston to Philadelphia, New York, Brooklyn and Cincinnati for a make-up game before returning to Chicago on June 20.

On their trip to Boston, Johnny Evers stopped off at his home in Troy, New York, which was on the train route. He joined the team in Boston and was back in the lineup on June 1. Overall pitched 8⅔ innings before a sore arm forced him out. Richie finished a 5–1 victory over the Boston Doves, which had been bought in 1906 by George and John Dovey, and had been renamed after their owners. Soon after this series, John Dovey, the surviving brother, sold the team for $100,000 to William Russell. After the sale, the team was renamed the Rustlers. Russell was one of the most successful owners in baseball history based on short-term return on investment. He held the team until after the 1911 season, selling it for $175,000.[1] Whatever they were called, the Boston NL team was in the midst of four straight last-place finishes (1909–1912). The Cubs took three of four games, losing the last game, 1–0, in 12 innings. Both pitchers (Brown and Al Mattern) threw complete games, and the time of game was two hours, ten minutes.

As the next day was Sunday, the Cubs played an exhibition game en route from Boston to New York. Reulbach, still regaining his strength, pitched. Four regulars (Evers, Schulte, Hofman and Tinker) played. Chance finally returned to the lineup in the second game in

Philadelphia. The Cubs still did not have their regular lineup, with Evers suspended for three games. The Cubs were shut out, 1–0, by a pitcher they had traded to the Phillies earlier in the year, Eddie Stack. In the eighth inning, the Cubs lost two runners on the bases. Chance was very upset with the baserunners, Beaumont and Zimmerman. The Cubs came back to win the last two games in Philly, splitting the series. In the final game, the umpire announced before the 3 pm start that the Cubs had to catch a train at 6 pm. Fortunately, the game took only two hours ten minutes, even though the Cubs used two relief pitchers (Richie and Brown), and the Cubs caught their train to New York.[2]

Even though the Pirates were the defending World Champions and had been close in the epic 1908 pennant race, the Giants were the Cubs' biggest rival at this point. The June series started with the teams in a virtual tie, the Cubs 27–15 and the Giants 28–16. It was scheduled for four games with Sunday off in the middle. The Cubs were supposed to go to Bridgeport, Connecticut, to play an exhibition game on that Sunday, but it was cancelled. The series started on June 10 with a game that looked in the bank for the Giants after seven innings. Pfiester had started for the Cubs, but was knocked out in the third inning after giving up five runs. Richie relieved for the second day in a row, holding the Giants scoreless through the seventh. He was pinch-hit for in the eighth. With the aid of an error by Merkle, the Cubs loaded the bases against Mathewson with two out. Chance drove a single to right which went through the legs of right fielder Murray, scoring all four Cubs. This gave the Cubs a 6–5 lead, and for some reason McGraw did not go to the third base coaching box in the eighth and ninth, even though he had been there the first seven innings. Brown came in for the second day in a row to save the game, retiring the Giants in order the last two innings.[3]

The momentum from this game continued through the rest of the series, despite two days off due to a rainout and Sunday. Brown pitched a complete game on June 13, winning because the Giants allowed five unearned runs. On the 14th, Richie came in after four innings, finishing a 9–4 win where all the Cubs' runs were scored after the sixth inning. This concluded a four-game stretch where Richie won three games in relief, Brown saved two, and the other game was a complete game victory by Brown. In the evening of June 14, Kling played in a billiard tournament in New York, winning his match. The Cubs had a three-game series scheduled in Brooklyn next. The middle game was rained out on a field with no tarpaulin. The two games played went to extra innings, the teams splitting them. On June 15, both Cole and Cy Barger threw 14-inning complete games in a two-hour 40-minute game. Barger singled in the winning run in the 14th and went 4-for-6 at bat. Brown won the second game of the series in relief after Pfiester pitched ten shutout innings. The Cubs won on a wild pitch by Nap Rucker in the 13th inning of a two-hour, 20-minute game. The road trip concluded with a make-up game in Cincinnati on June 19. The Cubs won, 10–3, in a two-hour, 32-minute regulation length game. Lardner said in his article that the Cubs "could have scored a million times if the P. L. had stayed wide awake." He noted the unusual fact that the Reds used 16 players in this game.[4] Brown pitched a complete game on a very hot day. On this road trip, Brown showed his Hall of Fame credentials by winning four games and saving two others. The two games he lost were 1–0 complete games. Overall was out with a sore arm, and Reulbach was just getting back into good form, so other pitchers were stepping up. Richie, Cole, Kroh and McIntire won games on this trip. When the Cubs started their next home stand (with the Reds, after traveling on the same train to Chicago), the Cubs had a 3½-game lead over the Giants.[5]

 The A's continued their road trip, traveling from Boston to Detroit on June 1, to be greeted by a rainout on June 2. The *Philadelphia Bulletin* listed all the pitchers and batters in the American League on June 3. The batters were listed in order of batting average. Among the regulars, Lajoie was batting .406 and Cobb .373. They were well ahead of everyone else in the race for the Chalmers automobile. The pitchers were listed in order of winning percentage, as earned run average was not yet an official statistic. The leading pitcher in the league was Russell Ford of the second-place Highlanders. The A's had six of the top 21 pitchers in this list.[6] One, Eddie Plank, started off the series in Detroit with a complete game but lost, 6–1. The Tigers swept three games from the A's, who lost the first game in Cleveland for a season-high four-game losing streak. One of the Naps' runs scored when Lajoie grounded out with a runner on second on a close play and got into an argument with the umpire. Harry Davis listened to the argument and ignored the runner, who scored. The A's won the next game in Cleveland, 13–1, with Bender throwing a complete game. The final game in Cleveland had a time limit due to the A's train for St. Louis. The teams completed nine innings but were tied, 4–4, after both scored in the eighth inning.

Coombs threw a complete game with no decision. On this day, Mack acquired Pat Donohue to help a catching corps ravaged by injuries. The A's were one game behind the Highlanders. They won three of four games in St. Louis, with Bender and Coombs getting complete-game victories. The western part of this trip ended in Chicago, where the first game went 14 innings. Plank started, faced two men and left per Mack's plan. Morgan pitched the rest of the game, opposing Ed Walsh. Walsh had a walk-off hit in the 14th inning for a 4–3 win, which probably pleased umpire Bill Dinneen. Dinneen made a decision in the top of the 14th that displeased the White Sox fans, who showered him with glass soda and beer bottles, an occupational hazard for umpires in these times. Russell Ford won his eighth straight decision for the Highlanders, putting them back in first ahead of the A's by percentage points. The four games in Chicago were split. The A's headed to New York for a six-game series with the Highlanders in a virtual tie, one-half game behind Detroit. The A's were 31–17, and the Highlanders were 30–16.[7]

This series ended the A's long road trip, six games in four days starting with two doubleheaders. The A's swept those first four games. Morgan, Plank, Coombs, and Bender threw complete games, and the A's outscored the Highlanders, 31–7. Russell Ford lost his first game of the year in the opening game. Ford must have had some trouble with his glove, the key to his success this year. Stories about baseball during this time stress that the ball was different from the new, white, lively ball in use today. According to Fred Snodgrass of the Giants in *The Glory of Their Times*:

> We hardly ever saw a new baseball, a clean one. If the ball went into the stands and the ushers couldn't get it back from the spectators, only then would the umpire throw out a new one. He'd throw the ball out to the pitcher, who would promptly sidestep it. It would go around the infield once or twice and come back to the pitcher as black as the ace of spades. All the infielders were chewing tobacco or licorice, and spitting into their gloves, and they'd give the ball a good going over before it ever got to the pitcher. Believe me, that dark ball was hard to see coming out of the shadows of the stands.[8]

Ford figured out a way to gain even more of an advantage. While in the minors, working through a sore arm in 1909, he slipped a piece of emery board into a finger of his glove and wore a small hole into that finger where the emery board showed through. He showed this only to his catcher and told the catcher he would scuff the ball with the emery. Ford and his usual catcher, Fred Mitchell, kept this secret the entire 1910 season. His emery ball was the key to his outstanding 26–6 season, which kept the Highlanders in contention.[9] The Highlanders came back to win the last two games of the series, and the A's returned home with a 12–12 record on this trip, in first place by one game.[10]

During the Deadball Era, pitching was paramount. Connie Mack was one of the biggest believers in this "small-ball" style of play. However, he was not a puppet master as manager. As shown by Harry Davis in his listing of the duties of a captain, leadership during the game was supplied by the players, while Mack kept score and made notes on the scorecard. One of his enduring and famous mannerisms was shifting players' (particularly outfielders) position in the field by waving his scorecard. This was an infrequent event. His continual effect on the players was achieved in two ways. The first was an innovation by the players that he adopted. In 1909 spring training, the regulars and youngsters played against each other in separate units. The youngsters, called the Yannigans, were led by Sam Erwin, a 75-year-old liquor distributor and friend of Mack. Erwin was mainly a chaperone, not expected to manage the team on the field where they were on their own, but guiding the youngsters to get through training camp. Erwin noted that the players were constantly talking about new plays to try. He suggested they hold evening meetings to go over the prior day's game and come up with new strategies. The youngsters, led by Collins and Barry, embraced this idea. After two weeks under Erwin, Mack left the veterans to be led by Harry Davis on their barnstorming trip north, and joined the Yannigans for their trip north. He let the evening meetings continue and saw the results on the field. By the end of this two-week trip, Mack agreed with the judgment of Ira Thomas, the veteran catcher playing with the Yannigans. Thomas said they were "the brightest bunch of ballplayers I've ever been around."[11] On Opening Day 1909, Mack called a team meeting before the game, complimented the young players on their ideas, and said there would be a meeting before each game to go over the upcoming game. This was the introduction of the daily meeting to baseball.[12] The other meeting he had was with the battery before each game. He would go over the opposing lineup and make recommendations on how to pitch each hitter, and how to play the hitter in the field. In both of these procedures, Mack was talking with the players about the best way to play to win. During the games, he did not give hitting or running signs. They were left to the players to initiate and implement. He did not give pitching signs. That was up to the pitcher and catcher. Mack gave guidance and led, then let the players play. If mistakes were made, he would talk to the player the next day, avoiding talking to the player in anger.[13]

The key to this approach was always pitching. Going into 1910, Mack had two anchors of his pitching staff, Eddie Plank and Albert Bender. Edward Stewart "Eddie" or "Gettysburg Eddie" Plank was senior in terms on continuous service on the A's. He made his debut with the A's on May 13, 1901, eight days before Harry Davis. Plank made a late start as a pitcher, not starting until his mid-20s. As his nickname indicates, Plank was from Gettysburg, Pennsylvania. He was a farmer, working his land while attending Gettysburg College in their "Preparatory Department," or high school. As he was too old for the department's baseball team, the college let him pitch on the varsity team. Mack heard about Plank from several sources and invited Plank to try out during the 1901 season. After Plank's relief appearance on May 13, he returned to Gettysburg and pitched a complete game on May 15. Mack joined the A's for good on May 17. He would stay with the A's through 1914. As a pitcher, Plank was a man before his time. He immediately established himself as the slowest-working pitcher in the major leagues. The fans in Washington, where he made his first start on May 17, 1901, made their

Eddie Plank in 1909.

feelings known by counting aloud until he threw his next pitch. Plank used these delays to good effect, making the batter as nervous as possible. Plank was a sidearming left-hander. His out pitch was what he called a "slant ball," probably some kind of slider.[14] He was reliable, completing almost 80 percent of his career starts. But since he started later than most, he needed more rest than other pitchers. When he knew he was going to start, he ate tomato soup before the game. He was a remarkably consistent pitcher who was not afraid to try something different if he thought it was necessary. Eddie Collins told this story of a situation in the 1909 pennant race, A's ahead of the Tigers, 3–1, in the ninth inning, runners on second and third, Ty Cobb at bat:

> In a discussion of whether to walk Cobb, Plank said "If I get two strikes on Ty, I'm going to throw a spitter." Livingston [the catcher] didn't know whether to laugh or argue. Plank didn't throw spitters, and the inexperienced catcher had rarely caught one. But Plank was serious, so all Livingston said was "I'll be looking for it."
> The first two pitches were balls with Ty tense and anxious. Then, after stalling around extra long, Plank shot over a strike catching Cobb off guard. Cobb was vexed. Next, a nice tantalizing curve, and the ball was slammed down the right field line, foul by inches. The next pitch was a ball, making the count three and two.
> As Livingston returned the ball on that pitch, Plank moistened his fingers and no one saw him. He fiddled around, changed his pose, then changed back, until at last he pitched. That spitter sure broke. It would have been a credit to Walsh [the best spitball pitcher in the American League] and it went over the pan for a perfect strike.
> Though Livingston had given the sign he had not anticipated the terrific break and the ball knocked him over as he blocked it.
> Cobb, however, was paralyzed and Livingston pounced on the ball and touched him out. The game was over. It was Plank's first and last spitter.[15]

The right-handed half of Mack's consistent pair of pitchers was Charles Albert Bender. Bender's father was German, his mother half-Chippewa Indian. Like most players at this time with Indian blood, he was nicknamed "Chief." Most newspaper accounts called him the "wily Redskin" and other names we would consider offensive today. Players often greeted him on the field with war whoops. All this treatment never had any external effect on Bender, who was cool and unflappable on the field. Bender had been living in white society since the age of seven, when he left the White Earth Reservation in Minnesota to attend an Indian school in Philadelphia. He moved to the Carlisle Indian School, where he played football for Pop Warner. His education at Carlisle gave him experience in many activities that became lifelong interests for Bender: shooting, billiards, golf, oil painting, and gardening. He was acknowledged to be the best marksman and golfer on the A's.[16] But he earned his living at baseball. After leaving Carlisle, Bender played ball for the Harrisburg Athletic Club. A friend of Mack's saw Bender pitch an exhibition game against the Cubs on June 17, 1902. This friend recommended Bender to Mack, and Mack signed him after the season to a contract for $300 a month for 1903.[17]

Bender, whom Mack always called Albert, made the team in 1903 as a 19-year-old. In 1910, he was a 27-year-old in his eighth year with the A's. Bender was not quite as consistent as Plank, as he suffered more injuries. Some suspected him of drinking a bit too much, but that was never a huge issue with Mack. Bender's first game for the A's came against Cy Young, in relief of Plank on April 20, 1903. Bender pitched six innings of relief and won the game. Forty years later, Bender called this day "my biggest thrill in baseball." By the end of the 1903 season, Bender was established as a starter for Mack. He had a mediocre year in 1904, but bounced back in 1905. He was called the speediest of all pitchers in 1905, even though he was a teammate of Rube Waddell. Bender and Plank each pitched two complete games in the 1905 World Series. Bender notched the A's only win in that series, with a four-hit shutout in Game 2. Bender had

Albert (Chief) Bender in 1909.

decent years in 1906, 1907, and 1909, and an injury-marred-year in 1908. He pitched slightly fewer innings than Plank, but was still a cornerstone of the pitching staff. In 1910, Bender got off to a great start with a record of 8–1 on June 3. One of those wins came on May 12 against the Cleveland Naps. There was no headline noting this accomplishment in the *Philadelphia Bulletin*, but there was a mention in the story that the Naps had not gotten a hit in the last 16⅔ innings against the A's.[18] Per Bill James, there were no specific mentions of a no-hitter until 1915. The *Reach Guide*, a leading annual baseball publication, started listing "Low-Hit Games" after the 1911 season.[19] Even though Bender faced the minimum on May 12 (walking one batter, who was thrown out stealing), no special note was taken of the no-hitter, the 12th in American League history. Bender was another pitcher who threw a slider, which he called a nickel curve. Ty Cobb called Bender the "brainiest pitcher I ever faced." Mack complimented Bender by saying, "If everything depended on one game, I'd use Albert."[20] All these good qualities owned by Chief Bender were not present in his brother, John C. Bender. John showed some emotional problems during his baseball career. While John was with the Columbia, South Carolina, so team in 1908, he had some harsh words with his manager. He pulled a knife on the manager and used it. He was suspended from Organized Baseball for two years and went back to the minor leagues after his suspension was served. On September 25, 1911, he died on the mound while pitching for the Edmonton, Alberta team.[21]

    The Cubs had three pitchers comparable to Plank and Bender on their roster, as well as Mordecai Brown, who will be discussed later. Orval "Orvie" Overall, John Albert "Jack" Pfiester, and Edward Marvin "Ed" Reulbach had all been on the Cubs since the start of their great run in 1906. These pitchers all performed well during this stretch, compiling records of 70–32 (Overall), 63–33 (Pfiester), and 79–25 (Reulbach) from 1906–1909. All had physical problems in 1910. Overall and Pfiester got off to good starts, but hurt their arms. After Overall pitched on June 1, he went to see the arm specialist of the day, Bonesetter Reese, in Youngstown, Ohio. Overall would come back later in the year, making 21 starts as opposed to his average of 28 the last four years. Pfiester started his last game on June 17, threw ten shutout innings in his 13th start, then was out the rest of the year. Pfiester had averaged 26 starts the last four years. Reulbach's case of diphtheria kept him out of the starting rotation until June 9. He had averaged 28 starts the last four years. A case of diphtheria could not be predicted, but it seems Overall and Pfiester showed the wear and tear of pennant races.[22]

Orval Overall took a path to the major leagues similar to Frank Chance's. Born in Visalia, California, in 1881, he went to the University of California, played football and baseball there, and graduated in 1903. He played one year in the minors before signing with Cincinnati. He was a workhorse for the Reds in 1905, starting 39 games, completing 32 with a record of 18–23. After Overall got off to a slow start in 1906 (4–5 in ten starts, with a 4.26 ERA), the Cubs traded pitcher Bob Wicker to the Reds for Overall. Wicker finished the 1906 season with

Orval Overall in 1910 at West Side Park.

the Reds, compiling a 6–14 record there. That was Wicker's last season in the majors. Overall helped the Cubs in 1906 with a 12–3 record. He pitched twice in relief in the 1906 World Series and followed this up with his best year in 1907. His record was 23–7, and it is an indication of the strength of the Cubs' pitching staff that Overall's ERA of 1.68 was the fourth-best on the staff. Overall "slumped" in 1908 to a 15–11 record.[23] By this point, he was a main cog in the Cubs' machine.

There is a good story about how the team viewed each other. In spring training in 1908, the Cubs held an intersquad game on St. Patrick's Day. The team self-divided into ethnic Irish and German squads. Those not fitting either background chose a side. Overall dubbed himself "O'verall" and joined the Irish team. The game ended in a 4–4 tie, which helped keep the peace for the rest of spring training.

On August 10, 1908, Overall pitched the best game of his career under trying circumstances. He had married earlier in the year, and his wife had taken ill in Chicago while the Cubs were in New York. He knew she would have to undergo surgery and left the team after that game, in which he pitched a one-hit complete game against the Giants but lost to Mathewson, 3–2. He returned to the team and rejoined the starting rotation for the stretch drive. He lost a game to his old team, the Reds, on a bottom-of-the-ninth, bases-loaded, two-out, two-strike hit. The pitching heroes for the Cubs this stretch drive do not include Overall.[24] However, he came into his glory in the World Series of 1908. In Game 1, he pitched one-third of an inning of relief in a 10–6 win. The next day, Overall started and pitched a complete game in a 6–1 victory. In the final game of the World Series on October 14, Overall shut out the Tigers in a 2–0 complete game. Hence, Orval Overall was the winning pitcher the last time the Cubs clinched a World Series title.[25] Overall had another fine year in 1909, with a 20–11 record and 1.42 ERA. We will see how he finished the 1910 season after the arm injury he suffered on June 1.

Jack Pfiester has been known since the 1908 season as the Giant Killer. He was from Cincinnati, born in 1878. Pfiester started in the minors in 1898 and served a lengthy apprenticeship. He had two short stints with the Pirates in 1903 and 1904, going 1–4. The Pirates let him loose, and Pfiester spent the 1905 season in the minors. The Cubs picked him up before the 1906 season, and Pfiester blossomed. During the Cubs' run from 1906 to 1910, Pfiester was the only left-handed pitcher on the regular staff. He pitched sidearm and was known for having a good pickoff move.²⁶ But he made his name against the Giants. During the 1906–8 seasons, the Giants featured three left-handed batters in their regular lineup. Chance would save Pfiester to pitch against the Giants. In a series in Chicago against the Giants in 1908, Pfiester won two games (on August 27 and 30). After these games, Pfiester was dubbed the Giant Killer. He would go on to start and finish the famous Merkle game against Mathewson, and start the make-up game. He had good years from 1906 to 1908, with a record of 46–27, and pitched in all three World Series. In 1909–1910, the Giants' regular lineup featured three or four left-handed hitters. Hence, Pfiester continued to get more starts against the Giants than anyone else. He finished the 1910 season with a career record of 15–4 against the Giants. As his record with the Cubs through 1910 was 102–66, his record against the Giants was not everything, but it was what Pfiester was known for.

Ed Reulbach was born in Detroit in 1882. He went to college at nearby Notre Dame for a couple of years. He played for Notre Dame under his own name and in the minors under an assumed name. He moved on to the University of Vermont, doing the same thing. Reulbach studied engineering and took pre-med classes, but never graduated

Jack (the Giant Killer) Pfiester, 1910.

from either institution. His future was in baseball. Reulbach was signed by George Huff and made the team in spring training 1905. Reulbach was a regular starter in 1905, ending with an 18–14 record and completing 28 of 29 starts. One of his complete games in 1905 lasted 20 innings. He led the National League in winning percentage the next three years with records of 19–4, 17–4, and 24–7. In the 1906 World Series, Reulbach threw a one-hitter against the White Sox, the fewest hits in a World Series game until Don Larsen's perfect game in the 1956 World Series. Reulbach had a 17-game winning streak covering the end of the 1906 season and the beginning of the 1907 season. He also won a game in the 1907 World Series. Reulbach's reputation was for two things—a great curveball and poor control. Even with his fine record, most articles about his pitching stress his problem finding the plate. It turns out that the reason was poor vision in his left eye. When the weather was overcast, he had trouble seeing the target. Sometimes his catcher would paint his mitt white to help him out. But the negative attitude of reporters regarding Reulbach is puzzling. He certainly won, and won in crucial situations. After the Merkle game, when the 1908 National League race was airtight and everyone was tired, Reulbach preformed a unique feat for baseball after 1900. He pitched two complete game shutouts in one doubleheader. Many pitchers threw two complete games in doubleheaders in those days, including two other pitchers during the same week. But Reulbach's performance on September 26, 1908, against Brooklyn has never been matched. These games were part of a 44-inning scoreless streak.[27] Reulbach started the first game of the 1908 World Series and finished the third game, the only game the Cubs lost in either the 1907 and 1908 Series. He had another good year in 1909, with a 19–10 record. After recovering from his case of diphtheria, Reulbach was ready to help the Cubs the rest of the year.

The Cubs returned from their road trip on June 20. On this date, the lineup of regulars the Cubs expected to use after Kling returned made its first appearance of the season. In 1931, a terminally ill Ring Lardner wrote an article called "Insomnia" that was published in May by *Cosmopolitan*. He goes through some of the various things he thinks about while trying to fall asleep. One of these is what Lardner called counting sheep: "Sheckard, Evers, Schulte, Chance, Steinfeldt, Hofman, Kling, Brown." That was the starting lineup on June 20, except Cole was the pitcher and Lardner reversed the order of Sheckard and Evers.[28]

5. June

It was a testament to the team that the Cubs were in first place by 3½ games anyway. This lineup lasted three games, which the Cubs swept from the Reds. Two games were won by relief pitchers. Richie relieved Cole in the first game, and the Cubs came back to win, 6–4. Reulbach threw six shutout innings in the second game before being relieved by Brown. The Cubs won this game in an unusual manner. The only hitter to get any hits for the Cubs was Sheckard, who got three. In the fourth inning, Sheckard led off with a double. Schulte sacrificed him to third, a normal play in this era even though Schulte was the third-place hitter. Chance came up and was beaned. Chance was out cold, and the umpire called for a doctor from the stands (teams did not have team doctors in those days). Lardner wrote: "The response to the umpire's call was a wonderful thing to behold. If all the people who dashed out on the field were doctors it's a good thing there weren't many sudden illnesses just at that time in other parts of the city, for it's a cinch there wouldn't have been enough medical aid available to look after half of them."[29] Chance went to the bench, had Luderus run for him, and called a squeeze play. Steinfeldt got the bunt down, and Sheckard scored. The final score was 1–0.

The Cubs went for the sweep the next day with their regular lineup. Chance had to come out in the third inning due to headaches. Tinker strained his back and came out. The Cubs were down 4–2 in the bottom of the ninth, and scored three runs to win it. McIntire got the win with a complete game. The Cubs had won 24 of their last 29 games to take a 4½-game lead. The schedule called for a couple of make-up games wrapped around a two-game trip to Pittsburgh. The Cubs beat the Pirates, 9–0, in a make-up game in Chicago on June 23, with Brown throwing a complete game three-hitter. The teams traveled on the same train to Pittsburgh for two games, which the Pirates swept. One person had a very unusual fielding line in the first game. Artie Hofman, playing first base for Chance, played the entire game on June 24 and had no putouts. The Cubs lost the game on a two-out, three-run triple in the sixth inning by the best player in the National League, Honus Wagner. The Cubs lost on Saturday, June 25, then returned home for a Sunday game against St. Louis, which the Cubs won. Kroh started the game, left in the sixth inning with sore arm, and Cole finished the game. A double steal netted the winning run, Kling stealing second leading to Hofman stealing home.

The final two games at home this month were against the Reds.

The Cubs split them, Reulbach losing a complete game, 2–0, and Brown winning a complete game 11–1. Tinker stole home twice in this final home game of June. The Cubs went to St. Louis for five games in five days. The June 30 game was an unusual one for the Deadball Era. The Cubs scored five runs in the top of the first inning, the Cards nine in the bottom, leading to a 13–9 Cards win. The Cubs won the last two games of the series, with a rainout on July 2. This rainout had to hurt, as the Cubs were up 7–0 in the top of the fifth when the rains came. This game was to be made up as part of a morning-afternoon doubleheader on July 3. The managers agreed before the morning game that the grounds were too wet to play, as the Cardinals did not have a tarpaulin. The grounds crew got the grounds into shape for the afternoon game, which started around 3 pm. As the Cubs had to catch a train for Pittsburgh at 6 pm, only one game was possible. Cole had pitched four innings in the rained-out game, but volunteered to pitch the next day. He threw a complete game, winning 5–3. After this game, the *Chicago Tribune* followed its regular procedure and switched baseball correspondents. Hence, this was the final regular season game article written about the Cubs by Ring Lardner.[30]

The A's finished the month with five games against Boston. Due to the vagaries of microfilm, the only facts I could determine about this series are that the A's won the first three games and the Red Sox won the last two. The A's finished June with a 38–21 record, one game ahead of the New York Highlanders. The Highlanders were coming into Philadelphia for a six-game series on July 1. Connie Mack was happy with his pitching and infield, but not yet sure about his outfield. He would go with the players he had for a bit longer.

Mack's outfield starting the 1910 season was Tully Frederick "Topsy" Hartsel, Reuben Henry "Rube" Oldring, and Daniel Francis "Danny" Murphy. While the infield was dominated by young players, all the outfielders were veterans by 1910. Topsy Hartsel was the second-oldest regular on the A's, 11 months younger than Harry Davis. Hartsel was from Polk, Ohio, and lived in Toledo. He became a pro in 1897 at the age of 23, making the majors the next year with Louisville. His nickname was an example of American racial attitudes around the turn of the century. In Indianapolis in 1899, a sportswriter wrote that Hartsel was as white as Topsy (a character in *Uncle Tom's Cabin*) was black. This name stuck.[31] Hartsel played in the National League through 1901 and spent the 1901 season with the Cubs, establishing himself as a top leadoff man by hitting .335, walking 74 times, stealing 41 bases and scoring 111 runs. Hartsel also set a record for putouts by a left fielder in one game in 1901 with 11. Mack was on the lookout for a leadoff man that winter and convinced Hartsel to jump to the A's. From 1902 through 1909, Hartsel was the A's regular left fielder. He was a part of two pennant-winning teams (1902 and 1905) and a solid leadoff man when healthy. He played 98 games in 1903 and 83 games in 1909. The other years he averaged 141 games. He led the American League in walks in 1905 through 1908, and led the AL in runs scored in 1902.[32] Bill James rated Hartsel has having the worst outfield throwing arm in the decade 1900–1909.[33] Mack was loyal to his veterans, but he was aware that Hartsel was slowing down. Mack still wanted Hartsel on his team, but preferably not as a starter.

Topsy Hartsel in 1906.

There was supposed to be a competition for the center field job in 1910 at the A's training camp. Amos Strunk was a 20-year-old speedster who had been on the A's roster the last two years, playing in 12 games in 1908 and 11 games in 1909. Mack intended for Strunk to compete with the incumbent, Rube Oldring. However, first Strunk had a job to do in training camp. Mack was trying to help pitcher Harry Krause learn how to hold runners on base. Mack assigned Strunk to lead off bases during drills and make Krause hold him on. During these drills, Strunk wrenched his knee badly enough that he was unable to play until late in the season. Hence, Rube Oldring was the center fielder for 1910. Oldring was from New York City and turned 26 in 1910. Mack heard about Oldring from an old associate in the late stages of the 1905 season and apparently bought his contract from the minor league team he was playing with. Oldring reported to Philadelphia after his minor league season ended. The A's were going to play in the World Series, so Mack told Oldring to go home and play in semi-pro games and earn some money. Oldring did so and was spotted by the New York Highlanders. Oldring ended up playing eight games for the Highlanders in 1905, hitting .300 and playing shortstop. In one of those mysterious transactions that were common in baseball during this decade, it was determined that Oldring was the property of the A's even though the Highlanders drafted him after the 1905 season. Mack intended to have Oldring play shortstop, but Oldring broke his ankle in 1906 training camp. When Oldring came back in July, he played all the infield positions as a utility man. Mack thought enough of his performance that Oldring was groomed to take over a vacancy in center field the next spring. Oldring won the job and was the regular center fielder from 1907 to 1910.[34] He had injury problems, playing 117 games in 1907, 116 games in 1908, and 90 games in 1909. His performance was adequate, but Mack was still on the lookout for improvement in center field. Oldring had remained healthy so far in 1910 and was having a good year.

Danny Murphy was another of Mack's older players. He was a 33-year-old Philadelphia native and had been a pro since 1899. After the court ruling in 1902 that deprived the A's of Napoleon Lajoie, Mack had tried various players to fill the second base vacancy. Mack heard of a player at Norwich in the Connecticut League and made a stop to see Danny Murphy during a train trip from New York to Boston on July 6. Mack bought Murphy's

Danny Murphy in 1905.

contract and directed Murphy to report to Boston two days later. When the game started, Murphy was not there yet. Mack had heard that Murphy was fond of the bottle, so he was worried. Murphy showed up in the first inning, got into uniform, and got six hits in a 22–9 A's win.[35] Murphy played second base exclusively from 1902 through 1907. In Mack's mind, he was not a good fielder, but his offensive production outweighed his defensive deficiencies. Murphy was a key player down the stretch in the 1902 pennant drive and in the 1905 pennant season. Except for Napoleon Lajoie, Murphy was the best hitting second baseman in the AL during these years. Mack was not looking to get Murphy out of the lineup, but he was looking for a better fielding option at second base. This better option became available in 1908, when Eddie Collins showed what he could do at second base. During the 1908 season, Murphy started 56 games at second base early in the season, and 84 games in right field.[36] As Murphy was a career .290 hitter with good power, he was a good fit in the outfield. In 1909, Murphy played 149 games and had a good year. Mack was satisfied with Murphy in right field, and Murphy was producing in 1910.

6

July

The A's started July with a six-game series against their closest pursuers, the New York Highlanders. The manager of the Highlanders was the opposite of Connie Mack while managing. George Stallings was known to have a split personality, somewhat like Frank Chance. Stallings graduated from Virginia Military Institute and studied medicine for a year before giving up medicine for baseball. Stallings entered the minors in 1891, becoming a manager in 1893. Stallings was known as a well-spoken, mild person off the field. On the field, he was a fierce, foul-mouthed fiend.[1] As his third baseman in 1910, Jimmy Austin, said:

> Stallings was a fine manager. One of the best. Like I said, we finished in second place in 1910, and you've got to say he deserved a lot of the credit for that. Talk about cussing! Golly, he had 'em all beat. He cussed something awful. Once, in a game, he gave me a real going over. Later that night he called me in and said "Jim, I'm sorry about this afternoon. Don't pay attention to me when I say those things. Just forget it. It's only because I get so excited and want to win so bad."[2]

Stallings was very superstitious, like many folks involved in baseball. He would stay in the same spot on the bench when a rally was ongoing, and move around when his team was not hitting. Stallings is the source of an old, often used, baseball expression about walks. He had a medical check-up while he was a manager, and the doctor told Stallings he had a bad heart, and asked what caused it. Stallings said, "Bases on balls."[3]

An example of how new and rough baseball was in this time is the name of the New York American League team. Most sources show the official nickname of this team as the Highlanders in 1910. Jimmy Austin, who was on the team that year, states this in *The Glory of Their Times*.[4] However, the *Philadelphia Bulletin* called them the Yankees in their articles in 1910. By whatever name, the New York team came to

6. July

Philadelphia on July 1 playing good ball, even in the loss column and one game behind the A's. This six-game series in Philadelphia would set the tone for the second half of the season. Even though by July 5 the A's would have played only 67 games of a 154-game schedule (the Highlanders only 65), July 4 was thought of as the halfway point of the season in the days before an All-Star break.

Mack had his pitchers ready for New York. On July 1, he started Coombs and Plank in a doubleheader. Coombs and Ford threw complete games in the opener, the A's winning, 2–0, on clutch hits by Oldring and Collins. Plank lasted seven innings in the nightcap, leaving with a 4–3 lead on Baker's homer in the sixth. Bender finished up. The A's swept New York again on July 2 behind Morgan and Krause. After a day off, there was another doubleheader on the fourth of July. Dygert started for the A's and was hit hard, and the A's lost, 8–3. Coombs returned for the nightcap, beating Ford, who was knocked out. Baker was spiked by New York first baseman Hal Chase but stayed in the game and hit well. As this was a holiday doubleheader, it was a morning-afternoon affair, with two admissions, as opposed to the earlier doubleheaders, which were one-admission, afternoon-only games.

Both teams had to leave after the game for short train hops. The Highlanders had another doubleheader on July 5. The A's went to Washington for three games, their only road games of July. The first game in Washington is a matchup of future Hall of Famers, Plank and Walter Johnson. Both threw complete games, and the A's won, 3–2, scoring three unearned runs. Morgan gave up 12 hits in the second game of the series but won, 3–2. Murphy stole home on a double steal and drove in another run. There was a story in the *Philadelphia Bulletin* that Detroit had offered $30,000 for Washington's Walter Johnson and catcher Gabby Street. Detroit owner Frank Navin denied the offer. The A's wrapped up their road schedule for July on the 7th with a 4–1 loss to the Nationals. Coombs threw a complete game but was let down by errors by Baker and Barry. The A's returned home for a home stand that would last until July 30 with a 5½-game lead.[5]

The Cubs traveled from St. Louis to Pittsburgh on the night of July 3. There was a story in the *Tribune* that Kling had perfected the organization of the National Amateur Three Cushion League, to start play in April 1911.[6] This turned out to be a pipe dream, and the Cubs still had to play the holiday doubleheader in Pittsburgh. They arrived in Pittsburgh just before the morning game and had to play in their unwashed uniforms from St. Louis. Not surprisingly, the Pirates won the first game, 5–2, with both teams using two pitchers. The Cubs won the afternoon game, 7–2, behind Reulbach. Chance showed his awareness of the condition of his club by playing 15 players in the opener, nine in the nightcap. Playing in the newest National League ballpark, Forbes Field, the two games drew more than 40,000 fans. After this road trip, the Cubs could see a modern concrete and steel ballpark in Chicago, but they would not play in it. Comiskey Park, the new home of the White Sox, opened on July 1, 1910, and was acclaimed as the best ballpark in America (mostly by Chicago boosters and White Sox fans). The Cubs split the next two games in Pittsburgh. On July 5, Brown threw a complete game. Chance batted five times, reached five times on one hit, an error, a walk, and two hit by pitch. Richie started the last game in Pittsburgh, losing an 11-inning complete game, 3–2. The Pirates tried to score the go-ahead run in the eighth, but Sheckard threw out Wagner at plate trying to score from second on a single. After the game on July 6, the Cubs headed home for an 18-game home stand.[7]

On the day the Cubs and A's each played doubleheaders, the one sporting event that could overshadow baseball in 1910 took place. Heavyweight boxing champion Jack Johnson fought ex-titleholder James J. Jeffries. This fight had been anticipated for months and was the only sports story that rivaled baseball in volume of coverage.[8] As Johnson was black and Jeffries was white, this fight was a microcosm of race relations in America. Even though Jeffries had been retired from the ring for six years, white bettors made Jeffries the 10–7 favorite. Jeffries hid himself away while trying to get back in shape, while Johnson trained in public and talked to the press constantly. The fight was scheduled for Reno, Nevada, on July 4. Racial tensions were such that guns were banned from the arena (a very rare occurrence then for the western U.S.) and alcohol was banned. Johnson dominated the fight, winning when Jeffries' corner threw in the towel during the 15th round, after Jeffries suffered the first two knockdowns of his career. Johnson earned $65,000 from the fight (over $1.6 million in 2014 dollars). Jeffries admitted after the fight that he had no chance against Johnson. Former champion John L. Sullivan commented that Johnson was the superior fighter and had fought fairly at all times. These comments would not stop racial unrest. There were race riots in 50 cities in 25 states. Some were between blacks and whites, and some started when police reacted violently to blacks celebrating Johnson's victory. Twenty people died, and hundreds were injured in these riots. The disturbances continued when the film of this fight was shown later in the year. There was a spontaneous movement to ban the showing of this film, which started three days after the fight. This led to a 1912 law banning the interstate distribution of fight films, which lasted until 1940.[9]

As baseball fans know, blacks were not allowed to play in the major leagues in 1910. Many players were identified by their ethnic background in this time. We have seen that players with Indian blood were usually called Chief. Some players with a German background were called Heinie, like Heinie Zimmerman. The nickname Rube was often applied to naïve country boys. But these folks could play in the big leagues, while blacks could not. Both the A's and Cubs played against black teams in the off-season, and both rented their ballparks to black teams when they were out of town. As a matter of fact, the first night game played in Philadelphia was played by a black team, the Philadelphia Giants, in the A's home park on June 4, 1902.[10] But baseball treated blacks per the 1896 Supreme Court decision in Plessy v. Ferguson. Blacks were separate but "equal." Of course, this equality did not exist. Great black players such as Rube Foster, John Henry Lloyd, Louis Santop, Bill Monroe, Pete Hill, Spottswood Poles and Jelly Gardner, who played during this era, never had the chance to play in the majors. Major league managers and players knew how good the black players were. John McGraw tried to pass light-skinned black players off as Cubans.[11] John Henry Lloyd was referred to as the "Black Honus Wagner." Connie Mack said you could put Wagner and Lloyd in a bag, pull out whichever one, and not go wrong either way.

Rube Foster claimed before his death in 1930 that the best team he ever saw was the 1910 Chicago American Giants, a black team that Foster pitched for. This team played in the ballpark the White Sox used before building Comiskey Park. The Chicago American Giants included Rube Foster, John Henry Lloyd, Pete Hill, and other fine black players. A small bit of progress was shown by Cap Anson, as discussed above. When Anson was in the majors, he made it clear he did not want to play against blacks. In 1907–1908, Anson's Colts (a semi-pro team in the Chicago City League) played against the Chicago Leland Giants, a black team. Anson took part in these games as player and manager, and made no difficulties.[12] Racial attitudes needed decades' more progress before the color line was challenged in organized baseball.

On July 8, the A's started their home stand. A story in the *Philadelphia Bulletin* just before their return discussed an activity conducted in the stands at the Philadelphia Ball Park (home of the Phillies), which applied to the A's as well. The magistrate in a case involving two fans arrested for gambling at a Phillies game suggested that the owner of the Philadelphia Ball Park be arrested as operating a gambling house. By the way, the owner of the Philadelphia Ball Park was Charles P. Taft, the same Charles P. Taft who was the silent partner of Charles Murphy in owning the Cubs, and half-brother of the President of the United States. Taft had supplied the money allowing Phillies owner Horace Fogel, the sports editor of the *Bulletin* before 1910, to buy the team. Murphy set up this deal, and Taft went along, seeing how well his investment in the Cubs had turned out. As has always been the case, if the amounts of money gambled were quite large and there was some property involved, it was business. If the amounts were smaller and bet on a game, it was gambling. Magistrate Monroe's comments on this case included this statement:

> The park is a public place of amusement, and the proprietors should certainly know what is going on there. That they do know, I think, is proved by the signs which they have posted forbidding gambling. It is up to the proprietors of places of this kind to prevent gambling. They can stop it if they wish. If they don't want to maintain gambling they have means to prevent it. Their own men could prevent betting about the grounds. The police are on duty there, it is true, but it is up to the proprietors to see that their premises are not used for gambling purposes.

The story goes on to say that the police at the local station got complaints about gambling every year, and nothing was ever done about it.[13] Some things do not change in sports. Gambling was a constant then and is a constant now. Baseball had a gambling scandal in the first year of the National League, when the Louisville team was accused of throwing the pennant by losing several games at the end of the 1876 season.[14] We have seen that the heavyweight boxing match in 1910 led to large gambling activity. The third most popular sport in the U.S., horse racing, was so popular because gambling on it was legal. The question of betting on sports is still being wrestled with, and there are different solutions all around the U.S. and the world.

Bender started the first game of the home stand, winning 4–3. The article in the *Bulletin* was very complimentary to Bender but was accompanied by a tasteless (to modern eyes) cartoon of Bender with a feather headdress and a scalp titled "Detroit." Statistics posted in the paper this same day showed that Lajoie led Cobb by 27 points in the race for the Chalmers automobile (.399 to .372). These statistics showed Bender as the leading pitcher in the American League with a record of 13–2.[15] The A's swept the four-game series with the Tigers, and the Tigers left town in fourth place. The A's stayed hot in series against St. Louis and Chicago. On July 13, Morgan and Browns pitcher Pelty threw 14-inning complete games, won by the A's on Barry's walk-off homer. The A's won three of four games, with Morgan throwing another complete game. Coombs started the series against the White Sox with his sixth complete game of July, a 5–2 win against Doc White.[16] Doc White was a real dentist who practiced in the off-season and was prosperous enough to send a very nice gift to his friend Ring Lardner when Lardner got married in 1911.[17] The A's took three of four games against the White Sox.

Even though the A's were 6½ games ahead of New York and Boston, Mack was still dissatisfied with his outfield. The doubleheader against the Cleveland Naps on July 22 made up his mind to take action. The Naps won, 7–6, against Morgan and Dygert in the morning game. In the afternoon game, Bender threw a 15-inning complete game that was called on account of darkness as a 1–1 tie. Mack was happy with his pitchers, but Hartsel and Heitmuller had bad games in the outfield, and Cleveland outfielder Bris Lord threw out three runners at home in the two games. Even though acquiring Lord would break one of Mack's rules, he traded for Lord after the game. The cost was utility infielder Morrie Rath, and Mack would give up his rights to an outfielder in the minors. It seemed like a small price to pay for a regular outfielder, except that the outfielder Mack gave up on was Joe Jackson. Jackson was not part of the trade, as Cleveland now had to buy Jackson from New Orleans. However, Mack was not convinced that Jackson could fit in with his team in Philadelphia. Cleveland paid $6,000 to New Orleans for Jackson, who came up with the Naps and hit .387 in 20 games in September.[18] Bris Lord was 26 in 1910, and was hitting .219 for the Naps. Mack made the move for defensive purposes, being familiar with Lord. The rule Mack broke was re-acquiring someone he had traded away before. Mack had signed Bris Lord as a 21-year-old in 1905, bringing him to training camp. Lord impressed Mack with the strongest throwing arm among the outfielders, but did not impress him at the plate. Lord was the utility outfielder on the 1905 pennant winners, playing 61 games and hitting .239. Lord was the regular center fielder in 1906, hitting .255. After Lord played 56 games in 1907 and was hitting .182, Mack gave up on him, selling him to New Orleans with no right of recall. New Orleans sold Lord to Cleveland before the 1909 season. Lord played 69 games in 1909, hitting .269.[19] Even though Lord had poor baseball instincts and was not hitting much in 1910, Mack thought his defense would help the A's.

The Cubs sent Brown and Tinker home from Pittsburgh a day early. The first series of their home stand was two games with Cincinnati, and neither Brown nor Tinker played in the first game. Cole pitched a fine game, losing 1–0 in an hour and a half. Cincinnati pitcher Bill Burns was better, allowing two hits and driving in the only run of the game. Burns would eventually become a major figure in the biggest gambling scandal in American sports history. After a scandal-free career in the big leagues that ended in 1912, Burns went into the oil business and gambled on the side. He got involved in the fixing of the 1919 World Series and testified against the Black Sox players in their 1921 trial. Brown relieved in the second game of the series, finishing a 3–2 Cubs win. Kling hit an inside-the-park homer for the winning margin. The Cubs had a 2½-game lead going into a scheduled four-game series with the Giants. The Giants won the first two games, getting the lead down to one-half game after the July 10 game. Brown was shelled in the first game after pitching in relief the day before. Pfiester came in and pitched well for seven innings, but the Cubs could not make up the deficit. The Cubs had their regular lineup together on July 10, Tinker returning from a sore ankle. The Giants won a hotly contested 10–9 game which ended with fans throwing seat cushions at umpire Hank O'Day. The teams used multiple pitchers, and the Giants scored three runs in the ninth inning to break a 7–7 tie. The Cubs came back with two runs in the bottom of the inning before the fourth Giants pitcher, Doc Crandall, closed out the game. A sub-headline in the *Tribune* called the game the "Greatest Game Ever," but as we shall see, something took place in New York this same day that had a greater historical impact on some Cubs players. The Giants ended up leaving town down 1½ games after the Cubs won the third game, 4–2. Richie threw a complete game, helping Chance out by saving the other pitchers. Chance helped Richie out by being involved in all the runs. The final game of the series was rained out and would be made up in September.[20]

6. July

On the day of the rained-out final game of this series, a humor and sports columnist from Chicago filled a small amount of column space with a poem about baseball. Franklin Pierce Adams wrote for the *New York Evening Mail*. He was a little short on material for his July 12, 1910, column, and filled it this way:

> These are the saddest of all possible words:
> "Tinker to Evers to Chance."
> Trio of bear cubs, and fleeter than birds,
> Tinker and Evers and Chance.
> Ruthlessly pricking our gonfalon bubble,
> Making a Giant hit into a double—
> Words that are heavy with nothing but trouble:
> "Tinker to Evers to Chance."[21]

Filling stories and columns with doggerel poetry was common for the newspapermen (and they were all men) covering sports in 1910. This "art" form reached its peak with the eight lines above. While the particular act described, turning a double play, was not something the Cubs infield specialized in, the observation that the Cubs were anchored by their infield was correct.

Both the Cubs and the A's featured all-time great infields in 1910. The three players listed in the poem above had first played together in 1902, and Harry Steinfeldt became the third baseman in 1906. In 1910, Chance was 32, Evers 28, Tinker 29, and Steinfeldt 32. They should have been in their primes, and the standings in the National League suggested they still were. However, as we have seen, Chance was on the downward side of his career, mostly due to injuries, but still sharp. In 1906, the Cubs were up by one run in the top of the ninth, two were out, and the Pirates had one runner on. The batter hit a ground ball to Tinker, who threw to Chance. Chance dropped the throw, but quickly picked it up and ran to the clubhouse. The fans were let on the field as soon as the throw got to Chance, as was common when the game ended. The umpire saw Chance drop the throw, but also saw him pick it up and leave. The writer covering the game thought the umpire was going to call the runner safe, but Chance faked him out of it. Just another example of how Frank Chance was always thinking about how to win games on the field.[22]

Harry Steinfeldt was the forgotten man of this infield, probably due to the poetic needs of Mr. Adams. He was not as good a player as the other infielders on the Cubs, but he was quite good. Steinfeldt was

Harry Steinfeldt, 1910. Note fielder's glove in his back pocket.

from St. Louis and had a bit of a career before he started in the big leagues. He may have run away from home and joined a minstrel show, Al Field's Minstrels, in his early teens. The personnel of this show played baseball against local teams during their travels, and Steinfeldt turned out to be a better ballplayer than actor. He started in the minors in 1895 at the age of 17, and made the major leagues with the Reds in 1898. Steinfeldt spent eight years as the Reds' regular third baseman, averaging 112 games a year from 1898 to 1905.[23] He was inconsistent, mixing in good and bad years. His best year there was 1903, when he hit .312 and led the league with 32 doubles. He had a poor year in 1904 and a decent year in 1905 before breaking his leg in August. Chance thought he needed a veteran third baseman to round out his infield for

1906. Chance targeted Steinfeldt, who was available because he did not get along with Garry Herrmann, the Cincinnati owner. Murphy investigated the possibility of acquiring Steinfeldt and came back to Chance with many stories from his Cincinnati contacts that Steinfeldt was a bad guy who never played his best. Chance had played with and against Steinfeldt during off-seasons in California and felt that Steinfeldt just needed to get out of Cincinnati. Chance went ahead with the deal, trading two young players for Steinfeldt. One of these young players, Hans Lobert, developed into a fine third baseman who played in the big leagues until 1917.

But the trade worked to the advantage of the Cubs. John Evers said of Steinfeldt, "He was slow, a heavy hitter, a good fielder and a wonderful thrower."[24] Steinfeldt had the attitude on the field of a player who came up in the 1890s, when dirty play prevailed. Two plays in big games show this. In the first game of the 1907 World Series, which ended in a 3–3 tie, Steinfeldt was the protagonist of an unusual play. He was at bat with two out and two on in the bottom of the tenth inning of a tie game, one of the runners on third. The pitcher threw a pitch that got by the catcher, who retrieved it and threw back to the plate with the pitcher covering. The runner was safe, but Steinfeldt had stayed in the batter's box and got in the way of the throw. The umpire called interference, and the run did not count. Steinfeldt made up for this by hitting .471 in the 1907 Series.[25]

In the 1908 pennant race, he helped his team win a game against the Giants with a small action that was common in the 1890s and becoming less common in the 1900s. In a game in July 1908, the Cubs won a one-run victory. During this game, Larry Doyle of the Giants was trying to score from second on a single. When he rounded third base, Steinfeldt gave him a shoulder, throwing Doyle off-stride. Doyle was thrown out at the plate. There is no record of protest from the third base coach and manager of the Giants, John McGraw. McGraw had been a third baseman for the Baltimore Orioles in the 1890s, who specialized in plays like this. As this pennant race ended up with a one-game margin for the Cubs, every play during the season was important.[26]

Steinfeldt's main contribution to the Cubs was with his bat. He had his best year in the majors in 1906, hitting .327 while leading the league in hits and RBI. He followed up with another good year in 1907, hitting .266 but leading the team in RBI (though not yet an official statistic) and doubles. Steinfeldt stayed healthy in 1908–1909, averaging 151 games from 1906 to 1909. His performance dropped off a bit, but Chance kept him in the starting lineup.[27] Heinie Zimmerman thought he was better than Steinfeldt and played 22 games at third in 1910 when Steinfeldt was out with various injuries. Zimmerman and Steinfeldt did not like each other, understandable considering one was a veteran and one was a youngster trying to take the veteran's job. Zimmerman finally got the third baseman's job in 1911. Ring Lardner took advantage of his knowledge of what Zimmerman and Steinfeldt thought about each other in 1912. Lardner introduced Zimmerman to a friend as Harry Steinfeldt. This friend of Lardner's said to Zimmerman: "I'm glad to meet you, Mr. Steinfeldt. I think you're the greatest third baseman in the world." Zimmerman responded by punching the unsuspecting fan.[28]

Other than Chance, the infielder who had been with the Cubs the longest was Joseph "Joe" Tinker. Like Chance, Tinker started with the Cubs at a position other than the one he played in 1910. Joe Tinker was born in 1880 and grew up in small towns in eastern Kansas. He signed with the Coffeyville, Kansas, club at the age of 18 for $35 a month in 1899. He had played for several teams around the Kansas City area before that, playing against and with John Kling. Tinker played for three teams in three years in the minors, ending up with Portland in 1901. After he helped Portland win the Northwest League pennant as a third baseman in 1901, two major league teams were interested in him. A teammate at Portland, Jack McCarthy, had played for Cincinnati and had not liked the experience. McCarthy told Tinker to ignore Cincinnati's offer and sign with the other team, the Cubs.[29] This was done before Frank Selee was hired to run the Cubs in 1902. Tinker went to spring training, and Selee recommended that Tinker move to shortstop. Tinker fought the move, but shortstop was the position open in the infield. In 1902, Tinker played 124 games at short, and eight at third base. He hit .273 and established himself as a regular. In 1903, Tinker led the National League with 73 errors in just 124 games played. That was the year Tinker achieved his highest batting average with the Cubs, .291. He was still finding his way at short, but Selee was convinced Tinker was his shortstop. Tinker remained the regular shortstop through 1912. Eleven years at one position for one team speaks to consistency.[30]

One amazing thing about the Cubs during their great early

6. *July* 95

Joe Tinker reaching base at West Side Park, 1910.

20th-century run was that their legendary double play combination couldn't stand each other by 1906. The other half of this combination, John Evers, joined the Cubs late in the 1902 season. The regular second baseman, Bobby Lowe, suffered an injury, and Selee asked a scout in upstate New York to send him the best second baseman available. When Evers arrived, few thought he would stick. Evers was 105 pounds and 19 years old. A left-handed batter, Evers played 26 games in 1902, hitting .225 with no power. On September 15, 1902, the official scorer of the Chicago-Cincinnati game wrote down "double play, Tinker to Evers to Chance" for the first time. Evers made the team the next year, playing 125 games and hitting .291.[31] Soon he earned his nickname "The Crab." This was partly for how he scuttled around the infield. Mostly it was for his disposition. Chance said several times that he wanted Evers on his team, but he wished Evers played the outfield so Chance would not have to listen to him all game in the field. Evers got on everybody's nerves, including his own. He claimed in April 1909 that he needed a complete rest and had asked the Cubs for the season off. While the Cubs were willing to let Johnny Kling take the 1909 season off, it did not work that way for Evers. He showed his true colors when he signed a two-year contract on May 11.[32] But Evers was very high-strung. Earlier in the 1910 season, he was involved in an automobile accident and took off about three weeks to recover mentally from that (Evers was not hurt physically in the accident, which killed a passenger in his car). Evers would play only 46 games in 1911 due to a nervous breakdown. Per Bill James:

> It was said of Evers that he was so full of electricity that he could not wear a watch. It was a common practice at that time to give watches at testimonial dinners. Evers was given several fine watches, but when you put a watch on Johnny Evers' body it would not keep accurate time. He'd always give the nice ones away and buy a cheap one, then throw it away when it stopped running.[33]

While Tinker and Evers were opposites in temperament, they worked together great on the field. Per modern statistical analysis, Tinker to Evers to Chance was not the best double play combination in the decade of 1901–1910. They were very good, averaging more double plays than they should have all years except 1903. One reason they did not turn too many double plays was that the Cubs' pitching was so good. The Cubs had fewer opposition base runners than poor teams, which figured in this calculation. But it was obvious to those who watched the Cubs in their great run that in their infield defense was above-average to excellent.[34]

The story of how Tinker and Evers reached their non-communicative state in 1906 is told a couple of ways. Evers claimed that in a game in 1906, Tinker threw a short throw very hard to Evers on a force at second. Evers complained about the throw and eventually they brawled on the field. Tinker claimed that a few players were waiting for a taxicab, a rare sight in 1906, when Evers got into the cab alone and rode off before the others could get in. In either case, the dispute led to them agreeing not to talk except for "I got it" or "You take it." They gave signals to each other on the field and played together well enough to help the Cubs win the pennant from 1906–1908 and the World Series in 1907–1908. They made up in spring training in 1909 and spoke during the 1909 season. When the Cubs finished second in 1909, Chance told them to go back to not speaking in 1910. They did not speak in 1910 and were in good shape in the pennant race in July.[35]

Both Tinker and Evers escaped from poverty-stricken childhoods. Tinker was a classic country boy, born in Mascoutah, Kansas. His family's economic situation compelled them to apprentice him to a paper hanger in Kansas City at the age of 14. Tinker was not a natural shortstop. Along with many others who excelled at the position, he started out making lots of errors. But he worked at his fielding and ended up leading the National League shortstops in fielding percentage four times. Tinker's accomplishments as a hitter were harder to quantify. His batting average with the Cubs peaked at .291 in his second year. From 1904 to 1909, his batting average was .250 with some power for the Deadball Era. His best traits were not measurable in the statistics of the day, as he was known for clutch hitting and his ability on the hit-and-run. In particular, he was known for hitting Christy Mathewson. Tinker's lifetime average against Mathewson was .291, and Mathewson called Tinker "one of the most dangerous batters I have faced." As he played in the same era as Honus Wagner, Tinker was never considered the best shortstop in his league, but he had a very good reputation as a winning ballplayer. Tinker stole home twice in one game and was a good base runner and stealer. His World Series batting average in 1906–1908 was .200, but he led the Cubs in runs scored in the 1906 and 1907 Series. Tinker hit a home run in Game 2 of the 1908 World Series to put the Cubs in the lead.[36]

As Evers (pronounced E-vers in Troy and Ev-ers elsewhere) was born to a poor Irish family in one of the many industrial small cities in the northeast U.S., working in a factory appeared to be his fate. Evers tried to escape the shirt factories of Troy by becoming a sign painter as a youth, but he suffered painter's colic. So Evers went to work in one of the 20 factories that gave Troy its name as "the Collar City," playing ball whenever he could. As his salary in the collar factory was $4 a week, baseball was an attractive alternative. As a small man (listed as 5'8" and 125 pounds by 1910), Evers had to use his smarts and competitiveness to make it. Evers was the number two man for the Cubs for most of his career. Evers' offensive skills were those of a small-ball leadoff man. His batting average was rarely outstanding, reflective of a .270 career average. He learned the value of a walk on his own, averaging 27 walks per year from 1903–1906 and 71 from 1907–1910. His runs total increased as his career advanced. Evers averaged 32 stolen bases

John Evers at West Side Park in 1910. A sign on fence says "No Betting Allowed."

a year from 1903–1910, with a high of 49 in 1906. After a poor World Series in 1906, Evers hit .350 in both the 1907 and 1908 World Series. One problem with Evers' intensity was that he was injury prone. Since 1903, he had three years when he played virtually every game (1904, 1906, 1907). The other years he averaged 120 games played. Hall of Fame umpire Bill Klem said: "Johnny Evers was the toughest man I ever saw on a ballfield."[37]

Even with their dispute, Tinker and Evers helped the Cubs win. Bill James selected both to his Gold Glove team for the decade 1900–1909.[38] Both made interesting comments on their relationship. Evers said, "Tinker and myself hated each other, but we loved the Cubs. That was one of the answers to the Cubs success." Tinker made a more low-key comment: "We used to get along apart."[39] Evers was clearly more verbal than Tinker yet, surprisingly, Tinker was the one who supplemented his baseball income by playing vaudeville theatres during the off-seasons. Remember that he was granted permission to report late to spring training in 1910. The reason he was late was theatrical commitments. Tinker also ran a successful saloon in Kansas City. Evers had a way he hoped to supplement his income as well. Evers opened a shoe store in Troy, where he still lived. The store was still open in 1910, but was having financial difficulties. After going through the 1908 pennant race, both infielders hated the Giants. Tinker said: "If you didn't honestly and furiously hate the Giants, you weren't a real Cub." Evers said: "If we didn't ride McGraw and his players, Husk [Chance] would have fined us and probably beat the hell out of us."[40]

The rest of the Cubs' July home stand was against the other Eastern teams: Philadelphia, Brooklyn and Boston. After the July 11 win, the margin over the Giants was 1½ games. The Giants went to Pittsburgh while the Cubs played four games against the Phillies. The Cubs split their four games and the Pirates swept the Giants, leaving the Cubs with a 3½-game lead on July 16. Evers was tossed out of the July 14 game, showing how he was viewed by people on the ball field: his teammates respected him, opponents hated him, and umpires despised him. This ejection led to a three-game suspension. Brooklyn followed the Phillies into Chicago. The Brooklyn team was an example of the fluidity of team nicknames. Just during this year, they were referred to as the Superbas, Dodgers, and in the story dated July 18, the Infants. The name Dodgers stuck for a couple of years, but by 1914 their name changed to the Robins, not going back to Dodgers until 1932. The Cubs beat the Brooklyn team four of five games, showing their pitching depth. Reulbach, Richie, Overall and Pfiester threw nine innings in their starts. Reulbach, Richie and Overall won their games, and Pfiester exited with a 0–0 tie. The best pitcher on the Cubs, Three Finger Brown, took the only loss of the series in relief of Cole when Zimmerman made an error in the tenth inning on July 19. Brown started the last series of the home stand against Boston with a complete game shutout in a one hour, 40-minute game. The Cubs swept this four-game series. Overall and Cole threw complete game victories. In the second game, Reulbach was roughed up for five runs in six innings, leaving with the Doves up, 5–0. The Cubs tied it up in the bottom of the sixth, and went on to win in the tenth on the kind of run that showed how bad the Doves were. Sheckard led off with a bloop double that fell among four Doves fielders. Hofman sacrificed him to third. Zimmerman grounded to short, and Sheckard was thrown out at the plate, Zimmerman taking second. Steinfeldt grounded to short, but the shortstop threw the ball into the stands, and Zimmerman scored. Even though both Chance and Tinker were out with injuries, the Cubs machine rolled on. The Cubs left Chicago with a 6½-game lead. Before their next game in St. Louis, the Cubs played an exhibition game in

Monmouth, Illinois. A crowd of 3,000 attended, the biggest crowd up to that date for anything in Monmouth. Chance let Evers manage the game, and the only regulars who played were Evers, Steinfeldt and Schulte.[41]

Due to make-up games, the series between the A's and Naps went from July 22 through 26 and included three doubleheaders, with Sunday off. The A's won on the 23rd, with Coombs throwing a complete game shutout. In the first game of the July 25 doubleheader, the oldest pitcher in the league faced the third oldest, both threw complete games, and 43-year-old Cy Young beat 34-year-old Eddie Plank for his 501st victory.[42] In the nightcap, Cy Morgan beat the pitcher who had been Cleveland's best, Addie Joss. Joss had joined the Naps in 1902. In his debut, on a pop fly to the right fielder, the fielder claimed he caught it, and the newspaper accounts agreed with the right fielder. The umpire disagreed, and it was ruled a base hit. Joss completed the game as a one-hitter. Joss was the best pitcher on the Naps from 1905 through 1908, going 20–11, 21–9, 27–11, and 24–11. On October 2, 1908, in the middle of a white-hot pennant race, Joss was the winner in a game that has been called the finest pitchers' duel ever. The Naps were one game up on the White Sox, and one-half game behind the Tigers. Joss faced Ed Walsh of the White Sox in Cleveland. Walsh struck out 15 batters and allowed one unearned run when he picked off a runner at first but the first baseman made a bad throw, the runner eventually scoring. Joss threw 74 pitches in a 90-minute game, and allowed nothing for a 1–0 perfect game.[43] Two seasons later, Joss no-hit the White Sox again on April 20, 1910. Until 2014, Joss was the only pitcher to throw two no-hitters against one team. However, Joss hurt his pitching arm in 1910, and his start on July 24 was one of only 12 this year.[44] The A's and Naps split the final doubleheader of the series on July 26. Cleveland clobbered Bender in the second game, but he took one for the team by pitching a complete game even though he lost, 8–2. The home stand ended with four games in four days against Washington. As there were no doubleheaders, it must have seemed like a breeze. Jimmy Dygert started the first game of this series.[45] Dygert is the one player in the major leagues who was considered smaller than John Evers. Dygert was described by Alfred H. Spink in *The National Game* as: "the toy pitcher of the Athletics of the American League. He only weighs 115 pounds, but this is made up mostly of nerve and muscle. Clubs who have opposed the Athletics say the little fellow has bluffed his way through the American League ever since Connie Mack discovered him at New Orleans in 1904."[46]

Dygert lost this game, but had won quite a few for the A's since coming up on August 31, 1905. The native of Utica, New York, was discovered by Mack while playing for the Utica minor league team in 1904. Mack bought Dygert's contract and sent him to New Orleans for the 1905 season. Even though there was a yellow-fever outbreak in New Orleans during this season, Dygert made New Orleans his home the rest of his life. A week after reporting to Philadelphia, Dygert won a game in relief. He learned his trade the rest of 1905 and 1906, with a combined 12–17 record for the A's. Dygert was known as a right-handed pitcher who could control all his pitches, which included a spitball. Everything came together for Dygert in 1907, his best year in the majors. He started 28 games, pitched in 42, and went 21–8. A small man, he was not quite the workhorse the other starting pitchers were. Even with his fine work in 1907, he completed 18 of 28 starts, a smaller percentage than the A's other pitchers. Mack commented well after the fact, in an *Atlantic Monthly* article in 1943: "The worst mistake I ever made was back in 1907, running nip-and-tuck with Detroit. I had a pitcher named Jimmy Dygert who could beat anyone for seven innings, then he was finished. If I had found this out in time, I could have won the pennant. I didn't realize it until after the season."[47] Mack may have known this, but acted on it too late in the July 27, 1910, game against Washington. Dygert was up 4–1 after seven innings and gave up three runs in the eighth before leaving for Plank. The Nationals scored one more run on a squeeze play, hanging the loss on Dygert. Dygert was not a main cog in the A's pitching staff in 1910, going 4–4 in eight starts and 19 total appearances. This was Dygert's last year in the majors.[48]

This same problem caused a loss the next day for the A's. Morgan had a 5–4 lead going into the ninth inning, but gave up one run in the ninth and another in the tenth to lose, 6–5. Coombs and Bender restored order in the last two games of the month, beating the Nationals, 4–0 and 7–5. The A's got seven runs off Walter Johnson on July 30, and hung on. Plank relieved Bender in the ninth inning to save the victory. At the end of July, the A's had a six-game lead over second-place Boston.[49] As with the Cubs, the A's strength was their pitching and infield. These were two of the most famous infields of early 20th century baseball. The Cubs' infield got their public nickname from the Tinker to Evers to Chance poem published on July 10, 1910. The A's infield would not get their nickname until August 1911, when they were dubbed the "$100,000 infield." We have already discussed Harry Davis, the first baseman in 1910. Davis was 36 in 1910 and wanted to manage. He knew Mack was manager of the A's for as long as Mack wanted. Davis was happy playing for Mack, and Mack intended to honor Davis' wish to manage at some future point. Because of that, Mack had two players on the 1910 roster as possible future replacements for Davis at first base. Ben Houser was the bigger, older and more experienced of the two. A left-handed thrower and hitter, Houser had played in the minors from 1902–1909. Mack signed Houser before 1910 training camp, and Houser made the team. Mack thought Davis would be fine in 1910, which turned out to be true. While Davis' hitting fell off a bit in 1910, his leadership was first-rate. Houser was the only other person to play first base, playing in 26 games. His hitting was not impressive, with a .188 average. Mack decided after spring training in 1911 to get rid of Houser, trading him to the Browns.[50] That left John McInnis. McInnis was from Gloucester, Massachusetts, one of five brothers whose mother ran a boarding house for fishermen. When the fishermen were in port, they would play ball, and the brothers were part of their games. When John was about eight, he took part in the warm-ups to the games. Whenever John made a good catch or hit, the fishermen would say "That's the stuff, John." This led to his nickname of "Stuffy." When Stuffy reached his full height of 5'8" at the age of 17, he was playing for Haverhill in the New England League and batting .301. Mack heard of McInnis through his brother Thomas Mack, and signed McInnis to a contract for 1909. Haverhill appealed to the National Commission that McInnis belonged to them, but lost their appeal. When McInnis made the A's in 1909, he was a shortstop, but Mack was content with his shortstop. McInnis played 14 games while Jack Barry was hurt in 1909, hitting .239. McInnis spent the year working out at all infield positions before games and sitting next to Mack on the bench during the games. Several minor league managers approached Mack during 1909, asking him to farm McInnis out. Mack declined, stating he was training McInnis himself. In 1910, Harry Davis taught McInnis how to play first base during infield practice. However, McInnis never played first base in 1910. He played in 38 games at short, second, third, pinch-hitter and one game in the outfield. Mack had not made up his mind who was going to replace Davis, but he had two players to work with in 1910.[51]

The rest of the infield was set. The double play combination was what Mack wanted in his ballplayers. Both were college men. During the 19th century, ballplayers had the reputation of being rough, drunk, uneducated carousers. While this reputation was probably overblown, there was some truth in it. Mack had lived through this time and wanted as many educated players as he could get. Eddie Collins of Columbia and Jack Barry of Holy Cross were part of a surprisingly large population of players who had at least attended college. Only five percent of the total population had attended some college in 1910. The percentage of major league players was closer to 25 percent. Some of these were like Eddie Plank, who probably never took a college level class at Gettysburg, taking high school level classes and pitching for the college baseball team. A partial list of players who attended college and were playing in the major leagues in 1910 was given by Harry Hooper in *The Glory of Their Times*:

> Bill Carrigan—Holy Cross, Jake Stahl—University of Illinois, Larry Gardner and Ray Collins—University of Vermont, Harry Hooper and Duffy Lewis—St. Mary's of California, Chris Mahoney—Fordham, Christy Mathewson—Bucknell, Frank Chance—Washington University, Hal Chase—Santa Clara, Buck Herzog—University of Maryland, Orvie Overall—University of California, Eddie Plank—Gettysburg College, Chief Bender—Dickinson College, Art Devlin—Georgetown, Ginger Beaumont—Beloit College, Andy Coakley and Jack Barry—Holy Cross, Eddie Collins—Columbia, Eddie Grant—Harvard, Fred Tenney—Brown, Bob Bescher and Ed Reulbach—Notre Dame, Jack Coombs—Colby, Harry Davis—Girard College, Chief Meyers—Dartmouth, Davy Jones—Dixon College, etc.[52]

Neither Barry nor Collins was with the A's because they went to college. They could play ball.

John Joseph "Jack" Barry was from Meriden, Connecticut. He went to Holy Cross at the age of 17 and was due to graduate in June 1908. Mack's brother Thomas lived in the town where Holy Cross was located (Worcester, Massachusetts), and scouted Barry his entire college career. Connie Mack went to Worcester after the 1907 season ended, and Tom Mack invited Barry to meet Mack. Barry's college coach recommended that Barry listen to Mack, and consider signing with Mack due to Mack's reputation for molding young players. Barry asked for a bonus, which was against Mack's policy. Mack agreed to the bonus ($300), but asked Barry to keep it quiet. Barry signed the contract, to take effect after the 1908 Holy Cross baseball season and graduation. Mack gave Barry the money and put the contract in his safe in Philadelphia. This was normal business practice in 1908. Barry went directly from

Holy Cross to the A's after his final game on June 16, 1908. Mack told Barry he would sit on the bench and observe. That lasted until July 4, when Barry pinch-ran. On July 15, in the second game of a double header, the starting shortstop was Barry and the starting second baseman was Collins. Even though the A's won that game, Mack was not convinced. The rest of the year Barry played second, short and third. After this 40-game trial in 1908 and 1909 spring training, Mack decided Barry was his shortstop. Barry played 124 games at short in 1909 in what would become a typical year for him. His batting average was not impressive at .214. He and Collins considerably tightened up the A's defense. Barry's real value was shown during the games he missed. Barry missed the first week of the season due an injury, and the A's had a losing record for that week. He played every day until the final game with the Tigers in the third week of September, when he was spiked by Ty Cobb. Barry was unable to play the rest of the year. The A's, who were in the race at this point, fell behind and lost the pennant. What appeared true about Barry was that he was a winner. His statistics were not too good, but all the teams he was on had winning records. Like Joe Tinker, Barry was known for clutch hitting, something that was hard to measure. His signature play was known as the double squeeze. This was a suicide squeeze with runners on second and third. Both were to start running on the pitch, and both were expected to score if the batter got the bunt down. Barry's hitting improved in 1910 and he was batting .276 on July 7, and making many other contributions to the A's success.[53]

The other two members of the A's infield were among the best young players in baseball. Edward Trowbridge "Eddie" Collins grew up just north of New York City, in Tarrytown, New York. He was an outstanding athlete. Collins went to Columbia University in New York City, starring on the football team as a 145-pound quarterback. Collins was not much of a baseball fan, preferring football. But he liked to get paid for playing a sport during his summers off, and in 1906 the best option was baseball. The Yale coach, Johnny Lush, asked Collins to join Lush's team in Plattsburgh, New York. Collins played there for three weeks, but the team folded and failed to pay the players. Collins moved on to Rutland, Vermont, where he was spotted by A's pitcher Andy Coakley, who was on his honeymoon. Collins was not the only college man playing summer league baseball for pay. Colleges were tolerant of this practice, as there were no athletic scholarships at this time and many of the players needed money for tuition. When the Rutland team completed its season (and the players were paid), Collins rejoined Johnny Lush in Rockville, Connecticut. Mack sent one of his catchers to look Collins over, and the catcher/scout said, "Get him quick. He's got the makings." Mack had played against Johnny Lush in the majors and asked Lush to bring Collins to see him when the A's were in New York. A meeting was arranged for September 9, 1906. Collins was not sure he wanted to pursue baseball as a career. He told Mack he was not sure he was good enough, and might go to law school. Collins had enough confidence in himself to ask for a guarantee he would not be sent to the minors. Mack agreed. He got Collins' signature on two documents. One was a 1907 contract for $400 a month. The other document read: "In consideration of Edward T. Collins signing for the season of 1907, the American League Base Ball Club of Phili does hereby agree not to farm or loan him to any base ball club without his consent."[54]

Collins joined the A's for the last three weeks of the season.

The A's infield in 1910. Left to right: Harry Davis, 1b; Eddie Collins, 2b; Frank Baker, 3b; Jack Barry, ss.

Sometimes he was called Eddie Sullivan to help keep his college eligibility. This turned out not to matter, as Collins' activity in Rutland and Rockville cost him his eligibility. Collins played in six games for the A's in September, batting .200. Collins returned to Columbia for the academic year. He was paid to coach the Columbia baseball team in the spring 1907 semester (he did not play football, which Columbia dropped after the 1905 season). After graduation, Collins reported to the A's in June 1907.[55]

Collins spent the rest of the 1907 season and all of 1908 learning his trade. Mack preferred to keep talented young players with him on the bench, as we have seen with Stuffy McInnis in 1910. Collins played a couple of games in June 1907 due to injuries to the regulars. He played shortstop and made several more errors than hits. Mack made a trade to replace the injured players and sat Collins next to him. In August, Mack got a request from the Newark, New Jersey, minor league team for Collins. Per their agreement, Collins had to approve going to the minors. Collins approved the move and played four games in Newark. Collins went 8-for-16, making three errors at shortstop in his first game. Newark asked Collins to finish out the season, but Collins exercised his right to go back to Philadelphia. This was the extent of Eddie Collins' minor league career. As the A's were in the 1907 pennant race until the final week of September, Collins saw what a pennant race was like, even though he played just 14 games with Philadelphia, hitting .348.

Collins missed spring training in 1908 due to pneumonia. When the season started, he played the outfield for ten games before moving to shortstop. Collins and the other youngsters on the team were featured during morning practices and were tutored by Mack and Harry Davis. Davis was one of the best in the business at picking up mannerisms of pitchers that would tell the hitter what pitch was coming. Collins picked up this knack quickly. Collins was an awkward baserunner in 1908, particularly his sliding. Mack told him, "Eddie, did you ever notice how Cobb slides? Very nice, isn't it?" Collins took the hint and worked on his sliding. Collins played 47 games at shortstop, 28 games at second base in 1908. His hitting improved, up to .273. When Mack played Collins at second base late in the year, he moved Danny Murphy to right field. After the season, Mack decided that Collins would be the second baseman, Barry the shortstop, and Murphy the right fielder in 1909.[56]

In spring training 1909, Collins and Barry were on the Yannigans, the team of youngsters who traveled north separately from the regulars. Both were instigators of the daily meetings, going over plays on both offence and defense. Mack soon appropriated these meeting, holding one himself before every game during the 1909 season. Collins announced his presence to the sports world in 1909. He had one of the great years in baseball history, per the advanced statistical analysis available today. In his *New Historical Baseball Abstract* (published in 2001), Bill James states that Collins' 1909 season was the second best ever by a second baseman, behind only Rogers Hornsby's 1922 season. Just the raw numbers for Collins in 1909 are impressive: .346 batting average, 198 hits, 62 walks, 104 runs scored, 56 RBI, 63 stolen bases, and per modern statistics Collins would have won the Gold Glove Award (which did not exist in 1909) as the best fielding second baseman in the American League.[57] There was no Most Valuable Player Award either. Collins would probably have come in second to Ty Cobb, who surpassed Collins in all the statistics listed above, and whose team won the pennant. Maybe because Collins was a college man, several of his superstitions were noted. When he got dressed for a game, the first item of uniform he put on was his cap. After the game, the last item of clothing he put on was his pants. He would not allow anyone else to touch his bat during a game, including the batboy. He chewed gum, but stuck the gum on the button on his cap when he went to bat. If the pitcher got two strikes on him, Collins took the gum off the top of his cap and put it back in his mouth. When the ball was thrown around the infield after an out, Collins returned the ball to the pitcher, not the third baseman. Collins and Barry were the leaders among the younger players on the A's.[58]

The other infielder for the A's in 1910 was a bit different than Davis, Collins and Barry. Those three had all attended college (Collins and Barry graduated, and Davis used his college background to work as an accountant when out of baseball in 1900). John Franklin "Frank" Baker was born near Trappe on the Eastern Shore of Maryland to a family that had been in this area over 200 years. Baker was born on a farm and lived on that farm his whole life. Baker typified the expression "country strong." He could lift a hundred pound sack of corn and put it on a wagon with one hand. He was discovered as a sandlot player by a major leaguer only a year older, Buck Herzog of the Giants. Herzog, a Baltimore native, was managing a semi-pro team in Ridgely, Maryland.

Herzog signed Baker for $5 a game and made him a third baseman. By 1908, the 22-year-old Baker was in the minors with Reading of the Tri-State League. In 1908, Mack sent two players to Reading in return for the right to take one player from the Reading roster. Baker was hitting .299, and Mack needed a young third baseman. Baker reported on September 20, 1908, in Chicago. Baker spotted Mack eating breakfast in the hotel, came up to the table and said, "I'm here, Mr. Mack." That was a long statement for Baker. After being shut out by the White Sox in a game where Baker sat, Mack started Baker in the second big league game Baker saw. It was against the White Sox, who were in the pennant race while the A's were well out of it, facing the best pitcher in the American League, Ed Walsh. Baker went 1-for-3 in that game, then 2-for-3 in his next game. Mack decided Baker was ready right away. Mack liked college men, but he liked really good ballplayers more. Mack thought Baker was a very good player, offensively and defensively. Baker hit .291 in nine games in September 1908, and Mack expected Baker to be his third baseman for 1909.[59]

Baker sprained his ankle running the bases against the Phillies just before the start of the 1909 season. He missed the first two weeks, then played 145 games. As Baker neither drank nor smoked nor chewed, Mack was confident in his ability to play every game. He was pleased with Baker as a hitter, batting him third in the lineup behind Collins. Baker produced. His production in 1909 was second only to Collins on the A's: .305 batting average, 27 doubles, leading the league with 19 triples, leading the team with 85 RBI, and 20 stolen bases.[60] Mack urged his young infielders to make all the plays they could and not to be afraid to throw the ball. Baker showed he was a good, if awkward looking, fielder. One of his fielding problems rose up on August 24, 1909. In an important game against the first-place Tigers, Baker tried to apply a tag to Ty Cobb. Baker had the ball in his right hand when Cobb slid. Baker missed Cobb, but Cobb spiked Baker while sliding in safe. Baker got the arm wrapped up and continued in the game, getting ten stitches after the game. Mack and Cobb had a newspaper dispute about the play after the game. Baker never complained. After his career, Baker noted: "I had no set way of handling Cobb at third base. He was so clever at sliding he kept the infielders off balance. You never know how he would slide. He could change direction in midair." The act of applying a tag brought out the awkwardness of Baker as a fielder. Later in his career, Baker tried to tag out a runner whose spikes

Frank Baker in 1910.

were nowhere near him. He missed the tag and came back to the bench with a spike cut. Mack looked at the hand and said, "What did he spike you with, Bake, his fingernails?" Even with these problems, Mack thought he had the infield he needed to win the pennant in 1910. On July 7, Baker was hitting .296 and Collins .286, both on their way to fine seasons.[61]

After their exhibition game in Monmouth, the Cubs arrived in St. Louis in a rainstorm. Their game on July 26 was canceled, even though the rain stopped by noon. Without a tarpaulin, the grounds were too wet to play on. This was the Cubs' last trip to St. Louis, so all remaining games needed to be played by Sunday, July 31. The Cards won an eventful game on the 27th, coming back from a 5–0 deficit. Schulte had two triples and a home run, and was victimized by a great catch in the outfield. Kling was called out for leaving early on a sacrifice fly, and Evers was ejected in the ensuing argument. The Cubs dusted themselves off and swept the rest of the series, winning five games in four days. The Cardinals were a bad team, part of the bottom-dwelling triumvirate of Brooklyn, St. Louis and Boston. After using three pitchers in the first game of the series, the Cubs use one in each of the remaining games. Overall, Reulbach, Pfiester, Brown and Cole all threw complete games. The final game of the series was the second game of a doubleheader on July 31. As both the Cubs and Cardinals had to travel to New York after the game, the Cardinals exercised their right to bat first in this game. There was as yet no rule that the home team had to bat last, and the home team had the choice to do either. This strategy backfired due to King Cole. He shut out the Cardinals for seven innings, at which point both teams had to leave to catch their train. As was noted in a small headline, Cole held them hitless. No big deal.[62]

The pitching staff was the Cubs' great strength during their run from 1906 through 1910. All great pitching staffs have an ace, and the Cubs had one. Mordecai Peter Centennial Brown was gifted with two middle names, two nicknames, and great ability. He had started two games against the Cardinals in the last series, losing the first game and winning the first game of the Sunday doubleheader. Brown had joined the Cubs in 1904 after a losing season with the Cardinals, a last-place team. Brown had a winning year in 1904, became the ace of the staff in 1905, and was still the ace in 1910. Brown started and relieved. In the heated pennant race year of 1908, Brown started 31 games and relieved 13 times. In 1909, he started 34 games and relieved 16 times.[63] So far in 1910, Brown was on track for similar numbers.

Mordecai got both of his nicknames in his youth. He was born in Nyesville, Indiana, in 1876, hence the middle name Centennial. At the age of seven, he inadvertently put his right hand into a corn shredder at his uncle's farm. He lost half his index finger, and the pinkie finger was damaged. A youngster, Brown quickly resumed his life. A couple of months later, he was running around with some friends when he fell and broke the fall with his right hand. The result of that fall was broken bones in the previously undamaged fingers, and the pinkie was paralyzed. The broken bones healed, but the middle and ring fingers on his right hand were bent and gnarled. This handicap did not keep Brown from the normal fate of many young men in this mining area. Brown entered the mines as a checker. When they had time, the miners played baseball. Brown played the infield, even though his throws to first sometimes took an erratic path. When the pitcher for his coal mine team showed up drunk one day, Brown was put in to pitch. He was successful enough to attract the attention of the local Terre Haute minor league team. Brown started off poorly with Terre Haute in 1901. The team was ready to release him when 600 of the local miners signed a petition stating that they would boycott Terre Haute games if their fellow miner was released. Hence, Miner Brown got another chance. He made good, eventually making his way to Omaha.

By this time, "Three Finger" Brown had decided that baseball was a fine alternative to the mines and kept himself in good shape. His workout routine in spring training made other players quit before he was done. Brown's signature pitch was an overhand curve ball. He could throw it three different ways. The most effective was the hook curve, which Ty Cobb called "the most deceiving, most devastating pitch I ever faced." While this pitch hurt batters' averages and confidence, it hurt Brown physically. Brown said he suffered excruciating pain every time he threw it. But it beat the mines. One of his fellow

Mordecai Brown in 1910. He batted left; note the damaged right hand.

miners, ex–minor leaguer Legs O'Connell, had shown Brown how to pitch when they played on the coal mine baseball team. By 1901, Brown was a known commodity. He was visited at his off-season home in Terre Haute by another young pitcher, Christy Mathewson. They became friends and stayed friends until Matty's death. Brown versus Mathewson was the most compelling pitching rivalry in the National League from when they first faced each other in 1904 until their final year in 1916. From 1904 through 1910, one or the other was the best pitcher in the National League.[64]

Brown's statistics are very impressive. He holds the record for lowest ERA in the National League for a starting pitcher since 1900, 1.06 in 1906. If there had been a statistic for saves, Brown would have led the league from 1908 through 1911. After establishing himself with the Cubs in 1904, Brown ran off five great years. He records were: 18–10 in 1905, 26–6 in 1906, 20–6 in 1907, 29–9 in 1908, and 27–9 in 1909. The Cubs led the league in ERA four of these five years and won the pennant in three of them. Brown had a somewhat unusual World Series record. He started and lost the first game of the 1906 Series, won Game 4 with a two-hit shutout, then lost the final game. Because he lost the first game of this Series, Chance would not start him in the first game of any World Series afterward. Brown did not pitch until the final game of the 1907 World Series, clinching the Series with a seven-hit shutout. Brown won the first game of the 1908 World Series—in relief. He pitched a four-hit shutout in Game 4 of a five-game Series. After the 1908 Series, Brown had a 4–2 Series record with one save and an ERA under 2.[65] Even with that record, it was known that superstitious Frank Chance would not start Brown in the first game of a possible 1910 World Series. That didn't bother Brown, who was going about his business in 1910 on the way to another outstanding season. The Cubs had a seven-game lead on July 31 when they traveled to New York to face the Giants.

7

August

By the time the Cubs' and Cardinals' train pulled into New York on August 1, their roster had changed. Fred Luderus had progressed through the minors for four years and started the season as the backup first baseman, an important job for the Cubs due to Chance's injury problems. During the first two months of the season, Luderus played 17 games at first base.[1] By June, Chance decided that there were better options on the roster to play first when he was out, even though Luderus was the left-handed hitting choice. On July 31, Chance sat out the doubleheader after playing three days in a row in St. Louis in July, which makes sense to anyone who has lived through a summer in this area. Hofman played first base, with Zimmerman taking Solly's normal spot in center. There were other games earlier in July when Archer played first. Luderus, a 24-year-old rookie, had not shown enough to gain Chance's confidence. Just before the Cubs left St. Louis, they made a trade with the Phillies. Luderus was sent to Philadelphia for pitcher Bill Foxen. Foxen was a left-hander, joining Pfiester and Kroh as left-handed pitchers on the Cubs staff. During this period of Cubs excellence, most young players on the Cubs would stick for a short while and get traded for a veteran. Other examples in the period 1905–1910 were Hans Lobert, Davy Jones, Frank Beebe, and Andy Coakley. Some youngsters established themselves as regulars, such as Solly Hofman, Jimmy Archer, and Rube Kroh. The Cubs were not interested in developing players at this point, they wanted to win now. With three consecutive pennants in 1906–1908 and a seven-game lead in 1910 it's hard to argue with their success.

Fred Luderus left the train in Philadelphia to join his new team. Bill Foxen stayed in New York, where the Phillies had just finished a series, and joined the Cubs on August 2.[2] Foxen had a career record of

15–19 after approximately two years with the Phillies. He got an opportunity in his first game with the Cubs. On August 2, Overall started against Mathewson. Overall had one of those games all pitchers, no matter how good, have from time to time. In the first inning, the Giants got four hits and three walks, which produced four runs. Chance went to a left-hander, but the left-hander was Rube Kroh. Kroh pitched shutout ball the rest of the way. The Cubs won, 5–4, using two-run singles by Hofman and Steinfeldt in the third inning, then an RBI single by Hofman in the sixth. Floyd Myron Kroh had been a phenom, making the big leagues for a cup of coffee with the Red Sox at the age of 19 in 1906. Several hard-throwing, left-handed pitchers were nicknamed "Rube" around this time, after the most famous left-hander of this time, Rube Waddell. That's what happened to Kroh, who was known as Rube for the rest of his career. Kroh played small parts of the 1906 and 1907 seasons with the Red Sox, ending up with a 1–4 record in eight appearances. He came up next in September 1908 with the Cubs. He was mentioned in some accounts of the Merkle game as the person on the Cubs who secured a ball that came to Evers to force out Merkle. Other accounts mention other Cubs, but it shows Kroh was with the Cubs during the finish of the hottest pennant race in NL history. Kroh made two appearances in 1908, with no record. He made the team in training camp in 1909, becoming the fifth starter at a time when four was the common number. Kroh pitched in 17 games in 1909, starting 13 and winning nine with an ERA of 1.65. Kroh had been used as a reliever and spot starter so far in 1910, and got the win on August 2. Chance still did not trust Kroh, using him very sparingly even though Kroh had been on the team since the start of 1909.[3]

    The Giants were hopeful that they could cut into the Cubs' lead during this series in New York. It did not work out that way. The Cubs won three of four games, leaving New York City with an eight-game lead over Pittsburgh and 8½ over the Giants. The second game of the series was a 3–0 shutout by Pfiester, and featured Evers-Tinker-Chance and Tinker-Evers-Chance double plays. It started raining in the fifth inning, but the umpires kept the teams playing and finished in one hour 35 minutes. Brown stopped the Giants in the third game, which featured a home run by Schulte. Kroh got another chance to pitch in the final game and was shelled in a 10–1 loss. The Cubs moved on to Philly for a scheduled four-game series. They lost two of three games, with a Sunday off and a rainout. Overall was smoked again in the first game, lasting one inning and giving up five runs. Fred Luderus had two hits against his old team, one a three-run triple. There was some activity on the Sunday off, August 7. Steinfeldt returned to Chicago for medical attention on a shoulder problem, with Zimmerman taking his place in the lineup. Kling gave out the schedule for his billiard league, which was printed in the *Chicago Tribune* on August 8. Several Cubs participated in the normal activity for a Sunday off in Philadelphia, a trip to Atlantic City. It was an indication of how popular Atlantic City was that King Cole ended up sleeping outside, as he could not get a room. After a rainout on Monday, the Cubs split a doubleheader. Cole showed no ill effects from his adventure in Atlantic City, pitching a complete game victory in the nightcap. Kroh did not return to Philadelphia and either quit the team or was cut, depending on which story you believe.

Their game on Wednesday was rained out as well, and the Cubs traveled to Boston. Their Thursday game in Boston was rained out, and both the Cubs and sportswriter Sanborn thought the game could have been played. Three games were played in Boston, and the Cubs swept them. Reulbach started the first game and Brown saved it. Overall pitched well in the second game before Richie came in and got the win. Cole threw a complete game in the finale.

On another Sunday off, the Cubs traveled to New York for a series with Brooklyn. The trip was supposed to be by boat, but the Cubs missed the boat and took a train. The weather was a major story on this trip. The Cubs split a doubleheader with the Dodgers in a steady drizzle. The next day the Dodgers called the game before it started, though the Cubs thought it could have been played. Several Cubs took the subway to the Polo Grounds and watched the Giants beat the Pirates. On August 17, the Cubs concluded the Eastern trip with another split doubleheader at Brooklyn. Cole had another outstanding game, a one-hitter where the one hit was a pop fly that Tinker fell down chasing. The Cubs and Dodgers got on the same train going to Chicago. The Cubs stopped off in Buffalo for an exhibition game, which was rained out. Some Cubs went to Niagara Falls before traveling on to Chicago. The Cubs went 14–6 on this trip, with four rainouts plus one rainout of an exhibition game. The Cubs returned to Chicago with a 5½-game lead over Pittsburgh and 7½ games over the Giants.[4]

After playing 30 of their 33 games in July at home, the A's set out on a Western trip on July 31. Coombs started the opener in Chicago and was shelled in a 6–1 loss. He could have been tired, because

Coombs had one of the greatest months in AL history in July. He tied the record for most wins in a month (set by Philadelphia pitcher Rube Waddell in 1902) with a 10–1 record. The one loss was a game where Baker and Collins made key errors. Even though the A's had veteran pitchers Plank and Bender, Coombs was the main man for the A's in 1910.[5]

John Wesley "Colby Jack" Coombs was a Down Easter from Maine. He went to Colby College in Waterville, Maine. As a freshman, he was the outstanding athlete on the Colby football, basketball, track and baseball teams. Thomas Mack tipped off his brother Connie about Coombs. Connie Mack scouted Coombs in 1905 and offered him a contract for the 1906 season in December 1905. Coombs signed the $2,400 contract and returned to school. Mack put the contract in his safe until the end of the school year. Coombs never played in the minors, reporting after graduation. Coombs came to Philadelphia on July 2, 1906, and got lost on Philadelphia streetcars trying to get to the ballpark. After Coombs arrived, he warmed up next to Rube Waddell, who showed Coombs what major league pitches looked like. Coombs said he was ready to pack up and go back to dad's farm in Kennebunk.[6] He appeared in 23 games as a rookie, starting 18, finishing 13 with a 10–11 record.

His most memorable game in 1906 was called

Jack Coombs in 1909.

"the greatest game in the history of baseball" in the next day's paper. After 23 innings the score was tied, 1–1. Some players asked the umpire to call the game because of darkness, and the umpire refused. In the top of the 24th inning, the A's scored three runs off Joe Harris. Coombs got the Red Sox out in the bottom of the inning. Both pitchers threw complete games. Since this game lasted 4 hours 47 minutes, the second game of the scheduled doubleheader could not be played.[7] In 1907 Coombs got off to a mediocre start. His record was 6–9 on July 27 when he tore a tendon in his right (pitching) arm and missed the rest of the season. At the start of the 1908 season, Coombs was one of the outfielders for the A's, having always been a good hitter. He played 47 games in the outfield in 1908, hitting .255. Coombs was often used as a pinch-hitter. Coombs was one of several A's who were known to spot mannerisms of pitchers that would allow him to call what kind of pitch was coming. He did this from the third base coaching box in games when he was not pitching. He appeared in 26 games as a pitcher, going 7–5 with a 2.00 ERA. The A's were in transition in 1908, and Mack was experimenting. Coombs came back in 1909 as a full-time pitcher. The A's used six starters this year, and Coombs was in the mix even though he had the worst record of the bunch at 12–11. Mack knew Coombs was still regaining his strength from his arm injury.[8] Even though the A's got off to a great start in 1910, Coombs did not win his first game until the last week in May. He threw his first shutout on June 22 and had five more in July. Even with his poor game on August 1, Coombs was the A's counterpart to Mordecai Brown as the ace of the staff in 1910.

The A's won the next two games in Chicago. Morgan started and Plank saved the game on August 2, and Bender threw a complete game on the 3rd in a 2–1 win when Baker scored the winning run on an error in the 9th. The game on August 4 was a classic, and I will let Ring Lardner (covering the White Sox for the *Chicago Tribune*) tell you about it:

> Sixteen innings. 0 to 0. That was the way the last game of the series between the Sox and Athletics wound up. People who left the park at the finish, four minutes before 7 o'clock, did not regret the loss of supper half as much as they would have regretted missing that ball game.
> Perhaps it was not the best ever played, but don't try to tell anyone who saw it that there have been many better. The book says there was just one longer runless contest in the big leagues and that was the one between Washington and Detroit in July last year. That one lasted eighteen rounds. Most of us missed that one, so we must be content to talk about yesterday's in the years to come.

And when we talk don't let us say that so and so could and should have scored in such and such an inning. Let us remember only that neither side had the shadow of a right to win against such pitching as that of Ed Walsh of Meriden, Conn., and John Coombs of Colby College. And don't let us say that Walsh was better than Coombs, or that Coombs was better than Walsh. They were both just about perfect. Coombs struck out eighteen men. Walsh made up for that with his feat in the first half of the sixteenth inning when he absolutely refused to allow a Philadelphia run with fast men on second and third, no one out and three of the Athletics' five best hitters coming up.[9]

As Lardner made clear many times in writing about baseball, he was a fan of baseball as played in this era. He liked good pitching, small ball, and good fielding. This game epitomized that kind of baseball for him in 1910.

Mack had regular players at seven of the eight positions. The exception was at catcher. Ira Thomas was the holdover catcher and played less than half the time. At the beginning of 1910, Coombs was having trouble finding the strike zone with Thomas catching. Coombs would not look at the batter when pitching, he concentrated on a part of the catcher's body. Thomas was six feet tall, and catchers did not go into a squat at this time, just crouched a bit, so Coombs was missing the strike zone high. The other main catcher, Jack Lapp, was 5'8". After a couple of poor starts in April, Lapp became Coombs' personal catcher. Two other catchers were used by the A's this year, but "Jawn" Coombs would not pitch to Thomas the rest of the regular season. (Most people called Coombs by his nickname, Jack, but Mack called him John, with Mack's Massachusetts accent came out as "Jawn").[10]

Ira Thomas made the majors with the New York Highlanders in 1906. He spent two years with the Highlanders as the backup catcher, catching 42 games in 1906 and 61 games in 1907. Thomas was sold to the Tigers before the 1908 season and caught 29 games for the pennant winners. Thomas was an established major league backup catcher when Mack acquired him for $4,000 from the Tigers in December 1908. As a matter of fact, he was established as a player like Mack. Connie Mack had been a major league catcher known for his defense and smarts, and any hitting was a bonus. Thomas had two poor hitting seasons in New York, batting .200 and .192. He had a good stretch in 1908, hitting .307 in 101 at-bats with the Tigers. Mack got Thomas mainly for his defense.[11] Before acquiring Thomas, Mack had secured John Walker "Jack" Lapp from Hazelton in the Atlantic League in August 1908. Lapp was a local kid, from Frazer, Pennsylvania. Mack played Lapp in 13 games in 1908 and thought that Lapp would be an acceptable backup catcher based on his defense. Lapp hit .143 in 1908, but his defense allowed him to make the team in 1909 even though there were already two catchers on the roster.[12] The Opening Day catcher for the A's in 1909 was "Doc" Powers, a 37-year-old veteran who had been in the majors since 1899 and with the A's since 1905. Powers got sick during the Opening Day game, finished the game and collapsed in the clubhouse. He was taken to the hospital, where the doctors diagnosed him with acute gastritis and said he would be back in a few days. They were wrong, and Powers was buried a few days later. It turned out he had an intestinal blockage which caused gangrene. Powers died on April 25.[13] A few days later, Mack purchased Patrick Joseph "Paddy" Livingston from Indianapolis. Livingston had been in baseball since 1901, mostly in the minors. He had played the 1906 season with Cincinnati, catching 47 games and hitting .158 before returning to the minors. These three catchers were on the A's in 1909 when the A's made their run at the Tigers. All were similar players, good on defense, smart, and any offense was a bonus. The A's got some good offense from catchers in 1909 when Lapp hit .337 in 19 games. Mack opted for defense first at catcher, playing Thomas in 84 games with a .223 average, and Livingston in 64 games with a .234 average.[14] Catchers being subject to injuries more than other players, Mack picked up another in 1910. Patrick William "Pat" Donahue had been a backup catcher with the Red Sox since 1908. He fit the mold of the other A's catchers, a light-hitting defensive specialist. Donohue played 14 games with the A's in 1910 before he was sold to the Naps.

As this review of the four catchers who played for the A's in 1910 shows, Mack was not looking for offense at this position. For example, Ira Thomas knew from playing with the Tigers that Detroit first baseman Claude Rossman had a psychological block about throwing. He often froze and would not throw, and if he did throw, threw poorly. Thomas showed the A's how to take advantage of this on May 22, 1909. Even though Thomas was slow, he took a long lead off first and started for second. The pitcher threw to Rossman, who would not throw to second even though he had plenty of time. Manager Hughie Jennings pulled Rossman from the game. The rest of this series, the A's ran wild on the bases when Rossman had the ball. Other teams picked up on this, and in July Rossman was traded to the Browns. After playing two games in the outfield, Rossman never played another major league game.[15] As a player, Mack was known for looking for an edge like this, and that is what he wanted from his catchers.

The A's arrived in St. Louis with a six-game lead which was extended when they swept the Browns in a four-game series. Plank, Bender and Coombs threw complete games, and the hitters gave them plenty of runs. Lord and Baker led the way with multiple RBI in the series. Collins stole home in the final game, and the A's scored a run on an infield fly where the umpire invoked the infield fly rule calling the batter out, and no one caught the pop-up. None of this was much of a surprise, as the Browns were terrible this year. They would win only 47 games and finish 57 games out of first place. The next stop on the trip was Detroit. The Tigers, three-time defending champions of the American League, were not having a good year and were 10½ games out of first. The main interest of Detroit fans was the batting race for the Chalmers automobile between Ty Cobb and Nap Lajoie. In a series where the A's won three out of four, several plays and actions show the difference between baseball in 1910 and today. A's pitchers threw four complete games. Plank started the first game of the series and the final game on two days' rest. The three home runs hit during this series were all inside-the-park home runs. The playing fields were so large that anyone could hit a home run this way, even Ira Thomas, the slowest player on the A's. Thomas performed this feat in the eighth inning of the final game, providing the margin in a 7–4 A's win after the Detroit catcher dropped a foul pop-up during Livingston's at bat. In the lone A's loss, Morgan had a 4–0 lead in the bottom of the eighth when he gave up five runs with two out. There was no pitching change. Manager Jennings was suspended for the final game after his behavior in the second game. Due to illness, only one umpire worked the second game of this series. Jennings and Cobb argued with the umpire during the early innings. Jennings was ejected and refused to leave the field for a while after being ejected. After the game, the players had to escort the umpire to the groundskeeper's shack, as there was no umpire's dressing room. Fans were trying to get at the umpire, and fans were allowed on the field after a game back then.

The road trip finished up in Cleveland with a six-game series. The A's were three outs from sweeping a doubleheader on August 13. Coombs threw eight shutout innings, going into the ninth with a 2–0 lead. A single, double, out, triple and sacrifice fly scored three runs for the Naps. The A's won the nightcap, 14–1. There was a story that Harry

Krause was put on waivers by the A's and claimed by the Naps. Mack denied the story and claimed that Krause would remain with the A's. Krause had not made this road trip due to a sore arm. After a Sunday off, there was another doubleheader on Monday. The first game was a battle of Cys: Cy Morgan versus 43-year-old Cy Young. Both threw complete games in a ten-inning A's win. Paddy Livingston drove in the tying run in the eighth inning and the winning run in the tenth. The second game was a hitting exhibition for the A's, who got 19 hits. Lord, Baker, Oldring and Murphy had three each, while Davis and Thomas two. The hitting continued the next day, when the A's won, 18–3. Another Cy, Cy Falkenberg of the Naps, took one for the team by pitching a complete game. Collins and Baker had four hits apiece as the A's scored eight runs in the eighth inning and six in the ninth. The Naps won the finale to give the A's a 13–4 record on this trip. The A's returned home with an 11-game lead over the Red Sox.[16]

    The A's played western teams the rest of the month. First up was three games with the White Sox, which the A's swept. Coombs, Plank and Bender threw complete game victories. Mack was rotating four outfielders: Hartsel, Lord, Oldring and Murphy. Livingston was also playing quite a bit. Morgan started the first game against Cleveland. He was in trouble the whole game, and Dygert was warming up sporadically from the second inning on. Morgan pitched nine innings and left with the score 4–4. Lajoie drove in the tying run in the ninth inning with a double. Dygert pitched the tenth, giving up two runs on walks. The A's tied it up in the bottom of the tenth, and Tommy Atkins finished the game. The A's won it in the 12th on Lord's RBI single. The A's won the next two games against the Naps behind Coombs and Bender. The Browns came to town next, winning the first game of the series. Four A's pitchers (Plank, Morgan, Dygert and Atkins) were shelled. The Browns led 5–0 until the A's tied it up in the bottom of the seventh inning. The Browns scored four runs in the last two innings. Murphy hit a home run in the bottom of the ninth to finish a great game. Murphy went 5-for-5 and hit for the cycle. Coombs and Bender restored order in the last two games of the series, both throwing complete game victories. Coombs struck out 14 in a shutout, and Bender threw a three-hitter to move his record to 21–3. The final series of this home stand was with Detroit. When the Tigers came to Philly in August 1909, it was a fierce series featuring Cobb spiking Baker and Mack calling Cobb a dirty player. This series was calm since the A's had a 12-game lead and the Tigers were in fourth place. The Tigers won two of three games, beating Plank and Bender. There was a newspaper story that Cobb had called the A's "quitters." Cobb denied this and picked the A's to win the World Series. He said Morgan would not pitch in the Series due to "lack of nerve." Cobb disclosed he was contracted to a magazine to cover the Series.[17]

In the first game of this series, Harry Krause made his first appearance since July. Harry William Krause was one of a limited number of players from the West Coast in the major leagues at this time. Mack had heard about Krause from an old friend in San Francisco, Krause's home town. Mack tried to sign Krause by mail right after the 1907 season, but Krause declined to sign. He was attending St. Mary's College, and his mother wanted him to finish school. Mack visited the family in November 1907 while on a scouting trip. An offer of $400 a month, to start after Harry graduated in May 1908, turned the trick. Krause signed and went back to school. He reported to Philadelphia after graduation, pitched two games and going 1–1, and was sent to Harrisburg for the rest of the 1908 season. He was successful there, going 17–4. Mack thought Krause would be a good left-hander for the 1909 season and he made the team even with the pressure of Mack calling him a young Rube Waddell. Krause lived up to this billing in 1909, pitching in 32 games. He started 21, completing 16. In a tight pennant race, he ended up with an 18–8 record and led the league with a 1.39 ERA. He won his first 11 decisions as a 21-year-old rookie, losing his first game on July 18. Krause was part of the A's starting staff leaving training camp in 1910. He got a sore arm in June and was used sparingly the rest of the year. Coombs and Morgan picked up the slack, and Krause's sore arm caused minimal damage to the A's. After the series with Detroit concluded this home stand, the A's headed out on the road again with an 11-game lead over Boston.[18]

With the American League pennant essentially sewn up, the remaining race in the American League was for the batting crown. When the prize of a Chalmers automobile was announced before the year, it was made clear that there would be one prize for all players, not one for each league. By the middle of August, it was clear that the race would be decided in the American League, where the three leading hitters were more than 30 points ahead of the National League leader. Some Detroit players thought Ty Cobb was playing just for this prize, as it was clear the Tigers would not win the pennant this year. In early

August, Cobb got into a dispute with Davy Jones, the leadoff man for the Tigers. According to Jones' account in *The Glory of Their Times*, Cobb was in a bit of a slump, and the opposing pitcher was Ray Collins, who always gave Cobb trouble. Jones was on first with Cobb at bat. Jones said he looked for the hit-and-run sign, which was initiated by the batter, and did not see it. After the first pitch, Cobb stepped out and yelled at Jones that he had missed the hit-and-run sign. On the second pitch, the same thing happened, and Cobb went to the bench and refused to continue. Cobb sat out the next game. Before the following game, Detroit president Frank Navin met with Cobb and told him he had to play.[19] Soon after this, Cobb regained his batting stroke, and by August 17 he was listed as 12 points ahead of Tris Speaker, with Nap Lajoie 19 points in arrears. The problem was that this was listed in a newspaper under the heading "Auto Chasers" and was not official statistics. Official scoring in 1910 was done by one newspaperman at each game. After the game, this reporter sent his official scorecard to league headquarters where everything was tallied. These numbers were not issued to the public until the end of the season. Various papers in major league towns published statistics throughout the season, based on their own reporter's scorecards and the box scores listed in their paper. There were discrepancies between these numbers and the official numbers, because no one outside the league office knew the official numbers. In late August, the Nationals played consecutive games against the Tigers and Naps. Cobb was jeered, and Lajoie was cheered. This feeling was prevalent for fans and players. Both factors would play a part in the race for the Chalmers.[20]

The Cubs returned to action at home on August 19. Brooklyn was the opponent, after a three-game series between the same two teams in Brooklyn. Four more games were scheduled in Chicago. The Cubs made quick work of the second-division Dodgers, sweeping the series. Brown threw a complete game in the first contest. Rube Kroh reported to Cubs headquarters before this game, asking to come back to the team. Chance turned him down, and Kroh would not be a part of the team the rest of the year. Reulbach threw a complete-game three-hitter in the second game, which was over after the first inning. In the Cubs' first, Evers made an out, but Sheckard, Beaumont and Chance singled, Zimmerman walked, and Schulte hit a three-run triple, scoring himself on the right fielder's error. That's five runs after six batters, and the Cubs coasted. The Cubs finished the sweep with a doubleheader on

Sunday. Overall started, but a sore arm forced him out after two innings. Richie finished and got the win when the Cubs scored two runs in the seventh inning to take a 3–2 lead. This rally started after two outs, when Tinker drove in Archer with a double and scored on Kling's RBI single. Cole pitched a complete game in the nightcap. One run scored off him when Beaumont misjudged a line drive in center, which went for an inside-the-park home run. The Cubs scored five runs in the seventh inning for a 6–2 win for acting manager Evers. The losing pitcher for the Infants (as named in the *Tribune* that day) showed what could happen to a good pitcher on a bad team. George Bell started 36 games for Brooklyn in 1910, finishing 25 of them. He had an ERA of 2.64, better than the league average. His record was 10–27, leading the league in losses.[21]

After playing the poor Dodgers, the Cubs played the awful Boston Doves and kept them in last place with a three-game sweep. McIntire, Reulbach and Richie threw complete games, and Boston scored three runs in the whole series. McIntire helped his own cause with a home run out of the park in his shutout win. After this game, Beaumont learned that his brother-in-law had drowned in Iowa, and he left the team to attend the funeral. In the final game of the series, the Cubs hit the Doves with a big inning. Thanks to four hits, four walks and two errors, the Cubs scored nine runs in the sixth inning. The Cubs went into the next series with the Giants with an 8½-game lead over Pittsburgh and 11 games over New York.[22]

So far in August, Chance had not been able to use his regular lineup. Hofman, Steinfeldt, Chance himself, and Pfiester were hurt. Even though the Cubs were an older team, they had sufficient depth to survive this rash of injuries. Sportswriter Sy Sanborn often called the Cubs the cripples in August. Several players helped overcome this problem. Two were Zimmerman and Beaumont, who were at opposite ends of their careers. Beaumont was in his 12th and final year. Zimmerman was in his third full season, and the first in which he played a lot. Other subs helped the Cubs weather their injuries. John Reid "Harry" McIntire became a pro in 1898 and made the majors with Brooklyn in 1905. A right-handed spitball pitcher called "Handsome Harry," his name was spelled McIntyre in the *Tribune* until he corrected the spelling in April 1910.[23] McIntire filled in when Reulbach was out with diphtheria early in the year, and when Overall and Pfiester had sore arms late in the year. McIntire started 19 of his 28 games in 1910.

The closest thing the Cubs had to a relief specialist (a job that did not exist in 1910) was Lewis A. "Lew" Richie. Richie was from Ambler, Pennsylvania, and was in the minors from 1903 to 1905. He was bought by the Phillies for the 1906 season, staying in Philadelphia through April 1909, when he was traded to the Boston Doves. The Cubs acquired Richie from Boston in May 1910 after he pitched twice for the Doves. He started 11 games for the Cubs, finishing eight, and relieved 19 times in 1910. On the better teams in the National League, only Doc Crandall (24 relief appearances) on the Giants and Deacon Phillippe (23 relief appearances) on the Pirates were used more in relief.[24] John Francis Kane was another substitute. A Chicago native, Kane was the nearest counterpart to Evers on the Cubs. They were of a similar size, Kane going 5'6" and 120 pounds. Kane had started in the minors in 1903, making the Cincinnati team in 1907. He played 79 games for the Reds in 1907 at second base, shortstop, third base and the outfield, hitting .248. The Reds made him their regular center fielder in 1908, and he hit .213 with 30 stolen bases. The Cubs acquired Kane before the 1909 season, and he played 20 total games at four different positions, hitting .089. Zimmerman supplanted Kane as the main utility man in 1910. Kane played in 30 games in 1910, hitting .242, usually sitting unless there was a blowout or rash of injuries.[25]

At the beginning of the

Harry McIntire, 1910.

year, catcher was the position that required the most finagling. John Kling was the Cubs' regular catcher from 1901 through 1908. Kling averaged catching 104 games a year, so more than one catcher was always a requirement. Remember that the only protection catchers wore before 1908 was a chest protector and a mask, which was not well padded. Even though shin guards were first used by Roger Bresnahan in 1908, Kling never used them. There is a picture of Pfiester pitching to Kling in the 1906 World Series showing Kling catching without shin guards. The shin guards used by Bresnahan were based on cricket shin guards. Several catchers tried these guards and went back to catching without shin guards. This same picture shows Kling ready to receive the pitch. He is not in the squat position we associate with catchers today. He is stooped, the normal position assumed by catchers in this time when the pitcher was ready to deliver.[26] Teams carried at least two catchers, and many times three. When the Cubs had Kling, he was the regular.

John G. Kling was born in Kansas City in 1875. He played semi-pro and minor league ball around Kansas City before joining the Cubs in 1900. He played with and against Tinker during this time. Kling beat out Chance for the regular catching job by 1902. When Selee held the election to select a captain in 1905, Kling and Chance were the main candidates. There seem to have been no ill effects between these two after Chance won the election and became manager. Kling had three nicknames. Evers said he was called "Silent John" because he never argued with umpires, getting good calls that way. Many sources call him "Noisy" because he talked to batters all the time. He was also called "the Jew" even though he was baptized Lutheran.[27] Kling was one of the best defensive catchers of this time and a good offensive player. John McGraw said his catcher, Bresnahan, was better on defense, but that Kling had the better arm. In one 1907 World Series game, Kling picked Davy Jones off second and threw out Ty Cobb stealing. As the Tigers hit .209 and .203 in their two World Series against the Cubs, they could not afford to lose any base runners.[28] Kling had two brothers who were successful in the real estate business in Kansas City, and he invested profitably with them. Kling sat out the 1909 season as discussed before, running a billiard hall he owned in Kansas City. He won a billiards world championship after the 1908 season and was trying to start a billiard league during the 1910 season.[29] When Kling was finally reinstated in 1910, he was not ready to play regularly until about the end of May. After that, he was the regular catcher for the Cubs.

At the start of the season, the Cubs' catchers were Jimmy Archer and Tom Needham. Thomas J. "Tom" Needham was a native of Ireland whose family immigrated when he was four. He played baseball, football and basketball as a young man, which is impressive considering that basketball was invented when he was 14. He started in the minors in

John Kling, 1910.

1898, making the majors with the Boston Beaneaters in 1904. He played there through 1907, catching about half the games. He was a good defensive catcher who hit poorly, averaging around .200 in these years. He went to the Giants in 1908, playing in 54 games. He joined the Cubs in 1909, teaming up with Archer to replace Kling. He played quite a bit early in the 1910 season, but his hitting stayed around the .200 level. After Kling rejoined the Cubs, Needham was the emergency catcher.[30]

James Patrick "Jimmy" Archer was also a native of Ireland. He was born in Dublin, and his family immigrated to Toronto when he was six months old. As a young man, Archer worked in a cooperage and fell into a vat of boiling tar. His right arm was seared nearly to the bone. Archer recovered from this accident, but his right arm was permanently bent and stiffened at the elbow. Even with this problem, Archer played semi-pro ball in Toronto until he was 20, when he signed with Fargo in the minors. After a year in the minors, he had a trial with Detroit, which he failed. He returned to the minors for most of three years, getting another trial with Pittsburgh at the end of the 1907 season. Archer failed this trial as well, returning to the minors with Buffalo. Chance spotted Archer with Buffalo during the 1908 season. Once it became clear that Kling was not going to play in 1909, Chance acquired Archer before 1909 training camp. Archer caught 80 games in 1909, sharing the job with Pat Moran, who caught 74. By the end of the season it was clear that Archer could play the position.[31] Two witnesses in *The Glory of Their Times* stated that Archer had the best arm of any catcher they played with or against. Al Bridwell, a shortstop with the Giants in 1910, played with Archer in 1913 with the Cubs. His statement about Archer's arm: "Best arm of any catcher I ever saw. He'd zip it down there to second like a flash. Perfect accuracy, and under a six-foot bar all the way down."[32] Chief Meyers, a catcher with the Giants in 1910, stated: "The best throwing catcher of them all was Jimmy Archer of the Cubs. He didn't have an arm. He had a rifle. And perfect accuracy."[33] Archer was known as the first catcher to throw out of a squat. It seems that in his earlier stops, the managers did not think he could do this with his slightly deformed arm. Chance let him try, and Archer was successful. He suffered a couple of injuries in the minor leagues that remind us that this was a different time. In 1905, he broke his collarbone while playing in the minors in Boone, Iowa, when he ran into a hitching post while chasing a pop fly. After he recovered from that injury, he was hurt later in the year. He was catching Bugs Raymond when Raymond crossed him up. Crossing a catcher up (throwing a different pitch from the signaled one) has happened since signals were first invented, and still happens. The difference is shown by the injury suffered by Archer. This pitch, a curveball thrown after a fastball signal, hit Archer on the kneecap, cracking it, as shin guards had not been invented yet.[34] Archer was one of the reasons that the Cubs felt Fred Luderus was expendable. After Luderus subbed for Chance early in the season with mixed results, Chance tried others at first base when he was injured. Archer and Solly Hofman played first quite a bit, and produced more than Luderus. A right-handed hitter, Archer was having his best year so far in the majors.

Before the Cubs started their series with the Giants on August 26 in Chicago, there was an indicator in the *Philadelphia Bulletin* as to how the Giants viewed the rest of the season. Under the sub-headline "Giants to Play Yankees":

> As to the post season series between the Yankees and the Giants nothing definite so far has been announced. Under officials of both clubs hint that the matter is as good as settled. Frank Farrell stands right where he has always stood. Ever since he put a team in New York, Mr. Farrell believed a series would be a benefit to both clubs. There is no one to speak officially for the Giants. President John T. Brush is in Chicago. He has made no statement as yet. Until he speaks the series is not assured.
>
> The Giant players are as anxious for the series as the Highlanders. McGraw, for some reason or other, has always frowned on the idea. But by playing the Boston Red Sox last fall he left himself open to censure on the part of his players if this year he puts any obstacle in the way of the proposed city championship. It means a lot of money to both McGraw and Brush and there is every likelihood that the Giant players will eventually press the management into action.[35]

The season was not done, and the first order of business was this series in Chicago. It was packed with drama, as most Cubs-Giants series were. After taking a 6–1 victory in the first game, the Cubs won the second game in unusual fashion for 1910. The score was 3–1 and the Cubs hit three homers. Schulte hit two over the fence. After Schulte's second homer, the next hitter hit one off the scoreboard in left. On his deep drive Joe Tinker got to third, where Steinfeldt, coaching third, tried to stop him. Tinker turned around, saw the throw to the third baseman, and took off for home. The third baseman turned around and saw a Cubs player near third, and tagged Steinfeldt while Tinker ran home. McGraw argued this play vehemently and was tossed for his efforts. Brown's pitching took care of the rest. The Giants got their revenge the next day, scoring 18 runs off four pitchers. Chance used every player in uniform, which totaled 19. Chance and Brown were at the park, but not in uniform, and Pfiester was out of town. Everyone else played. The Cubs completed a triple play in the game, which didn't help much. The series finished on August 28 with a 10–2 Cubs victory. Reulbach, who had been shelled out in the second inning the day before, pitched a complete game. Schulte and Sheckard each hit two home runs, all going out of the park. This series completed play between the Cubs and Giants in Chicago. The Cubs secured victory in their season series after this game, even though several games remained to be played in New York.

The Cubs split a doubleheader with the Phillies on August 29, Cole pitching in both games. He pitched the 11th inning in a 6–5 Cubs win in the first game, getting the decision. Cole started the second game and left with the game tied in the fifth inning. Richie finished the game, taking the loss, 9–5, the second game called on account of darkness after eight innings. On getaway day, the Cubs beat the Phillies, 3–1, behind a complete game by Brown that took one hour 35 minutes. The Cubs' winning rally was more like normal 1910 "small ball." In the eighth, they scored three runs

King Cole, 1910.

this way: Evers walk, sacrifice by Beaumont, Hofman walk, Evers to third on passed ball, Archer RBI single, Steinfeldt loads bases by reaching on error, Pfeffer two-run single. The only regulars playing for the Cubs this day were Evers, Steinfeldt, Hofman and Kling. As the Cubs were up by ten games after this win, Chance was trying to get everybody healthy. After this game, the Cubs left for a road trip to play two exhibition games.[36]

8

September–October

Even though the Cubs had two more games scheduled on their home stand, they left on a day off (August 31) for an exhibition game in Clinton, Illinois. The only regulars who played were Evers and Hofman, playing third base. Zimmerman, Kane, Beaumont and Needham started, and two pitchers filled out the eight positions. Foxen and McIntire pitched. Overall played first base, and Jeff Pfeffer played right.[1] Francis Xavier "Big Jeff" Pfeffer was another dividend from the Cubs relationship with George Huff, athletic director of the University of Illinois. Pfeffer was from Champaign, Illinois, and attended the University of Illinois, playing football and baseball there until 1905. He faced Reulbach while both were in college. Huff recommended Pfeffer to the Cubs, and Big Jeff (at 6'1", 185 pounds he was considered big) had a long trial with the Cubs in 1905, pitching in 15 games, 11 starts with nine complete games. After the season he was traded to the Boston Beaneaters. Pfeffer was a regular starter for the Beaneaters until he hurt his arm in July 1907 and pitched decently for a bad team. In 1906 he started 36 games, completed 33 and had a 13–22 record. He got off to a good start in 1907, pitching a no-hitter against the Reds on May 8. Pfeffer met and married his wife, a Boston woman, during this time. His arm injury was severe enough that he made only 19 appearances in 1907, and four in 1908. He was in the minors all of 1909, trying to regain his strength. The Cubs acquired Pfeffer over the winter of 1909–1910, and he was with the team all of 1910, making 13 appearances, mostly in blowouts as a reliever. Pfeffer also played in the outfield a couple of times in 1910.[2]

Someone, probably Chance, talked sense to Cubs President Charles Murphy, and the exhibition game scheduled in Iowa on September 2 was cancelled. The Cubs had an unusual travel schedule starting September 1. They went to Clinton for the exhibition game discussed above, though only 12 men traveled to that game. They had two games scheduled with the Cardinals in Chicago on September 3–4. The game on the 3rd got to the bottom of the third inning with the Cubs leading, 3–1, when the rains came. It rained hard enough that the game the next day was cancelled due to wet grounds. The Cubs traveled to Cincinnati for a make-up doubleheader to be played on September 5. With no game to report, Sy Sanborn wrote a story for the *Tribune* on the 4th with some remarkable statistics about the Cubs. As of their victory on August 30, the Cubs had won 500 games in the last five seasons (1906 through August 30, 1910), with just 222 losses. Twelve members of the team were on the roster this entire time: Chance, Evers, Tinker, Steinfeldt, Sheckard, Hofman, Schulte, Kling, Brown, Reulbach, Overall, and Pfiester. Kling missed the 1909 season, but was officially on the roster that year.[3] All healthy members of this 500 club played in the doubleheader on September 5. The Cubs and Reds split, Brown losing the opener, 4–3, on a three-run triple by Bob Bescher. Reulbach won the nightcap, 9–5, when the game was called after six innings due to both teams having to catch the train back to Chicago.

The Cubs had one more week at home before their final eastern swing of the season. They played the Reds three more times, sweeping them. Cole won the first game against Bill Burns, who had beaten the Cubs three times this year. The game was tied in the bottom of the eighth inning when the Cubs scored three runs this way: Evers walk, sacrifice, Hofman RBI single, taking second on the throw to the plate, Steinfeldt RBI single, stole second, Zimmerman RBI triple. Overall was knocked out in the first inning of the next game, and McIntire pitched the rest of the game. The score was tied 6–6 in the Cubs' ninth when Evers led off with a triple and Sheckard knocked him in with a single. Reulbach's complete game, 8–3 win completed the sweep. The substitutes, along with Evers and Hofman, traveled to Ottumwa, Iowa, after this game for an exhibition game, which they lost, 10–1. Chance's 33rd birthday present was that he didn't have to go along on this trip. The home stand ended with two games against the Cubs' closest pursuers, Pittsburgh. Brown lost the opener when the normally sure-handed Cubs infield made two errors leading to the tying and winning runs in the ninth inning. Of course, the infield was not the normal one. Chance was still out and did not attend the game, allowing Evers to be acting manager. Evers was ejected from the game in the third inning, leaving an infield of Archer, Zimmerman, Tinker and Steinfeldt. Archer and Steinfeldt made the errors that cost Brown. Cole finished the home stand with a 5–2 win in which he held Honus Wagner hitless in five at-bats. Evers scored three runs, and the Cubs were cheered on by their biggest home crowd of the year. As was common in 1910 when there was a crowd bigger than the seating capacity of the stands, fans stood in the outfield behind ropes. Any ball hit into these fans was a ground rule double this day. The Cubs had a day off on the 12th, when they left for Philadelphia. Chance took all his players, hoping to get everyone healthy by the end of this 17-game trip.[4]

The A's started September with a Sunday off and a Labor Day doubleheader in Washington. Coombs won the first game with a complete game and support from Danny Murphy. The second game went seven innings before being called for darkness. Morgan allowed one run in the second inning. The A's tied it in the fourth on Davis' RBI single, and Collins drove in winning run in the sixth with an RBI double. The Nationals took the final game before the A's went to New York.

In the morning game of a double header, Russell Ford beat the A's again, when Morgan got wild in the third inning and the Yankees scored three times without a hit. A walk and two hit batsmen filled the bases. Morgan threw a wild pitch that scored two runs. Mack pulled his catcher, Livingston, for poor effort chasing the wild pitch. A grounder scored the third run. Plank, Dygert and Bender finished up the game, but the A's lost, 5–2. Coombs threw a complete game in the afternoon game, winning 2–1. Approximately 35,000 attended these two games, which was about one-tenth the total home attendance for the Highlanders this season. The series finished with a Plank defeat. New York right fielder Birdie Cree hit a two-run home run in the eighth inning for a 3–2 win. This was one of four home runs hit by Cree this year.

The A's headed to Boston for three games with the second-place Red Sox, who dropped to third after the A's swept. The A's scored seven runs in this series, the Red Sox three. The A's won 2–1, 3–2, and 2–0. Complete games by Bender, Coombs (another shutout) and Krause turned the trick. Small ball was the rule in this series. The A's scored the winning run in the opener on an error in the tenth inning. In the second game, another Boston error led to the lead run in the ninth. In the 2–0 shutout, one run scored on a squeeze bunt with the bases loaded, the other on a ground out.

8. September–October

The A's returned home for a three-game series with Washington before heading out on their final Western swing. When they headed west, it was with a six-game winning streak and a 15½-game lead. Morgan, Coombs (a shutout, of course) and Dygert threw complete games against the Nationals, and Baker was the hitting star. On the last day the A's were in town before heading west, the *Philadelphia Bulletin* had a story about how the A's and Cubs matched up in the World Series. This was on September 13, more than one month before the National League season was to end. As the A's lead on that date was 14½ games and the Cubs' lead was 8½, the matchup looked inevitable.[5]

One A's player did not figure in Connie Mack's plans. There was a story in the *Philadelphia Bulletin* on September 2 which listed the players who would play in the World Series, as only players on the major league roster on September 1 were eligible. All players were listed except one, William "Heinie" Heitmuller, another player from the West Coast signed by Mack on the trip that netted Harry Krause. Heitmuller was from San Francisco and attended the University of California. He spent 1908 in the minors and made the A's in spring training in 1909. A left-handed-hitting outfielder, he was part of the Yannigans squad that traveled north in 1909. Mack was impressed enough with Heitmuller to play him in 60 games in 1909, and he had a .286 batting average with little power and less speed. Early in 1910, Heitmuller played in 27 games before the acquisition of Bris Lord. His performance did not impress Mack. After the Lord trade, four outfielders played for the A's. Heitmuller was the odd man out, as Hartsel, Lord, Oldring, and Murphy got all the playing time. He was still on the team, but was not included in the September 2 list of players eligible for the Series.[6]

Mack spent this road trip setting up his pitching for the World Series. Against the Tigers in Detroit, Plank started and finished the first game, a 7–1 win. Coombs continued his stellar month with another shutout before the A's lost the third game. Dygert won the final game against Detroit, which clinched the A's winning their season series against every AL club. It helped that Cobb missed the entire series with eye trouble, though some of his teammates thought he sat to keep his lead in the batting average race. That strategy backfired, as his only legitimate competitor, Napoleon Lajoie, was hot. The A's saw this in their series with the Naps. In the first game on September 19, Morgan threw a complete game and lost. Lajoie got three hits to make the batting race close, even though no one was sure what the official numbers were. The Philadelphia paper said Lajoie was ahead, but that was using their statistics, not league figures. Mack was reminded of one of his former players in this game. Joe Jackson drove in the winning run and made an outstanding catch to save the game in the ninth inning. A victory on September 20 clinched at least a tie for the pennant with 14 games left. Plank got the victory in relief. The final game in Cleveland was a 0–0 tie, which continued Coombs' shutout streak, now at 46 innings. The Yankees/Highlanders lost this day, which clinched the pennant. There was no indication in the newspaper coverage of a celebration by the A's.[7]

The New York American League team changed managers at this time. George Stallings had been the manager since the start of the 1909 season and had taken a last place team to a fifth-place finish in 1909 and second place as of September 21, 1910. Stallings was extremely intense and hard on his players, most of whom had no problem with this as long as the results were good, and the results were good. One player had a problem, first baseman Hal Chase. Chase was an important figure in baseball at this time. He was thought to be a great player, but with marginal morals. Jimmy Austin, in *The Glory of Their Times* calls Chase the finest fielding first baseman he ever saw.[8] A California native, Chase made the Highlanders in 1905 as a 22-year-old. He was established as a good hitting first baseman with little power. Chase was thought by many teammates and by Stallings to be giving less than his best effort. The first charge that Chase was "laying down" was made in 1908. Chase left the team and played with an outlaw team in California. After a suspension, Chase rejoined the team in May 1909. Chase and Stallings did not get along at all. In July 1910, Stallings accused Chase of trying to throw a game, which caused a near-fight between them. By mid–September, Stallings said he would resign if Chase was not replaced. Chase was friendly with Frank Farrell, the Highlanders' owner. Both were fond of gambling and associated with the same people. Chase went to Farrell and said Stallings needed to go. Even though Chase was under investigation from the earlier charge of throwing a game, Farrell fired Stallings and appointed Chase as manager with 14 games left in the 1910 season, after the Highlanders were eliminated. On that same day, Ban Johnson issued a statement that Hal Chase was cleared of all charges. Baseball would hear more about Hal Chase's morality.[9]

The A's moved on to Chicago and were greeted by a rainout. That game was made up as part of a doubleheader the next day, swept by the White Sox. Rube Oldring sprained his ankle and was replaced by Amos Strunk, a 21-year-old who had been injured most of this year. Mack was high on him, keeping Strunk around even though he could not play until late in August. Strunk would end up playing 14 games in 1910, hitting .333 and giving Mack another left-handed bat. There was another doubleheader on Sunday, September 25, with 33,000 fans in attendance, the biggest crowd for the White Sox this year. Plank started, pitched eight innings and left with the game tied, 1–1. Coombs, scheduled to pitch the second game, came in and pitched six shutout innings. The A's won it in the 14th inning when Coombs and Hartsel singled, Lord sacrificed, Collins RBI groundout advanced both runners, and a wild pitch scored the second run. Walsh threw a complete game for the White Sox. Coombs started the second game and threw one more shutout inning before the White Sox scored in the second. This concluded a 53-inning scoreless streak, the longest in American League history at this time. The A's lost the final game in Chicago.

The last stop on this western swing was St. Louis. The A's went there minus Coombs, Plank and Livingston, sent home by Mack to rest. Oldring went to St. Louis with a sprained ankle and sat out the series. Morgan and Dygert pitched complete games in a doubleheader, swept by the A's. Eddie Collins passed Ty Cobb's record for stolen bases in the American League. This record was 76, set in the 1909 season. Collins would end up the year with 81 stolen bases. The A's also tied the American League record for wins in a season with 98. They lost their final game in St. Louis, on a day that Walter Johnson broke the American League record for strikeouts in a season.[10]

The Cubs started their final Eastern swing in Philadelphia on September 14. As this was an off-day for the A's before they went west, Mack and several A's players attended the doubleheader with the Phillies. The lead story on the *Philadelphia Bulletin* sports page on September 14 was about the upcoming World Series, comparing the teams.[11] After the Cubs and Phillies split the doubleheader, the *Philadelphia Bulletin* sports page caused lots of talk. Mack and Bender said the A's would beat the Cubs easily in the World Series if the Cubs played like they had that day.[12] The Cubs' response was to win the final two games in Philadelphia, though in contrasting fashion. On September 15, they were behind until the eighth inning, when they took the lead. Evers and Sheckard walked, Hofman hit an RBI single, Archer had an

RBI groundout, and Steinfeldt made the second out. Schulte swung at a pitch that hit him for a strike, and on the next pitch hit a home run. The next day the Cubs scored four runs in the first inning and hung on. After this game, they headed to New York for series against the Dodgers and Giants.[13]

Back when the American League was starting up, many players jumped between leagues. The players who moved were known as "jumping frogs." The player most associated with this kind of movement would be playing in the 1910 World Series. James Tilden "Jimmy" Sheckard was from York City, Pennsylvania. He turned pro at the age of 17 in 1896 and made the majors in 1898 with Brooklyn. He was traded to Baltimore, where he played with John McGraw in 1899, then back to Brooklyn for the 1900 season.[14] Before the 1901 season, Sheckard signed with Baltimore (and McGraw) in the new American League in January for $2,250 and a $200 advance. In February, he signed a similar contract with Brooklyn. In March he reported to spring training with Baltimore. In April he went back to Brooklyn and stayed. Sometimes referred to as "Jumpin' Jimmy,"[15] he was a 5'9", 165-lb. left-handed hitter, Sheckard was consistently inconsistent in Brooklyn. After all the movement before the 1901 season, he showed he was worth the fuss with a .353 batting average and 42 stolen bases. His batting averages for the rest

Jimmy Sheckard in 1910.

of his time in Brooklyn: .273 in 1902, .332 in 1903, .239 in 1904, and .292 in 1905.[16] Chance had been playing against Sheckard for several years and wanted Sheckard to complete his outfield in 1906. The Cubs traded three players plus $2,000 cash to Brooklyn for Sheckard in the off-season. Schulte had been playing left field and now moved to right to make room for Sheckard in left. Sheckard lost his inconsistency in Chicago between 1906–1910. His batting averages these years were .262, .267, .231, .255, .256. The low point of Sheckard's Chicago career was the 1906 World Series, where he went 0-for-21. He batted .238 in both the 1907 and 1908 World Series. Sheckard was a fine outfielder and baserunner who got on base more than his average indicated. Even though his statistics were not outstanding in Chicago, the Cubs were happy with him.[17]

The center fielder between Sheckard and Schulte was Arthur Frederick "Solly" Hofman. Hofman was from St. Louis and started playing ball there. St. Louis was home to outstanding amateur baseball around the turn of the century, and Hofman worked his way up to the top semi-pro league there, the Trolley League. His four older brothers had played in this league. Even at this level, there were contract jumpers like Sheckard. Hofman was one of these jumpers. Once he had a contract with East St. Louis in the Trolley League for $8 a game, weather permitting. There was a game scheduled one day when the weather was great, but the grounds had been flooded by the Mississippi River and were unplayable. Hofman showed up and claimed his pay, which was denied him. He got so angry he jumped to the Belleville team. While he was with Belleville, the Pirates signed him. As a 20-year-old, Hofman played in two games for Pittsburgh in 1903. As the Pirates were three-time pennant winners at the end of 1903, they did not need Hofman and sold his contract to Des Moines. During the 1904 season, Cubs president James Hart sent George Huff to Des Moines to scout outfielder Harry McChesney. Huff thought McChesney was okay, but was very impressed by the Des Moines shortstop, Solly Hofman. Both were purchased by the Cubs. McChesney got a 22-game trial in 1904, hit .261, and never played in the majors again. Hofman played in seven games, hit .269, and stayed with the Cubs until 1912. For the next four years, Hofman was the best utility man in the majors. He was not happy about that, always trying to secure a regular position. He even told Chance that he should be put at first base, Chance's position. Evers was so concerned with the possibility that

Artie (Solly) Hofman in 1910. Note the lack of shin guards on the catcher.

Hofman could take his job at second that Evers told Chance to put Hofman in center.

During his time as the main utility man, Hofman played all positions except pitcher and catcher.[18] In 1905 and 1906, he played in 86 and 64 games respectively. In 1907 and 1908, he played in 134 and 120 games. He may have been the most valuable player on the Cubs in the 1908 pennant race, as he filled in for all the position players except the catcher. Due to the injury status of regular center fielder Jimmy Slagle, Hofman played all the games of the 1906 and 1908 World Series, and not at all in the 1907 World Series. He hit .304 in 1906 and .316 in 1908 World Series. Hofman became the regular center fielder on the retirement of Slagle after the 1908 season, playing 153 games there in 1909 and hitting .285. In 1910, Hofman was having his best year in the majors. He played 110 games in the outfield, 24 games for Chance at first base, and one at third base. He led the Cubs in several major hitting statistics in 1910: batting average .325, slugging percentage .461, triples 16, RBI 86, and stolen bases 29.[19] After covering the Cubs as a beat reporter in 1910 and 1911, and as a columnist for several years in the later teens, Ring Lardner said the outfield of Sheckard, Hofman and Schulte was the "best outfield I ever set eyes on."[20]

The Cubs continued their road trip with a four-game series with the Giants. Jack Pfiester lived up to his nickname in the first game of a doubleheader on September 22, beating the Giants, 5–1, with a complete game. Fred Merkle got a small measure of revenge against Evers by catching him off base with a hidden ball trick in the fifth inning. The Giants won the rest of the games in this series, beating Reulbach and Cole. The final game was the marquee pitching matchup in the National League for the past five years, Three Finger Brown against Christy Mathewson. The Cubs saved Brown from a rare loss against Mathewson by scoring two runs in the eighth and ninth innings to tie the game at 5–5. Brown pitched six innings before being replaced by a youngster on trial, Orlie Weaver. The Giants scored in the bottom of the ninth to give Mathewson the win. In this game, the Cubs had their regular lineup for the first time in over a month, as Chance returned to the lineup. The Cubs moved on to Boston up 11½ games. On their travel day, September 25, Evers, Chance and Hofman went to Troy, New York, Evers' hometown. The Cubs finished their National League business on the East Coast with a four-game split against the last-place Doves. Brown and McIntire won, but Overall and Reulbach lost. Before this series started, the two beat writers who covered the Cubs in 1910, Sy Sanborn and Ring Lardner, wrote articles predicting the Cubs would beat the A's in the World Series.[21] The Cubs left Boston with a 10½-game lead and expected to clinch in Cincinnati. On arrival in Cincinnati, Chance was assured by National Commission head Garry Herrmann (owner of the Reds) that all his players would be eligible for the World Series. There had been talk by a promoter, D. A. Fletcher, who said he had signed contracts from several players, including Kling, Brown, Evers, Overall and Hofman, for an exhibition series to be played after the World Series. Herrmann said there was nothing to these charges. It turned out that the first game of this series, on October 1, was the last chance the Cubs had to trot out their regular lineup—except Chance, as Archer started at first. The Cubs won, 9–6, but lost Johnny Evers for the year with a broken ankle suffered when he scored in the fifth inning from second base on a Hofman single and made a bad slide into home though no throw was made. Evers was operated on in Chicago on October 3. The Cubs had clinched the pennant on the 2nd, beating the Reds, 8–4. Evers' replacement, Heinie Zimmerman led the way with three hits, and the Cubs clinched their fourth pennant in five years. Chance shared a bottle of wine with his wife, his way of celebrating. The rest of the team celebrated enough that most sat the next day. Weaver pitched, and Chance, Schulte, Tinker and Kling sat. The Reds made 11 singles, and Zimmerman matched their total bases with two homers and a triple. The Cubs finished their regular road season on October 4 with a 3–2 win in a rain-shortened, five-inning game. The Cubs headed home to Chicago for the rest of their games, except one make-up game in Pittsburgh.[22]

The rest of the schedule for the A's was at home except a make-up doubleheader in Washington. Coombs started the first game against the Red Sox on September 30, winning his 30th game with another complete game. Collins knocked in one run with his 15th triple of the year. Lapp had an RBI triple later in the game. The total of triples and home runs hit in the major leagues was a good indicator of how dead the ball was, and how big the parks were. No team in either league had more home runs than triples. The A's led the American League in triples with 105, and the Red Sox led the league in home runs with 43. The Cubs led the National League with 84 triples and 34 home runs. Just as Chance tried out young players after clinching, Mack trotted out his recent $12,000 purchase, Lefty Russell, for his first start on October 1. Russell shut out the Red Sox with a 3–0 complete game in his only appearance this season. The A's finished a four-game sweep of the Red Sox with complete game victories by Dygert and Krause. The final two games were against the second-place Highlanders, now managed by Hal Chase. Before the first game, the players presented Mack with an automobile, a Bergdoll touring car. The Highlanders won both games, as Mack cleared his bench. One of the bench players was his son, Earle Mack, in the only game of his big league career. Coombs lost the first game of this series in relief. The A's went to Washington for a make-up doubleheader on September 8. This was so important that Mack decided not to go, and Captain Harry Davis missed the train. Hartsel was going to run the team, but the games were rained out.[23] Even though the A's played only 150 games to conclusion (plus five ties), they set an American League record with 102 wins against 48 losses. The four remaining games did not have to be made up, as they had no bearing on the final standings. The Yankees/Highlanders hurried through a victory in their last game in just 72 minutes.[24] In

1910, the two leagues were separate entities, under the supervision of the National Commission. One National League owner, Charles Ebbets of Brooklyn, had persuaded his league to extend the schedule to October 15 to take advantage of the Columbus Day holiday. That meant the World Series could not start until October 17. How could the A's stay sharp? We will see later.

The Cubs swept three games from the reigning world champion Pirates from October 6–8. Richie shut out the Pirates, beating 1909 World Series hero Babe Adams. Brown continued the shutout streak against the Pirates the next day in a 1–0 win. All the regulars played except Kling. The finale was in Pittsburgh, where Connie Mack watched the game. The Cubs won their 100th game and won the season series against Pittsburgh, 12–10. That gave the Cubs season series victories against every team in the National League. Their season concluded with six games against the second-division Cardinals in Chicago. The Cubs won four of the six, getting everyone who figured to play in the World Series some innings pitched or at-bats. There was an interesting mistake by the scoreboard operator on October 9. The game was tied at 3–3, the scoreboard said in the bottom of the eighth inning. The Cubs scored a run on a bases-loaded hit by Kane with two out. The man on first started to run to the clubhouse, and was intercepted by Steinfeldt (coaching first) and instructed to touch second to avoid a Merkle play. The lone umpire checked with the sportswriters, who verified this was really the bottom of the ninth, and the game was over. Cole threw a complete game for his 20th victory. In a couple of the remaining games, the regular lineup started for the Cubs, and subs came in during the game. The Cubs ended up with a 104–50 record and a 13-game margin over the second-place Giants. The final game for the Cubs was on October 15, and the World Series was to start on October 17 in Philadelphia.[25]

The final game for the A's was scheduled for October 8 and was rained out. The A's returned to Philadelphia and spent most of the time before the World Series at Shibe Park. By the beginning of the 1910 season, several A's players had established residences in this neighborhood. Jack Barry and his wife rented an apartment on 20th Street, one of the streets bordering the ballpark. Jack Coombs boarded with ex–A's player Monte Cross, who lived a couple of blocks away. Chief Bender bought a house seven blocks north of the park, and Harry Davis and his family lived four blocks west of the park. Eddie Collins and Eddie

Plank boarded with the Davis family during the season. Rookies boarded with families on 20th Street, beyond the right field wall. Connie Mack purchased a rowhouse two blocks from the park, within walking distance of his office and of the players' residences.[26] The A's played games in Shibe Park on October 9, 10, 11, 12, and 13. The first was an intrasquad game, Regulars v. Yannigans. The regular lineup was: Lord LF, Oldring CF, Collins 2B, Baker 3B, Davis 1B, Murphy RF, Barry SS, Thomas C, Dygert P. The substitutes' lineup was: Hartsel LF, Strunk CF, Castle RF, McInnis 3B, Houser 1B, Derrick SS, Monte Cross 2B, Livingston C, Morgan P. Castle and Derrick were youngsters who each played one game at the end of the year, and Monte Cross had retired in 1907 and lived in the neighborhood. Mack managed the Yannigans, and Davis the regulars. Both pitchers pitched the entire ten-inning game, won by the subs, 5–4. Players on both teams moved around to different positions during the game. With the help of American League president Ban Johnson, Mack recruited an all-star team to play against the A's for the next five days. This was a genuine all-star team of American Leaguers, who would split the proceeds with the A's. The A's won the first game on the tenth innings, but the All-Stars swept the rest of the games. In the game on September 11, Walter Johnson beat the A's, 8–3. More importantly, Rube Oldring twisted his knee and was done for the season. Bender, Plank and Coombs each pitched three innings. This same trio each pitched three innings the next day, as the A's lost to the All-stars and Ed Walsh, 5–1. Ty Cobb stole home on the back end of a double steal. Doc White beat the A's, 6–3, next, with Bender, Coombs and Krause each pitching three innings for the A's. The final game of this World Series warm-up was played in Washington on the 14th. Walter Johnson won, 4–1. Morgan threw six innings, and Dygert finished up.[27] To show the quality of the All-star team, here was their normal lineup: Clyde Milan, Nationals, RF; Harry Lord, Red Sox, 3B; Tris Speaker, Red Sox, CF; Ty Cobb, Tigers, RF; Kid Elberfeld, Nationals, 2B; Jake Stahl, Red Sox, 1B; and George McBride, Nationals, SS. There were three pitchers: Walter Johnson of the Nationals and Ed Walsh and Doc White of the White Sox, and two catchers: Gabby Street of the Nationals and Billy Sullivan of the White Sox. The pitchers threw to the catcher from their own team. After the series, Mack presented each of the All-stars with a gold watch. Mack got what he wanted from this series. All his pitchers got some work. The batters got some at-bats, and there was only one serious injury. Oldring was out for the

World Series. Each team would go into the World Series healthy except for one injured regular: Evers for the Cubs and Oldring for the A's.[28]

There was another contest going on during the last weekend of the American League season, the batting contest between Ty Cobb and Napoleon Lajoie. Figures in various newspapers showed Cobb with a lead of eight points or so when the final series of the season started. The Tigers were in Chicago playing the White Sox, and the Naps were in St. Louis playing the Browns, both four-game series. The first games were played on Thursday, October 6. Cobb went 2-for-4, and Lajoie went 3-for-4. As far as they knew, the averages at the end of this game were Cobb .382, Lajoie .376. On Friday, the game in St. Louis was rained out. Cobb went 2-for-3 with a walk. He had been invited to play in the series against the A's and left the Tigers, along with manager Hughie Jennings, after the Friday game. This was done with the approval of Tigers ownership. Cobb thought he had a seven-point lead in the batting race, with three games left for Lajoie to catch up. Cobb thought there was no way Lajoie could do this. Some Detroit writers claimed Cobb was hurting, but Cobb never said he was, and always owned up to leaving for the two reasons given above.

Now Lajoie had three games in two days to catch Cobb. The newspapers listed the batting averages of the two participants, but with the caveat that these numbers were unofficial. The official averages would not be released until after the season ended by the league office. Lajoie was hurt and helped in his quest on Saturday. He batted four times, and per most observers did not get any hits. The one person who mattered, official scorer E. Victor Parrish of the *St. Louis Republic*, gave him a hit on a fly ball to the center fielder that was dropped. All the newspapers that commented on this, except the *St. Louis Republic*, thought the play should have been scored an error.

This led to the final day of the season, a doubleheader in St. Louis which normally would have drawn a crowd of around 2,000. The newspapers ran stories showing that Lajoie could catch Cobb if he went 8-for-8 or 7-for-8 per their best guess. Fans had been following this race, and the possibility of Lajoie catching Cobb lured a crowd of about 10,000 to the park on Sunday, October 9. There was no question Lajoie was more popular than Cobb. Two years before, the Naps had ended their season in St. Louis. That last game was even more important for Lajoie, as a win would have put the Naps into the World Series. The Browns won, upholding the tradition of competitive play at all times.

Thirteen members of that Browns team were on the 1910 team. Would any sentiment for Lajoie or against Cobb come into play? The question was answered in the games.

Lajoie's first at-bat netted a triple on a line drive over the center fielder's head. In his second at bat, he grounded to short and beat the throw. Most observers thought the throw was poor and could have been an error. The official scorer, Mr. Parrish again, scored it a hit. By his third at-bat, the crowd was cheering for Lajoie. He noticed that the rookie third baseman, Red Corriden, was playing deep. That was the normal position for a third baseman when facing Lajoie, who was known for hitting vicious line drives. In his last two at-bats in the first game, Lajoie got bunt hits down the third base line. He was 4-for-4 in the first game. It is not known if Corriden played deeper in the last two at-bats than the first two. Either way, Corriden stayed there the entire second game. In his first at-bat, Lajoie got another bunt hit. In his second at-bat, Lajoie bunted with a runner on first. The bunt was harder, and Corriden fielded and fumbled it. The scorer thought it was an error, but scored it a sacrifice as the runner advanced. Lajoie batted in the fifth, seventh, and ninth innings. He got bunt singles down the third base line all three times. The crowd thought that Lajoie had won the batting title, and joyously surrounded him on the field after the game. Most of the reporters thought there was something rotten about how this happened, and would make their views known. No one knew the final averages yet. The *Philadelphia Bulletin* published a story, along with a picture of Nap Lajoie, stating that Lajoie won the batting crown, but that there was a scandal that needed to be cleared up.[29] The *Bulletin* published their final statistics for the batting race on October 14 and showed Lajoie three points ahead of Cobb.[30]

9

The World Series

Before the World Series started, the teams filled the roles the public expected them to fill. The Cubs were the veteran group, loose and confident. There was a story in the *Chicago Tribune* that Orval Overall turned down the chance to buy tickets for the sixth and seventh games, as he thought the Cubs would finish off the Series before then.[1] Chance, with three World Series in the last four years behind him, indulged in his World Series superstitions. In 1906, Chance thoroughly scouted the White Sox and started Brown in the Series opener. After the Cubs lost the 1906 Series, he changed both of these procedures for the 1907 and 1908 Series. As the Cubs won both these Series, he continued these practices. The A's had not been scouted by the Cubs, and Brown would not start the first game. Chance thought the number 13 was lucky and always got berth 13 on the Pullman car.[2] The Cubs traveled to Philadelphia after their last game on the 15th. The A's stated in public that they were happy to be there. In private, Mack thought the A's were better, but wanted to do everything he could to keep their edge. He asked all the players to take a pledge not to touch alcohol during the Series. All took the pledge. Then Mack said, "Keep Chicago crossed, boys; do the unexpected. Outguessing them will win."[3]

As would become normal in baseball and other sports, the payrolls for these clubs showed which was the veteran team and which the younger team. Unofficial salary lists showed the Cubs with the highest payroll in the majors, around $120,000. The A's were next to last at $50,000.[4] Both teams had excellent players at the top of their games. Chicago pitchers led the National League in ERA with a figure of 2.51. This was higher than any of the last four years, mostly due to injuries and illness. Brown and Cole led a balanced staff with 25 and 20 wins, respectively. The offense was balanced as well. Two players, Schulte and Hofman, hit over .300, and Schulte tied for the league lead in home runs with ten. A dozen members of this team had been on the Cubs since their great run started in 1906. Missing Evers was a concern, but Heinie Zimmerman had played 99 games, hitting .284. He appeared to be a capable replacement.

The A's had the same concern with Oldring out. Mack had the choice of two replacements. Topsy Hartsel, who had been a teammate of Chance and Kling on the Cubs in 1901, was the older option. Amos Strunk was the younger option. As Oldring had the second best average on the team, this was a problem. But the other young offensive stars of the A's were healthy and unknown to the Cubs. Collins, Barry and Baker built on their breakout years in 1909 with good years in 1910. The rest of the A's lineup was experienced, and Davis, Murphy and Hartsel had played in the World Series in 1905. Mack thought his big advantage was in pitching. Jack Coombs was the best pitcher in the big leagues in 1910. His record was 31–9, with a league record 13 shutouts plus 12 starts in which he allowed one run. Bender was almost as good, with a 23–5 record. Bender gave up one home run all year, which was one more than Coombs. The other pitchers were steady and productive, as the A's team ERA and strikeout total led the American League. They led the majors in complete games with 123.[5]

One constant in sports is the struggle between offense and defense. Baseball had been through this pendulum a couple of times since the National League formed in 1876. Back then, fielding gloves were just coming in, and errors were very common. Offense had an advantage over defense. Over the next decade, better fielding gloves and overhand pitches changed the advantage to the defense.[6] By 1892, the rules makers felt that the time had come to make a change to help the offense. This change was major, moving the pitching distance to the present distance of 60 feet, 6 inches. After this change, the hitters took over. Averages and other offensive statistics increased greatly in the 1890s.[7] By the beginning of the new century, the pendulum had swung back to the defense. Pitching and defense had improved, and the offensive strategy used by all big league teams in the 1900s reflected this. Deadball baseball was small ball. Teams played for one run at a time, certainly taking big innings, but not expecting them. Sacrifices were very common. Stolen bases were important. Pitching was dominant. Oral history accounts of this time, like those in *The Glory of Their Times*, stress the fact that the ball was kept in play as long as possible.[8]

9. The World Series 149

The players rarely saw a new, white baseball. Many players said the ball was no longer round when they caught it. One reason was the normal practice of getting the ball back from the crowd after a foul ball reached the seats. This continued until 1923, when an 11-year-old boy, Reuben Berman, was jailed overnight for refusing to return a ball at a Phillies game. The judge hearing the case ruled that "a boy who gets a baseball in the bleachers to take home as a souvenir is acting on the natural impulse of all boys and is not guilty of larceny."[9] After this decision, balls in the stands were fair game. Even with this, the storytellers exaggerated how few balls were used. The average number of balls used in 1910 was between six and ten per game. The umpires got three new balls at the beginning of the game. If those were used up, it was incumbent on the home team to supply more. The kind of ball supplied depended on the score. If the home team was ahead, the balls were old and mushy. If the home team was behind, the balls were new. Obviously, the ball was a major component of the game, and a change to the ball would cause a change in the way the game was played.[10]

The ball changed in the 1910 World Series. Before this World Series, the ball had a rubber, cushioned-wood center. Balls manufactured by the Spalding Company were used in the National League. Balls manufactured by the Reach Company were used in the American League. Ben Shibe, half-owner of the A's, was half-owner of the Reach Company. In 1909, Ben Shibe invented a cork-centered baseball, getting a patent on it in 1910. According to George Reach, this new ball had not been used in the 1910 season. His exact quote, from the *Philadelphia Bulletin* in 1949: "We used our newly patented cork center ball for the first time in the 1910 World Series. Nobody knew about it except a few people in the factory. Not even Ban Johnson or Connie Mack knew about the different ball."[11] One other innovation took place in the 1910 World Series. Four umpires were used in this series for the first time. The umpires were: Cy Rigler, NL; Tommy Connolly, AL; Hank O'Day, NL; and Jack Sheridan, AL.[12]

The World Series of 1910 was scheduled to start in Philadelphia on Monday, October 17. The home team for the first two games was determined by a coin flip, won by the A's. The World Series schedule had not yet become the 2–3–2 format we are familiar with today. The original schedule was two games in Philadelphia, two games in Chicago, one game in Philadelphia, one game in Chicago, and the last game to be determined by another coin flip.[13] Remember that the

American League season ended on Sunday, October 9, and the National League season ended on Saturday, October 15. During this time, the two biggest stories in baseball competed for newspaper space. One was acceptable to all the powers in baseball, the upcoming World Series.

The other story, the Chalmers Race for the highest batting average in baseball, was not welcome to the baseball establishment. The Chalmers Automobile Company loved it. The National Commission, headed by Cincinnati Reds owner Garry Herrmann, determined that this was an American League problem, and turned it over to the American League President, Ban Johnson. Johnson, a newspaperman before he became AL president, knew that the publicity about this batting race took attention away from the World Series. He did a quick investigation into any possible scandal, talking to St. Louis manager Jack O'Connor, third baseman Red Corriden, and owner Robert Hedges. He got written reports from official scorer E. Victor Parrish and umpire Billy Evans. He waited for his secretary, Robert McRoy, to finish going over the score sheets for Cobb and Lajoie for the whole season and come up with official batting averages. Earlier this week, Hugh Chalmers of the Chalmers Automobile Company had offered to give a car to both Cobb and Lajoie if there was any controversy. Chalmers met with Johnson on Saturday, October 15, to renew this offer. Johnson issued a statement to the press that day, along with the final statistics. Johnson cleared Red Corriden but not Jack O'Connor, asking Robert Hedges to investigate further. The statistics issued showed these final results: Cobb, 196 base hits in 509 at-bats, average .385069; Lajoie 227 base hits in 591 at bats, average .384095. Johnson said Cobb won the batting title, but both Cobb and Lajoie would get Chalmers automobiles due to the offer of the Chalmers Automobile Company. The cars were delivered to Philadelphia and awarded before the second game of the World Series. Cobb, who was covering the Series for a newspaper syndicate, accepted his car. Lajoie was playing in an exhibition series against the Reds and got the car later. The National Commission's feeling about this race for the automobile was stated by Ban Johnson after he issued his press release: Never again. The Chalmers Automobile Company loved the publicity and interest created by this race, and wanted to continue. The parties compromised by instituting a Most Valuable Player Award for each league, starting for the 1911 season, voted on by the writers.[14]

Predictions for the Series followed league lines. American Leaguers picked the A's, National Leaguers picked the Cubs. The Cubs were the favorite in the betting, particularly in Chicago. When the Cubs arrived in Philadelphia, one of the Chicago writers tried to get a bet down on the Cubs. He was surprised to make an even money bet in Philly, as all the bets in Chicago had the Cubs as the favorite. Johnny Evers said he would not travel with the Cubs in the Series. Evers had opened a shoe store in Chicago on the last day of the season, and the crowd around the store had to be sent home by the police because they were blocking traffic. Ring Lardner asked Evers if his leg was the reason he could not travel to the games in Philadelphia. Evers replied: "It's my brains I'm afraid of. I'd go crazy sure if I had to sit up in the stand and watch those games.... A fellow sitting in the stand can see things that the men on the field can't see. If I went to Philadelphia I'd be trying to tip off Chance to some things, and I probably would go wild in the effort or get put out of the place for yelling too loud."[15] The *Chicago Tribune* had players from each league cover the Series. Solly Hofman wrote an article each day from October 16 through 24. Doc White, pitcher for the White Sox, wrote an article each day as well. Hofman picked the Cubs, White the A's.[16]

Connie Mack had not let slip his pitching plans for the Series. However, he had no doubt who was going to pitch. With Evers out, the Cubs were an overwhelmingly right-handed lineup, as only Sheckard and Schulte were left-handed batters among the starters. Mack had known this for a long time, not starting Chief Bender since September 7. Coombs was going so well that Mack let him pitch in his regular turn. If one thought that two pitchers were too few to win a World Series, Connie Mack knew better. In their only appearance in a World Series prior to 1910, the A's were beaten by the Giants, who used two pitchers, Christy Mathewson and Joe McGinnity. Mack was quoted once saying, "If everything depended on one game, I'd use Albert." So, even though Plank and Bender warmed up before the lineups were announced, Bender was his choice to start the first game of the 1910 World Series.[17] Chance countered with Overall, who had a 3–0 record in seven World Series appearances.

Bender was known for keeping a cool head. He had two chances to show this before the first game started. The only Cub who had played against Bender was Tinker, back in 1902. Tinker was coaching third in the first inning when Bender walked out to start the game. As Tinker recalled, "When he passed me, I said 'Big Indian, this is where you get

Crowd shot of the first game of the World Series in 1910, Shibe Park, Philadelphia.

yours good and plenty.' Bender stopped and looked at me for a second. With one of those cold grins he said, 'My word, do you think so?' and walked on. I left him alone after that."[18] Then there was a dispute at home plate. The National Commission had sold movie rights to film the World Series for the first time ever, and the cameramen had secured Ban Johnson's permission to be on the field during the game. Still photographers joined the movie cameramen on the field, which was okay in the American League, but banned in the National League. Manager Chance and Umpire Hank O'Day wanted to clear everyone off. This dispute was settled by letting the movie cameramen stay and making the still photographers leave. All this took time, while Bender was waiting on the mound.[19] When he started pitching, Bender had his good stuff and motivation. The last time the A's were in St. Louis, Bender spotted and cut out an article from a local paper. This story included the line, "The Cubs will triumph over the Athletics and will have no trouble beating Bender." He had this article in his pocket while pitching Game 1 of the World Series, per his testimony in 1942. Bender moved the defense around to suit his pitching pattern and struck out eight

9. The World Series

Cubs. He faced the minimum over the first eight innings. Schulte, the fastest Cub, got two hits. He was thrown out stealing each time on a pitchout. By the time Bender weakened in the ninth, the A's had a comfortable lead.[20]

The A's broke through in the second inning. Baker led off with a ground-rule double and scored on Murphy's RBI single. Murphy stole second (the only successful steal by the A's in four attempts), took third on Barry's groundout, and scored on Bender's bad-hop single. The A's scored again in the third. Lord had a ground rule double and scored on Baker's single. Overall finished the third inning and was replaced by McIntire, who finished the game for the Cubs. McIntire was effective, giving up only one unearned run in the eighth inning. Collins had a leadoff single, went to third on McIntire's error on a pickoff throw, and scored on Baker's single. The Cubs scored in the ninth. Tinker led off and lifted a foul pop to the catcher that Thomas dropped for an error. Tinker then singled, and Kling followed with a single to center. Strunk, playing center, booted the ball allowing Tinker to score while Kling held first. Kane ran for Kling, and advanced to second on a hot shot by pinch-hitter Beaumont to Collins that became the first out. Sheckard struck out and Schulte walked, leaving Hofman up with men on first and second. Hofman hit a hard grounder to Baker, who fielded it and stepped on third for the final out. This was fitting, as Baker was the hitting star of the game, involved in three of the A's runs. Bender pitched a complete game, allowing only one unearned run.[21] The crowd of 26,891 went home happy. Later that night, according to Chicago sportswriter Hugh Fullerton, an investigation took place in his hotel room. Some of the Cubs thought the ball was different. Fullerton said in 1941 that he obtained two of these balls after the game and took them to his room. He cut them in half and discovered the cork center, which neither he nor the Cubs had ever seen before. This account can be taken with a grain of salt, but it was true that the ball was new and different.[22]

Chance and the Cubs were not too discouraged by the loss of the first game. Chance had taken a gamble on Overall, and lost. Now he had his ace ready, Mordecai Brown. Mack countered with Jack Coombs. Brown had been the Cubs' best pitcher since the start of their great run in 1906. He was the second-best pitcher in the National League in 1910, exceeded only by Christy Mathewson. Coombs, the best pitcher in baseball in 1910, threw 353 innings and got better as the year went along. He thrived on work. His last start in a meaningful game was on

September 30, and his last work during the season was finishing a game for Plank on October 4. He had pitched in two of the exhibition games against the All-Stars, but just three innings in each.[23]

There was lots of activity, good and bad, before the second game. The crowd was slightly smaller at Shibe Park, but the rooftops across the street from the outfield were more crowded. The A's asked the police to curb the neighborhood seating, with minimal success. There was a display board showing the game in progress at the building of the *Philadelphia Inquirer*, which drew thousands in downtown Philadelphia. There was a counterpart in Chicago, in Orchestra Hall.[24] Four of the Cubs were in an automobile accident on their way to the game. In another example of how different things were in 1910, the players made their own way to the park, as there were no busses to take them from the hotel to the ballpark. Kling, Kane, McIntire and Reulbach shared a cab to Shibe Park, and the cab was in an accident while traveling 30 mph. Only Kane was injured and missed the game, but all were shaken up.[25] Before the game, the Chalmers automobiles were presented. The A's had a batboy/mascot named Louis Van Zelst, who had been with them since the last game of the 1909 season. Louis had a twisted spine and a hump on his back from a fall when he was eight. He was now 16, and had been the home batboy all season. Mack gave Louis the lineup card, and he carried it out to the home plate umpire Cy Rigler.

When all this was done, Coombs started for the A's. He was rusty and wild, not helped by Mack using Ira Thomas instead of Coombs' normal catcher, Jack Lapp. In the first inning, Coombs could not get his fastball over, relying on curves and changeups. He walked two, Chance got an infield hit off Baker's glove, and Zimmerman drove in a run with a sacrifice fly. Coombs struck out Steinfeldt on a pitch that Ring Lardner wrote was over Steiny's head. In the dugout after this half-inning, Mack told Coombs, "The only way you can lose is for you to beat yourself. I am satisfied they can't hit you effectively."[26] Coombs tried to beat himself. He threw 153 pitches, gave up eight hits, walked nine and committed two errors. He was able to win and finish the game due to his defense, even though the A's committed two more errors. Collins had ten assists and received praise from his fellow second sacker, Johnny Evers, who had come to Philadelphia in spite of his comments on October 15. Evers told Chicago sportswriter W. A. Phelon that "Collins is the greatest second baseman I ever saw, darned if I can explain why he is, but he is, just the same."[27] The Cubs were foiled by

Collins on a play in the second inning. Tinker led off by reaching on Davis' error. He saw how the A's were positioned in the infield and signaled a hit-and-run play to Kling. Tinker and Kling expected Collins to cover, as he was closer to second. Tinker took off, Barry covered, and Kling's line drive went right to Collins for a double play.

After Brown got the A's out in the first two innings, with the only blemish a bloop hit and steal of second by Collins in the first, the A's went to work in the third inning. Steinfeldt's error put Thomas on first. After Coombs struck out, Strunk bunted between Brown and Chance and beat it out. Lord forced Strunk at second, bringing Collins up with men on first and third. Collins grounded a double down the left field line. Thomas scored on the hit, and when the Cubs fumbled the throw, Lord scored as well. Baker made an out, leaving the A's ahead, 2–1. Tinker got on in the fourth and was out trying to steal second. The A's got two hits with two out in the fourth, but Coombs struck out to end the inning. Coombs made two errors on bunts in the fifth and walked Hofman to load the bases with one out. Chance flied to short right, and Murphy threw out Brown trying to score to end the inning.

In the A's half, Collins was on first with two outs. He waited through two pitchouts and stole second. In the press box, Ty Cobb told reporters that the A's were reading the Cubs pitchers, not Kling's signs. Kling was changing his signs every game, but that made no difference to the A's. The reason Cobb could make this assertion was that Cobb was reading the Cubs pitchers as well, predicting the pitches in the press box with impressive accuracy.[28] Baker walked and Davis singled in Collins before Murphy made the last out. Neither team scored in the sixth. The Cubs pulled within one run in the top of the seventh. Sheckard hit a ground rule double with one out, and Hofman walked with two out. Chance singled Sheckard in, making the score 3–2, before Zimmerman made the third out.

Brown was tired and showed it in the bottom of the seventh. Collins led off with a walk and took third on Baker's single. Davis hit a ground rule double, scoring Collins and sending Baker to third. Murphy hit one to the same place, scoring Baker and Davis. Barry sacrificed, and Thomas knocked Murphy in with a single. Coombs grounded out, sending Thomas to second, and Strunk doubled Thomas in. Lord lined to Sheckard in left, who dropped the liner, scoring Strunk. Lord was thrown out stealing but the A's were up, 9–2. Beaumont batted for Brown in the top of the eighth, striking out. The Cubs scored a consolation run in the ninth. Hofman singled and took second on Chance's ground out. Zimmerman hit a ground rule double, scoring Hofman. Coombs finished the game, even though he stated after the game that he pitched poorly. In his story in the *Chicago Tribune* about this game, Artie Hofman said that he thought Bender was a much better pitcher than Coombs. He acknowledged that the A's hammered Brown in the seventh, but stressed that the Cubs left way too many (14) men on base. He said the Cubs would switch the momentum in Chicago during the next games. He said that the Game 3 starters would be Reulbach and Bender.[29] Gamblers in Chicago did not agree. An article in the *Chicago Tribune* stated that the A's were now favored, as opposed to before the Series when the Cubs were the favorite.[30]

Both teams took their own special trains to Chicago. On the A's train, reporters asked Mack who was going to pitch the next game. Most thought Plank would get his chance. Mack's response was, "I think I'll use Jawn (Coombs) again." One reporter asked if it was wise to use Coombs on one day's rest, particularly when that day was mostly spent on a train. Mack restated his intention to use Coombs in the next game.[31] The two trains arrived at the same station ten minutes apart. The A's got a polite reception from the fans present. The Cubs were greeted warmly and encouraged to go ahead and get back in the Series. All Cubs interviewed and writing in the press (Hofman for the *Tribune* and Evers for the *Philadelphia Bulletin*) said the Cubs would play much better in Chicago.[32] A Philadelphia fan on the special train brought a crate of pineapples. There had been a time during the season when some of the A's had a good day after eating pineapples for breakfast. This fan thought bringing the pineapples would help the A's win in Chicago. Pineapples were now on the A's breakfast menu at the LaSalle Hotel in Chicago.[33]

Chance had to make a choice between Reulbach and Cole. He made the choice often made by managers, going with experience. Cole was a rookie, Reulbach a veteran of six years and three World Series. Reulbach had started four World Series games, winning two, and relieved in two other games without a decision. Reulbach had authored the lowest-hit start in World Series history in 1906, winning the second game, when the Cubs were down 1–0, with a one-hitter. However, the weather indicated that Chance should have chosen someone else. Reulbach had problems when the weather was overcast, and the weather was overcast and spitting rain on October 20 in Chicago. The A's got off to a good start with a run in the first inning. Strunk led off with a walk and was sacrificed to second by Lord. Collins flied out, but Baker grounded a single to center, driving in Strunk. Baker was out stealing. The Cubs answered in the bottom of the inning. Sheckard singled on a pitch half a foot outside, and Schulte got a ground rule double on the next pitch, putting men on second and third. Hofman flied to left, advancing both runners and scoring a run. Chance struck out, and Zimmerman flied out. The teams matched results in the second. Davis led off with a walk and took second on Murphy's ground out. Barry had an RBI ground rule double. After Thomas flied out, Coombs hit another ground rule double for a two-run inning. The Cubs responded right away. Tinker doubled with one out, and pinch-hitter Ginger Beaumont walked with two outs, taking Reulbach out of the game. Sheckard walked to load the bases, followed by a ground rule double by Schulte, scoring two runs. The game was tied 3–3 after two innings.

McIntire came in to pitch the top of the third. After getting Lord on a flyout, things got tough for him. Collins singled off Steinfeldt's glove. Baker tripled to right, allowing Collins to score. After hitting Davis, McIntire grooved one to Murphy, who hit it for an opposite field home run, over the crowd and into the permanent bleachers. That finished McIntire. Chance brought in Pfiester while arguing with the umpire that Murphy's hit should have been a ground rule double because it did not reach the permanent bleachers. The umpire disagreed and threw Chance out of the game. Archer replaced Chance. Another run scored when Barry's ground rule double was followed by Tinker's throwing error on Thomas' ground ball, which allowed Barry to score. Coombs faced the minimum over the next five innings, allowing one hit which was erased on a double play. Pfiester shut out the A's for three innings. In the Philadelphia seventh, the A's put the game away after the first two men were out and the third batter, Baker, hit a grounder to third. Steinfeldt booted the ball and opened the floodgates. Davis singled, and Murphy followed up with a grounder for a single. Barry followed this with a two-run single. Thomas walked, and Coombs finished the A's scoring with a two-run single. Now that the score was 12–2, the bugs in the Chicago stands lost hope. The Cubs scored two runs on a wild pitch in the bottom of the eighth, but got no closer. The 12–5 win put the A's one game away from their first World Championship. Coombs was wild early, throwing 44 pitches in the first two innings. He settled down to complete a 120-pitch game. Hofman admitted in his article the next day that he was impressed by Coombs' curveball, which had not been good against him in the first game. Now the Cubs needed some serious help.[34]

The Cubs' doubts about the ball being used in the Series were shared by another Chicagoan, who was rooting for the A's. White Sox owner Charles Comiskey shared his opinion about the ball in the *Chicago Tribune* on October 21. Comiskey's manager, Fielder Jones, told Comiskey about the new ball after the first game. After seeing a game in Chicago, Comiskey went public with his concerns.

> The balls used in that game yesterday were not like the balls batted by the White Sox this season. They were livelier. That's the only way to explain to my own satisfaction the amount of clean, hard hitting, which was greater than I have ever seen in one game between two high-class teams. I've been watching ballgames a good many years. It seemed to me that those balls did not bound as I expected them to. The only way I can understand it is that they were livelier than the ones the American League used this year. Of course, it is just as fair for one club as another, and it is my explanation of why so much good hitting was done off good pitching.[35]

As always happens when news gets out before the parties involved want it to, the Reach Sporting Goods Company denied any change in the ball.

The Cubs got help from the weather. The fourth game was rained out on the 21st[36] and would be played the next day, with the fifth game in Chicago on Sunday the 23rd, if necessary. This was because there was no Sunday ball in Philadelphia. The weather was still cold and dark on Saturday but the game went ahead. Bender started for the A's, and Chance used Cole. A small crowd of 19,150 showed up, hoping against hope that the Cubs could start a comeback. The Cubs took the lead for the second time in the Series in the first inning. Sheckard walked to lead off. Schulte struck out, but Sheckard stole second, and Hofman singled Sheckard in. Chance grounded to short, and Hofman's slide into Collins resulted in an interference call that ended the inning with a double play. In the A's third, Bender walked with two out. Strunk followed with a triple, scoring Bender before Strunk was caught off third. In the fourth, the A's took the lead even though Cole struck out three. Between the strikeouts, Collins singled and Baker doubled, putting men on second and third. Murphy drove one to left that Sheckard got a glove on, but could not hold for a two-run double. The Cubs answered in the fourth with three leadoff singles. Chance got the RBI, and men were on first and second. Zimmerman failed on two sacrifice attempts, grounding to Bender for a 1–5–3 double play. Steinfeldt's long fly ended the inning.

The score remained 3–2 A's until the ninth inning. Cole was pinch-hit for in the bottom of the eighth, and Brown came in to shut the A's out in the ninth. In the bottom of the ninth, Schulte led off with a double. Hofman sacrificed him to third. Chance was hit by a pitch, but the home plate umpire, Tom Connolly, ruled that Chance did not try to get out of the way. Chance tied the game with a triple. Zimmerman popped up to Collins, and Baker leaned into the stands to catch Steinfeldt's foul pop. Brown got the A's out in the tenth inning after Davis doubled. In the bottom of the tenth, Archer doubled with one out. After Brown made an out, Sheckard won the game with a single to center.[37]

Artie Hofman wrote in the *Tribune* that this game showed the Cubs had not quit. Connie Mack was disappointed as he wanted the A's to become the first team to sweep a World Series. The Cubs had won four straight against the Tigers in 1907, after the first game ended in a tie. Mack had a couple of issues with Topsy Hartsel. The first was Mack's own fault, as he acknowledged. After letting Thomas talk his way to the plate in the eighth inning the day before, Mack vowed (not for the first or last time) "never again to let sentiment interfere with my judgment." Later that night, Mack met with Hartsel alone after a team meeting in his suite. Hartsel had a cold, and he told Mack, "Connie, I'm a sick man. If I don't take something to brace me up, I'll be in bed tomorrow." Mack asked if Topsy wanted a drink, and Topsy nodded. Mack said, "All right, go ahead, do as you think best. But, by golly, if it was me I'd die before I took a drink." Hartsel promised not to drink that night.[38]

Mack was not just enforcing a temperance pledge. He was thinking about starting Hartsel in left field, moving Lord to center, and sitting Strunk. Mack, even after his vow not to be influenced by sentiment, was thinking about starting Plank. After talking to Plank, he decided not to start him. This was because Plank said he felt great. Mack had learned over the decade Plank had pitched for him that Plank pitched best when he was complaining about something. So when the lineup was announced for the next game, Coombs was the starting pitcher. Hartsel was the leadoff man, and Coombs' normal catcher, Jack Lapp, started. Chance stayed with his normal lineup, with the exception of Archer catching instead of Kling, which had been the case in Game 4 as well. Brown was the starting pitcher, after finishing and winning the game the day before.[39]

A much larger crowd came out for Game 5 on Sunday. More than 27,000 fans were present in what would turn out to be the last World Series game at West Side Park. Mack's change to Topsy Hartsel paid off in the first inning. Hartsel led off with a single, stole second, and scored on Eddie Collins' single. The Cubs came back in the second. Chance led off with a double and scored on Steinfeldt's single. In the fourth, the Cubs had a great chance to take the lead, loading the bases with one out. Mack wanted to talk to Coombs, so he called Coombs to the dugout. Mack gave his advice, and Coombs said he would handle the situation. Coombs was up to the task, striking out Tinker and Archer on six pitches. The A's took the lead in the next half-inning. Murphy led off by reaching on Steinfeldt's error, and Barry sacrificed him to second. The other new player in the A's lineup, catcher Jack Lapp, singled Murphy home.

The 2–1 score held until the top of the eighth. Brown had been pitching well but suddenly tired. Coombs led off with a single and was forced at second by Hartsel, who stole second on a disputed call. Then

Sheckard starts to first in the fifth game of the World Series in 1910. Hank O'Day is the umpire, Jack Lapp the catcher (with shin guards).

the game was decided. Lord drove Hartsel in with a double, and Collins followed with another RBI double that Chance argued was foul. Collins stole third. Baker grounded to Zimmerman, and Collins was out at the plate. Davis walked, and Murphy drove Baker home with a single. Zimmerman's relay throw was wild, sending Davis home and Murphy to third. Brown's wild pitch scored Murphy. This ended their scoring, leaving the A's up, 7–1. The Cubs were down to their last two at-bats. In the bottom of the eighth, Sheckard led off with a double, and two outs later Chance drove him in with a single. Coombs cruised through the ninth, and the last out was made by Barry on a force-out at second.[40] Connie Mack had won his first World Series in his second attempt, and used only 12 players in the Series, tying the all-time low set by the New York Giants when they beat Mack's A's in 1905.[41]

The complete statistics from the World Series are included in Appendix 2. These statistics reflect that the A's won this Series decisively. The A's took advantage of the new livelier ball to hit very well. Their .316 team batting average set a record that lasted

Chance scores in the second inning of the fifth game of the World Series in 1910, as umpire Hank O'Day and catcher Jack Lapp look on.

until 1960. Baker and Collins led the way, with averages of .409 and .429 respectively. Murphy hit .350 and had nine RBI. Davis, Bender, and Coombs also hit over .300. Bender pitched quite well, with a 1.93 ERA and a 1–1 record. Coombs pitched less well, but had better support to become the fifth pitcher to win three games in one World Series. The Cubs had four hitters who had a good Series. Chance hit .353 and led the team with four RBI. Schulte matched Chance's batting average, and Tinker hit .333. Sheckard hit .286 and led the Cubs with four runs scored. But the Cubs' pitching and defense were poor in the Series. The Cubs committed 12 errors, and their ERA was 4.70. Pfiester was the only pitcher who had good statistics, and he gave up four (unearned) runs.[42]

Epilogue

The Cubs were disappointed in their loss, but handled it with class. Hofman noted in his final newspaper story that the A's were better than the Cubs during the Series and congratulated them. Evers said the same thing in his *Philadelphia Bulletin* article.[1] Another thing both of them agreed on was that the A's had the Cubs' signals. This was the cause of Chance's change of catchers in Game 4. Kling caught the first three games of the Series, and Chance switched to Archer for the last two games. The opinion was expressed that the A's got pitching signals from Kling. This opinion continued to be expressed even though the A's scored seven runs in the final game, with Archer catching. As it turned out, blaming Kling was incorrect.[2] Ty Cobb had shown in the press box during the Series that he could tell what pitch was coming by reading the pitcher. The A's were doing the same thing. The Cubs had changed their pitching signals each game, to no avail. Topsy Hartsel was in the third base coaching box during the first four games of the Series. He was given credit by the A's as having figured out what kind of pitch was coming, and getting that information to the batters. This stress on figuring out how the pitcher tipped off his pitches was something Mack had done his whole playing and managing career. This would continue per the testimony of other players. The A's played the New York Giants in the 1911 and 1913 World Series, winning both. In *The Glory of Their Times*, Giants catcher Chief Meyers talked about how the A's knew what pitch was coming. The third base coach for the A's was Harry Davis, and he was correctly calling all fastballs. Meyers went to his pitchers and told them to pitch without signals. Davis still called fastballs correctly, from looking at the pitcher before he threw. Davis had learned this skill from Mack, and he passed it on to his teammates.[3]

Epilogue

The A's celebrated in low-key fashion on their train trip from Chicago to Philadelphia. Mack was happy that there were no shenanigans, such as he experienced when Rube Waddell and Ossee Schrecongost were on his team. The team knew there would be a big celebration in Philadelphia. There was only one Sunday afternoon paper in Philadelphia in 1910, the *Philadelphia Evening Times*. That paper had the field to itself and printed 300,000 copies of a special edition right after the final game concluded. The celebration dinner was scheduled for Monday evening, October 24. The train arrived shortly after 5pm at Broad Street Station. The players made their way through the thousands of well-wishers as best they could. Remember there was no bus to take them to the banquet. The players got into taxis, which were immediately surrounded by fans. The dinner started a little late, but all present got a good meal and were in a mellow mood when Mack rose to speak. Mack was famous for his New England taciturnity in after-dinner speaking. He was expansive this day. He went through each game, getting cheered when speaking about A's highlights. He went through his entire roster, praising all the members of the team. His final praise went to his captain. Mack said, "There was not a move made on the field that was not directed by Davis. He has not been appreciated to the extent his work merited by the Philadelphia baseball public." This went over well, particularly since Davis was a Philadelphia native.[4]

The players left this dinner and went to Keith's Theatre, where the actors put on a special show honoring the champions. The next day, the A's met at Shibe Park to divide the World Series money. The A's voted a share to everyone, including Lefty Russell and Claud Derrick. Russell pitched one game in October, and Derrick played in one game and had one at-bat. Each got a full share of $2,062.74. This amount was larger than the salary of several of the A's.[5] The losing share was $1,315.78. The Cubs awarded 23 full shares and two half-shares.[6] Another indication of how different the times were in 1910 came in the *Chicago Tribune*. The writer itemized how much money the National Commission made from all the approved post-season series. We would think this came from just the World Series. That was where about three-fourths of the money came from.[7] Two other approved post-season series went on during the World Series. One was between Cincinnati and Cleveland, for the championship of Ohio. The other was between the Giants and the Yankees/Highlanders for the championship of Manhattan. Both series went seven games, and the players received shares of about $800 from the Manhattan series and about $400 from the Ohio series.[8] Many of the players from all major league teams, including the Cubs and A's, went on barnstorming tours after the World Series finished. The appetite for baseball was such that players could make a significant portion of their income from these barnstorming tours. There were articles in the *Chicago Tribune* about exhibition games in late October and November featuring several Cubs. Many of the A's went on a tour of Cuba in December, each of them picking up an additional $375.[9]

The managers spent their time after the Series in different manners. Frank Chance stayed in Chicago for a week after the Series. The Cubs signed King Cole to a new, three-year contract. Chance met with president Murphy about his roster. Chance was still optimistic about the Cubs continuing at their championship level. He had concerns about two positions, catcher and third base. However, he felt that the Cubs had adequate replacements for Kling and Steinfeldt in Archer and Zimmerman. Whether the Cubs kept all their players would be determined next spring. Chance and his wife attended a farewell party at the South Shore Country Club on the Thursday following the World Series, before leaving for California on Saturday. Chance was a substantial landowner near the growing city of Los Angeles and spent his winters there.[10]

Connie Mack had something bigger on his mind than baseball right after the World Series. Mack was 47 when the World Series finished in 1910. He had been a widower for 18 years. Since he had been widowed, Mack spent most of his winters traveling around, scouting and signing baseball players. His three children from his first marriage had been raised mostly by Mack's mother, with Connie's input when he was around. Mack had not been a recluse during his widowhood. He often went to the theatre, prize fights and football games. When he went to the theatre, he usually had a date. Several women had accompanied Mack at various times, but by 1910 his constant companion was Margaret Holahan (or Hoolahan). Margaret was one of five girls in a nine-child family. Her father was a saloon owner who drank a good bit of his product. It is thought that Connie and Margaret (known as Nan) met in the spring of 1910. Connie knew one of Nan's sisters and came to the house with two tickets for a show. The other sister was unable to go with him. Mack invited Nan, and they hit it off. Soon, marriage plans were being made. These were kept secret. Reporters asked them, while they were together, about an engagement. Both denied one. One of Mack's quotes read, "If friends of mine have spread the report abroad that I am to marry Miss Hallahan [Nan had asked him to use this spelling] in October, I can only repeat that it may never take place." This was not true. They had agreed on getting married right after the World Series but kept it quiet and personal. Mack took out a marriage license on October 26, 1910. When contacted by reporters, he said he was not sure when the wedding would take place. However, he had already booked passage to Europe for two leaving New York on November 3. Connie Mack and Margaret Holahan were married on October 27, 1910, at her parish by her parish priest. Two church workers were the only witnesses. They went from the ceremony to Mack's home and informed his mother and sister of the news. They then went to her home and informed her mother. Right after that, the newlyweds left for New York. Connie Mack's only trip to Europe was this honeymoon, which lasted until late January.[11]

As stated in the introduction, the 1910 World Series was the changing of the guard in baseball. The Cubs had been the best team in baseball during the regular seasons covering 1906–1910. The A's had a similar record in 1910 and decisively won the 1910 World Series. While the Cubs remained competitive for a couple more years, their pennant-winning days with this group of players were over. One overriding fact needs to be stressed. The 1904–1913 Cubs had the most wins in consecutive regular seasons of any team in major league history—for one, two, three, four, five, six, seven, eight, nine, and ten seasons.[12] Only one of these records has ever been matched. The 1906 Cubs' 116 wins was matched by the 2001 Seattle Mariners. The Cubs won this total in a 154-game season, and the Mariners needed a 162-game season. Their record in winning pennants and championships was not as good as later great teams. The Cubs won four NL pennants and two World Series in this run. The Yankees had several runs which exceeded these numbers (1932–1941, 1949–1958, and 1996–2003), and the A's record will be explored below. But the Cubs were a legitimately great team in this era. The only players who were on the Cubs for all these years were Johnny Evers and Frank Schulte. But the players discovered and developed by Selee and Chance had long careers with the Cubs. Here is a list of the years played with the Cubs of the main actors on the 1910 Cubs:

Chance 1898–1912
Evers 1902–1913
Tinker 1902–1912 and 1916
Steinfeldt 1906–1910
Sheckard 1906–1912
Hofman 1904–1912 and 1916
Schulte 1904–1916
Kling 1900–1908 and 1910–1911
Zimmerman 1907–1916
Archer 1909–1917
Brown 1904–1912 and 1916
Cole 1909–1912
McIntire 1910–1912
Pfiester 1906–1911
Overall 1906–1910 and 1913
Reulbach 1905–1913[13]

    This is remarkable continuity in any era of baseball and the reason for the Cubs' great record. Owner Charles Murphy thought he could continue the Cubs' success without much help. Murphy fired Chance after the 1912 season and named Evers as manager. Evers guided the Cubs to a good record in 1913 but butted heads with Murphy, who traded him after the season. Other owners in the National League persuaded Charles Taft to buy out Murphy. Murphy was willing to sell for his price of $500,000. Considering that Murphy originally invested $15,000, that's a very good return on investment.[14]

    The A's team that won the 1910 World Series was a great team at the start of a five-year run of success. The A's won the American League pennant in 1911, 1913 and 1914. They had a disappointing year in 1912, winning 90 games with the team Connie Mack would claim later was the most talented he ever had. But that year was offset by World Series victories against the New York Giants in 1911 and 1913. The team that played in the 1910 World Series was mostly intact during this run. Harry Davis was replaced halfway through the 1911 season at first base by Stuffy McInnis. This created the "$100,000 infield" of McInnis, Collins, Barry and Baker. The outfield would change some, but Oldring and Strunk remained for the entire run. Mack had his eye on a great young catcher and kept Thomas and Lapp around until Wally Schang established himself in 1913. Coombs, Plank and Bender were the main pitchers through 1912. Coombs hurt his arm in 1913 and had only one decision in the 1913–1914 seasons. Mack found plenty of other pitchers to replace Coombs. In 1914, the A's had seven pitchers with ten or more wins, and only Plank and Bender were over 23 years old.[15] But the 1914 regular season was the last hurrah for this group of A's. There were two main reasons for the breakup of this team, both financial. The Philadelphia public got tired of winning baseball for some reason. Attendance at Shibe Park went from 588,905 in 1910 to 605,749 in 1911, 517,653 in 1912, 571,896 in 1913, and 346,641 in 1914.[16] Mack's entire income came from baseball, so he was seriously affected by this decline. There was no other large source of income for a baseball owner in this time—no radio or TV rights fees, and concession income was based on attendance. The A's made a profit through 1913, but not in 1914. Salaries had risen because of the team's fine performance. The other reason was the existence and actions of the Federal League. The Federal League had operated in 1913 as a high minor league and had made clear its intention to be the third major league in 1914. As had happened in other wars between leagues, salaries rose. Even before the 1914 World Series, Mack knew some of his players had been approached by the Federal League, and the money being offered was beyond his means. In the 1914 World Series, the A's faced the Boston Braves. George Stallings was the manager and Johnny Evers was the National League MVP, winning the Chalmers car. Stallings got under Mack's skin before the Series, and the Braves became the first team to sweep the World Series in four games. The Braves, who had been in last place on July 4, were ever after known as the "Miracle" Braves.[17]

After building this great team, Mack determined to tear it down. After the 1914 season, he let Bender and Plank sign with the Federal League. Coombs was released and signed with Brooklyn. Collins was sold to the White Sox. Baker held out the entire 1915 season. Mack thought his youngsters would keep up the winning tradition, but that did not work out. After a bad first half of 1915, Mack continued unloading valuable players. Good young pitchers Bob Shawkey, Bullet Joe Bush and Herb Pennock were traded. Jack Barry was sold to the Red Sox. The A's would finish last every year from 1915 to 1921.[18]

Let's see what happened to the main players in the 1910 season over the rest of their lives. For many of these players, I will be including Bill James' positional rank from his *Historical Baseball Abstract*, 2001 edition. Statistics in this book were the ones used in 1910. The rankings done by Bill James used modern sabermetric analysis. The ranking listed is as of the end of the 2000 season.

Jimmy Archer remained with the Cubs until July 11, 1917, the last player from the 1906–1910 era to be let go. Archer threw out 105 base stealers in 1912 and 105 in 1913. He retired after the 1918 season and became a hog buyer for Armour in the Chicago Stockyards. After 14 years of that, he became Promotional Director of the Congress of Bowling Alleys in Chicago. Archer got a lifetime pass to major league games in 1936. He was selected to the Canadian Baseball Hall of Fame in 1940. He died in Chicago in 1958.[19]

Frank Baker got his nickname in the 1911 World Series. He hit two crucial home runs, one off Christy Mathewson, and was nicknamed "Home Run." He sat out the entire 1915 season in a holdout, was traded to the Yankees before the 1916 season, and played there the rest of his career. Baker sat out the 1920 season due to his wife's illness, then death. Baker's production decreased significantly after each of the breaks in his career. He managed the Easton team in the Eastern Shore Baseball League and is credited with discovering Jimmie Foxx. Baker lived on his farm in Trappe, Maryland, until his death in 1963. He was elected to the Baseball Hall of Fame in 1955.[20] Baker was ranked the fifth-best third baseman by Bill James and the 70th-best player of all time.[21]

Jack Barry continued his winning ways after leaving the A's. He was the first player to play in six World Series, two with the Red Sox after playing in four with the A's. He could have played in another in 1918, but chose to join the Navy. Barry was the baseball coach at his alma mater, Holy Cross, for 40 years, winning the NCAA baseball championship in 1952. He died in 1961.[22] Barry was ranked the 90th-best shortstop by Bill James.[23]

Ginger Beaumont was released by the Cubs in March 1911, and retired from baseball. He moved back to his farm in Honey Creek, Wisconsin. Beaumont had twice lost his life savings because of bank failures in Pittsburgh and decided to buy a farm. He lived the rest of his life there, becoming a town supervisor for many years. He died in 1956.[24] Beaumont was ranked the 39th-best center fielder by Bill James.[25]

Chief Bender pitched in the majors through 1917. He was in the Federal League for the 1915 season but called this move "the biggest mistake in my life." Bender pitched in the minor leagues until 1924. He started his coaching career with the White Sox in 1925, pitching his last big league inning that year. Bender was a coach in the big leagues and college until he rejoined the A's in 1933. He spent the rest of his life working for the A's organization, dying in 1954. Bender was elected to the Baseball Hall of Fame in 1953.[26]

Three Finger Brown stayed with the Cubs through 1912, then played for the Reds and three Federal League teams before returning to the Cubs in 1916. His career ended with a start against his great rival, Christy Mathewson, now of the Reds. In the last start for both pitchers, Matty's Reds beat Brown's Cubs, 10–8. Brown pitched in the minors until 1920. He was then hired by Texaco as a "fire inspector," which allowed him to manage Texaco's baseball team, called the "Havolines," from 1921 to 1935. He worked as a service station attendant in Terre Haute until his death in 1948. The corn shredder that took part of his finger was on exhibit at this station while Brown worked there. Brown was elected to the Baseball Hall of Fame in 1949.[27] He was ranked the 20th-best pitcher by Bill James and 83rd-best player of all time.[28]

Frank Chance had his last decent year in 1910. All those beanings caught up with him. Even though he managed the Cubs through 1912, he played only 33 games for the Cubs after 1910. After the 1912 season, Chance sold his stock in the Cubs to Harry Ackerland of Pittsburgh for $40,000, after declining to sell to Charles Murphy for $20,000. Chance returned to California and underwent an operation to clear up blood clots in his head. While Chance was recovering, Murphy fired him as manager. Chance managed the Yankees in 1913–1914 and the Red Sox in 1923. As those teams had poor players, his record was not good. He was much more successful off the field. He bought a one-third interest in the minor league Los Angeles Angels in 1915 and successfully invested in Southern California real estate. He was named manager of the White Sox for the 1925 season, but died in Los Angeles in September 1924, leaving an estate of $300,000. Chance was elected to the Baseball Hall of Fame in 1946.[29] He was ranked the 25th-best first baseman by Bill James.[30] In the *Bill James Guide to Baseball Managers* (which considers records through 1996), Chance was ranked 22nd. In this same ranking, Frank Selee was 12th.[31]

King Cole signed a three-year contract with the Cubs right after the 1910 World Series concluded. He had a good year in 1911, then a bad year in 1912 with the Cubs and Pirates. He was out of baseball after the 1915 season and returned to his home town in Michigan, where he died of cancer in 1916.[32]

Eddie Collins tied Jack Barry's record of playing in six World Series by the end of the decade. Collins had great success with the White Sox and returned to the A's to finish his career. He won the 1914 Chalmers MVP. Collins worked for Connie Mack for a short time after retiring as a player in 1930. He became Red Sox general manager in 1933, lasting in this job until 1948. He discovered and signed Ted Williams and Bobby Doerr while the Boston GM. Collins died in 1951 and was elected to the Baseball Hall of Fame in 1939.[33] Collins was ranked the 2nd-best second baseman and the 18th-best player of all time by Bill James.[34]

Jack Coombs was released by the A's in December 1914. He signed with the Dodgers and pitched in the 1916 World Series. Coombs ended up with a 5–0 record in the World Series. He pitched in the majors until 1920, retiring with a 158–110 record. He became a wholesale grocer in Iowa until the Depression. He spent the final 26 years of his working life as a baseball coach at Princeton and Duke. Coombs died in 1957.[35]

Harry Davis played with the A's in 1911 but was replaced as the regular first baseman that year. Mack knew Davis wanted to be a manager and arranged for him to be hired by Cleveland in 1912. He was player-manager there until August, when he resigned. Davis returned to the A's as a player-coach through 1917. After coaching baseball at Williams College in 1920, he returned to the A's as a scout and worked for the A's until he died in 1947.[36] Davis was ranked as the 60th-best first baseman by Bill James.[37]

Johnny Evers was correct to be worried about his brains during the 1910 World Series. He physically recovered from his broken leg but played only 33 games in 1911 due to a nervous breakdown. Evers recovered to have his best year in 1912, hitting .341. He managed the Cubs to a good 88–65 record in 1913 while playing full-time. Traded to the Boston Braves, he won the NL MVP for the World Championship team in 1914. He played regularly through 1917. Evers managed the Cubs in 1921 and the White Sox in 1924. While manager of the Cubs, he was punched out by the trainer, who quit over Evers' nagging. Evers had financial trouble later in his life, declaring bankruptcy in 1936, the same year he got a lifetime pass to major league games. He was elected to the Baseball Hall of Fame in 1946 and died in 1947.[38] Evers was ranked the 25th-best second baseman by Bill James.[39]

Topsy Hartsel returned to his hometown of Toledo, where Mack sent him during the 1911 season. He played in the minors until 1915 and resided in his hometown until he died in 1944.[40] Hartsel was ranked at the third-best leadoff man and the 47th-best left fielder by Bill James.[41]

Arthur "Circus Solly" Hofman was traded to the Pirates in 1912. He knocked around the National, Federal, and American Leagues until he retired in 1916. Hofman had moved to Akron, Ohio, when he was married just after the 1908 season. When his wife died, he moved back to his hometown of St. Louis, where he died in 1956.[42] Hofman was ranked as the 106th-best center fielder by Bill James.[43]

John Kling was blamed by some Cubs for the loss of the World Series in 1910. This perception made it difficult for the Cubs to bring Kling back, and he was traded to the Boston Braves during the 1911 season. Kling played there for two years and for the Reds in 1913, when he retired. He returned to his hometown, Kansas City, where he lived the rest of his life. Kling was very successful in the real estate business with his brothers. He was thought to be tied to the Prendergast political machine in Kansas City, but was never charged with anything. Kling bought the KC minor league team in 1933 and abolished segregated seating in that ballpark. He sold the team to Yankees owner Jacob Ruppert in 1937. Kling died in 1947.[44] Kling was ranked as the 48th-best catcher by Bill James.[45]

Harry Krause helped the A's win the pennant in 1911 but suffered a sore arm in 1912. He was traded to Cleveland and released. Krause returned to the West Coast and played in the minors until 1929. He died in San Francisco in 1940.[46]

Bris Lord stayed with the A's until August 1912, when he was traded to Baltimore of the International League. Lord played one more year in the majors with the Braves in 1913 and played in the minors until 1916. He became a probation officer in Baltimore and died in 1964.[47]

Stuffy McInnis took over as the regular first baseman for the A's in 1911. He played for five World Series champions (A's, 1910, 1911, 1913; Red Sox 1918, Pirates 1925), and had a lifetime batting average of .307. He played in the majors through 1926 and managed the Phillies in 1927. He was a college coach at various schools in Massachusetts from 1928–1954 and died in 1960.[48] McInnis was ranked the 68th-best first baseman by Bill James.[49]

Harry McIntire pitched for the Cubs through 1912. He had an arm operation that year and never regained his pitching form. He cut a mysterious figure after baseball, thought to make his living as a gambler. McIntire married a rich widow in 1938, living up to his nickname of "Handsome Harry," and died in 1949.[50]

Cy Morgan was with the A's through 1912. He finished his career in 1913 with a 78–78 record. His best years were with the A's, a 52–38 record. Morgan umpired in the minors from 1915 to 1938. He performed in vaudeville in the off-season. He was credited with telling Branch Rickey about Rogers Hornsby while an umpire in the Texas League. Morgan died in 1962.[51]

Danny Murphy was with the A's through 1913 but played little in 1913. He jumped to the Federal League in 1914 and retired in 1915. There is very little information on his life after baseball. Murphy died in 1955.[52] Murphy was ranked the 51st-best second baseman (his position before Eddie Collins joined the A's) by Bill James.[53]

Rube Oldring remained with the A's until 1916, when he was released and signed by the Yankees. He had threatened retirement after the 1915 season but came back. He sat out the 1917 season and played in 1918 for the A's. Oldring played and managed in the minors until 1926. Afterward, he worked as a PR man for a canning company in South Jersey. He died in 1961.[54] Oldring was rated the 123rd-best center fielder by Bill James.[55]

Orval Overall could not agree on a salary with Charles Murphy and sat out the 1911–1912 seasons. He came back, after requesting reinstatement, for the 1913 season. A 4–5 season with a 3.31 ERA convinced him that his arm had not recovered from the injury suffered in 1910. He retired to his father's citrus farm, which he ran until 1921. He ran for Congress and lost in 1918. His father died in 1920, and Orval sold the farm properties in 1921. He became a banker in Fresno in 1922 and stayed with that career until his death in 1947.[56]

Jack Pfiester was another victim of an arm injury suffered in 1910. He pitched for the Cubs in 1911, but his record of 1–4 with a 4.01 ERA convinced him to retire. Pfiester won a lawsuit against Western Union in 1912 for $2,000. He returned to his hometown of Cincinnati and died in 1953.[57]

Eddie Plank remained with the A's through 1914. He signed with the Federal League and had a 21–11 record in 1915. Plank pitched in the majors until age 42, retiring after the 1917 season. His record, including the Federal League, was 326–194; not including the Federal League, 305–183. Plank returned to his farm in Gettysburg. He was a farmer and part-time guide to the Gettysburg battlefield until he died in 1926. He was elected to the Baseball Hall of Fame in 1946.[58] Plank was rated the 34th-best pitcher by Bill James.[59]

Ed Reulbach was with the Cubs until August 1913, when he was traded to Brooklyn. He pitched in the Federal League in 1915 and finished up with Boston of the National League in 1917. He posted a 182–106 career record. He led an attempt to form a union of ballplayers in 1914, which led to his release by Brooklyn. After his retirement from baseball, his son had a long, fatal illness, which bankrupted Reulbach. He returned to his hometown of Detroit and worked as the supervisor of a construction crew. During World War II, he worked in a shipyard. Reulbach died in 1961.[60]

Frank Schulte played in the majors through 1918. He was the last of the regulars from the Cubs' great run to be traded, in 1916. Schulte won the 1911 NL Chalmers MVP award, and was the last player to get 20 doubles, triples, homers, and stolen bases in one season until Willie Mays. Schulte was a forerunner of modern hitters in that he used a bat with a thin handle, gripped it at the handle, and broke around 50 bats a year. He managed in the minors until 1923 and went to his 627-acre farm in Georgia. He moved to Oakland later, and died in 1949.[61] Schulte was the 60th-ranked right fielder by Bill James.[62]

Jimmy Sheckard played in the majors through 1913. He set the National League record for walks in 1911 with 147, a record which stood until 1945. He lost his savings during the Depression. After 1930, he was a milkman and then a service station attendant in Lancaster, Pennsylvania. He died in 1947.[63] Sheckard was the 24th-ranked left fielder by Bill James.[64]

Harry Steinfeldt was sold by the Cubs after the 1910 season and started in the minors in 1911. He was purchased by the Boston Braves later in 1911 and played 19 games there. He caught typhoid fever and retired. He died of complications from this disease in 1914.[65] Steinfeldt was ranked the 57th-best third baseman by Bill James.[66]

Amos Strunk played in the majors through 1924. He was on four World Champion teams (A's 1910, 1911, 1913; Red Sox 1918). He had a .284 lifetime average and was known as a great fielder. He became an insurance salesman in Philadelphia after his retirement and pursued this career for 50 years. When Shibe Park (then known as Connie Mack

Stadium) hosted its last game at the end of the 1970 season, the Phillies asked Strunk, the last survivor of the first game played there on April 12, 1909, to throw out the first ball. Strunk declined. He died in 1979.[67] Strunk was ranked the 100th-best center fielder by Bill James.[68]

Ira Thomas remained with the A's until 1915. He was named captain after Danny Murphy retired, causing friction within the A's. Most of his teammates did not like Thomas, but Mack trusted him. Some members of the 1914 A's stated much later that Thomas being named captain was the downfall of that team. He coached at Williams College for a while and managed in the minors from 1921 to 1924. He became a scout for the A's and had a real estate business in Philadelphia. He died in 1958.[69]

Joe Tinker remained with the Cubs until Evers was named manager between the 1912–1913 seasons. Tinker asked to be traded and was sent to Cincinnati, becoming player-manager that year. He had his best year ever in 1913, batting .317. Tinker was the first prominent big leaguer to jump to the Federal League, playing for the Chicago entry in that league for both years of its existence. He became player-manager of the Cubs in their first year in what is now Wrigley Field in 1916. Tinker went to the minors the next year, managing Columbus. He liked to take credit for helping to ban the spitball. That year, when an opposing pitcher threw the spitball, Tinker had his pitchers take a file to the mound and scuff the ball. The ensuing brouhaha led to the league banning the spitter, a move soon followed by the major leagues. He managed in the minors until 1923, then moved to Florida and made and lost a fortune in Florida real estate that decade. He lived in Orlando the rest of his life and was ill with Bright's disease for much of the last decade before he died in 1948. He and Evers did not speak to each other until 1938. Tinker was elected to the Baseball Hall of Fame in 1946.[70] He was ranked the 33rd-best shortstop by Bill James.[71]

Heinie Zimmerman remained with the Cubs until August 1916, when he was traded to the Giants. He played second base in Evers' absence in 1911, moving to third base in 1912. Zimmerman had a great year in 1912, leading the National League in batting average (.372) and home runs (14) and in RBI (104, garnering him today's equivalent of the Triple Crown). He finished his career with the Giants from 1917 to 1919. Chance had charged him with "shadiness," and he fit that description while in New York. He was banned from baseball after the 1919 season, leaving with a .295 lifetime batting average. He was accused of being a partner of gangster Dutch Schultz in a speakeasy in the 1920s. His wife's brother was involved with Schultz, and Zimmerman was accused as well, without consequence. This brother-in-law was killed gangland-style in 1928. Zimmerman became a steamfitter in New York and died in 1969.[72] He was ranked 51st among third baseman by Bill James.[73]

Connie Mack remained the owner-manager of the A's through 1950. He remained as part-owner until the sale of the team in 1954. Mack rebuilt his gutted team in the 1920s, coming up with another great team which won three pennants and two World Series from 1929 to 1931, showing that Mack could still recognize great talent. This team featured four players from Bill James' top 100 players of all time: Lefty Grove (19th), Jimmie Foxx (29th), Al Simmons (71st), and Mickey Cochrane (72nd).[74] The Depression forced Mack to break up this team, just like he broke up the team that won his first World Series in 1910. Mack attempted to carry on using the methods that had worked to build up these two great teams, but baseball had moved on. Mack never developed a good farm system with the A's, and suffered accordingly. His major league managerial record has the highest numbers in all categories: games managed (7,755), wins (3,731) and losses (3,948). He tried to secure a local owner to buy the team but was unable to find one. The team was bought by Arnold Johnson, who owned the ballpark in Kansas City. Johnson moved the A's to Kansas City after the 1954 season. Mack attended the 1954 World Series, but broke his hip before the 1955 Series, causing him to miss that World Series. It was the only World Series played during his lifetime that he missed as a manager or spectator. Connie Mack died in February 1956. He was elected to the Baseball Hall of Fame in 1937.[75] In the *Bill James Guide to Baseball Managers*, Connie Mack is rated the 2nd-best manager of all time.[76]

Appendix 1

Appendix 1

1910 Philadelphia A's: 102 wins, 48 losses, .680 winning percentage, first by 14½ games, Connie Mack, Manager

Hitting Statistics

Name	G by Pos	B	Age	G	AB	R	H	2B	3B	HR	RBI	BB	SB	BA	SP
TEAM TOTALS					5154	671	1373	191	105	19	541	409	207	.266	.355
Harry Davis	1B139	R	36	139	492	61	122	19	4	1	41	53	17	.248	.309
Eddie Collins	2B153	L	23	153	581	81	188	16	15	3	81	49	81	.324	.418
Jack Barry	SS145	R	23	145	487	64	126	19	5	3	60	52	14	.259	.337
Frank Baker	3B146	L	24	146	561	83	159	25	15	2	74	34	21	.283	.392
Danny Murphy	OF151	R	33	151	560	70	168	28	18	4	64	31	18	.300	.436
Rube Oldring	OF134	R	26	134	546	79	168	27	14	4	57	23	17	.308	.430
Topsy Hartsel	OF83	L	36	90	285	45	63	10	3	0	22	58	11	.221	.277
Jack Lapp	C63	L	25	71	192	18	45	4	3	0	17	20	0	.234	.286
Paddy Livingston	C37	R	19	37	120	11	25	4	3	0	9	6	2	.208	.292
Bris Lord	OF71	R	26	70	279	54	78	13	11	1	20	23	6	.280	.416
Ira Thomas	C60	R	29	60	180	14	50	8	2	1	19	6	2	.278	.361
Stuffy McInnis	IF27,OF1	R	19	38	73	10	22	2	4	0	12	7	3	.301	.438
Ben Houser	1B26	L	26	34	69	9	13	3	2	0	7	7	0	.188	.290
Heinie Heitmuller	OF28	L	27	31	111	11	27	2	2	0	7	7	6	.243	.297
Morris Rath	3B11,2B3	L	23	18	26	3	4	0	0	0	1	5	0	.154	.154
Pat Donohue	C14	R	25	15	35	2	5	0	0	0	4	3	1	.143	.143
Amos Strunk		L	21	16	48	9	16	0	1	0	2	3	4	.333	.375

G by Pos, Games by Position; *B*, Left or Right; *G*, Games Played; *AB*, At Bats; *R*, Runs Scored; *H*, Hits; *2B*, Doubles; *3B*, Triples; *HR*, Home Runs; *RBI*, Runs Batted In; *BB*, Walks; *SB*, Stolen Bases; *BA*, Batting Average; *SP*, Slugging Percentage

Appendix 1   179

1910 Philadelphia A's: 102 wins, 48 losses, .680 winning percentage, first by 14½ games, Connie Mack, Manager

Pitching Statistics

Name	T	Age	W	L	PCT	SV	G	GS	CG	IP	H	BB	K	SHO	ERA	BA
TEAM TOTALS		27	102	48	.680	8	155	155	123	141⅓	1103	450	789	24	1.79	.183
Jack Coombs	R	27	31	9	.775	2	45	38	35	353	248	115	224	13	1.30	.220
Chief Bender	R	26	23	5	.821	1	30	28	25	250	182	47	155	3	1.58	.269
Cy Morgan	R	31	18	12	.600	0	36	34	23	290⅔	214	117	134	3	1.55	.141
Eddie Plank	L	34	16	10	.615	2	38	32	22	250⅔	218	55	123	1	2.01	.128
Harry Krause	L	21	6	6	.500	0	16	11	9	112⅓	99	42	60	2	2.88	.211
Jimmy Dygert	R	25	4	4	.500	1	19	8	6	99⅓	81	49	59	1	2.54	.083
Tommy Atkins	L	22	3	2	.600	2	15	3	2	57	53	23	29	0	2.68	.118
Lefty Russell	L	19	1	0	1.00	0	1	1	1	9	8	2	5	1	0.00	.000

T, Throws; *W*, Wins; *L*, Losses; *PCT*, Winning Percentage; *SV*, Saves (figured later, not a statistic in 1910); *G*, Games Played; *GS*, Games started as pitcher; *CG*, Complete Games; *IP*, Innings Pitched; *H*, Hits Allowed; *BB*, Walks; *K*, Strikeouts; *SHO*, Shutouts; *ERA*, Earned Run Average; *BA*, Batting Average as a Hitter

1910 Chicago Cubs: 104 wins, 50 losses, .675 winning percentage, first by 13 games, Frank Chance, Manager

Hitting Statistics

Name	G by Pos	B	Age	G	AB	R	H	2B	3B	HR	RBI	BB	SB	BA	SP
TEAM TOTALS			29	154	4977	711	1333	219	84	34	586	542	173	.268	.366
Frank Chance	1B87	R	33	88	295	54	88	12	8	0	36	37	16	.298	.393
Johnny Evers	2B125	L	28	125	433	87	114	11	7	0	28	108	28	.263	.321
Joe Tinker	SS131	R	29	134	473	48	136	25	9	3	69	24	20	.288	.397
Harry Steinfeldt	3B128	R	32	129	448	70	113	21	1	2	58	36	10	.252	.317
Frank Schulte	OF150	L	27	151	559	93	168	29	15	10	68	39	22	.301	.460
Artie Hofman	IF25,OF110	R	27	136	477	83	155	24	16	3	86	65	29	.325	.461
Jimmy Sheckard	OF143	L	31	144	507	82	130	27	6	5	51	83	22	.256	.363
John Kling	C86	R	34	91	297	31	80	17	2	2	32	37	3	.269	.360
Heinie Zimmerman	IF82,OF4	R	23	99	335	35	95	16	6	3	38	20	7	.284	.394
Jimmy Archer	C49,1B40	R	27	98	313	36	81	17	6	2	41	14	6	.259	.371
Ginger Beaumont	OF56	L	33	76	172	30	46	5	1	2	22	28	4	.267	.343
John Kane	IF12,OF18	R	27	32	62	11	15	0	0	1	12	9	2	.242	.290
Tom Needham	C27,1B1	R	31	31	76	9	14	3	1	0	10	10	1	.184	.250
Fred Luderus	1B17	L	24	24	54	5	11	1	1	0	3	4	0	.204	.259

G by Pos, Games by Position; *B*, Left or Right; *G*, Games Played; *AB*, At Bats; *R*, Runs Scored; *H*, Hits; *2B*, Doubles; *3B*, Triples; *HR*, Home Runs; *RBI*, Runs Batted In; *BB*, Walks; *SB*, Stolen Bases; *BA*, Batting Average; *SP*, Slugging Percentage

Appendix 1

1910 Chicago Cubs: 104 wins, 50 losses, .675 winning percentage, first by 13 games, Frank Chance, Manager

Pitching Statistics

Name	T	Age	W	L	PCT	SV	G	GS	CG	IP	H	BB	K	SHO	ERA	BA
TEAM TOTALS		29	104	50	.675	13	154	154	99	1379	1171	474	609	22	2.51	.183
Mordecai Brown	R	33	25	14	.641	7	46	31	27	295⅔	256	64	143	6	1.86	.175
King Cole	R	24	20	4	.833	1	33	29	21	239⅔	174	130	114	4	1.80	.231
Harry McIntire	R	31	13	9	.591	0	28	19	10	176	152	50	65	2	3.07	.258
Orval Overall	R	29	12	6	.667	1	23	21	11	144⅔	106	54	92	4	2.68	.122
Ed Reulbach	R	27	12	8	.600	0	24	23	13	173⅔	161	49	55	1	3.12	.107
Lew Richie	R	26	11	4	.733	4	30	11	8	130	117	51	53	3	2.70	.225
Jack Pfiester	L	32	6	3	.667	0	14	13	5	100⅓	82	26	34	2	1.79	.091
Jeff Pfeffer	R	28	1	0	1.000	0	13	1	1	41⅓	43	16	11	0	3.27	.176
Rube Kroh	L	23	3	1	.750	0	6	4	1	34⅓	33	15	16	0	4.46	.250
Orlie Weaver	R	24	1	1	.500	0	7	2	2	32	34	15	22	0	3.66	.154

He omitted Al Carson and Bill Foxen

T, Throws; *W*, Wins; *L*, Losses; *PCT*, Winning Percentage; *SV*, Saves (figured later, not a statistic in 1910); *G*, Games Played; *GS*, Games started as pitcher; *CG*, Complete Games; *IP*, Innings Pitched; *H*, Hits Allowed; *BB*, Walks; *K*, Strikeouts; *SHO*, Shutouts; *ERA*, Earned Run Average; *BA*, Batting Average as a Hitter

Appendix 2

1910 World Series—Philadelphia (AL) 4   Chicago (NL) 1

Game 1 October 17 at Philadelphia   R H E
Cubs   0 0 0 0 0 0 0 0 1   1 3 1
A's   0 2 1 0 0 0 0 1 X   4 7 2
Pitchers: Cubs: Overall, McIntire(4)   A's: Bender

Number in parentheses after pitcher's name indicates inning in which he entered the game.

Game 2 October 18 at Philadelphia
Cubs   1 0 0 0 0 0 1 0 1   3   8 3
A's   0 0 2 0 1 0 6 0 X   9 14 4
Cubs: Brown, Richie(8)   A's: Coombs

Game 3 October 20 at Chicago
A's   1 2 5 0 0 0 4 0 0   12 16 1
Cubs   1 2 0 0 0 0 0 2 0   5   7 2
A's: Coombs   Cubs; Reulbach, McIntire(3), Pfiester(3)

Game 4 October 22 at Chicago
A's   0 0 1 2 0 0 0 0 0   3 11 2
Cubs   1 0 0 1 0 0 0 1 1   4 10 1
A's: Bender   Cubs; Cole, Brown(9)

Game 5 October 23 at Chicago
A's   1 0 0 0 1 0 0 5 0   7   9 1
Cubs   0 1 0 0 0 0 0 1 0   2   9 2
A's: Coombs   Cubs: Brown

World Series Batting Statistics—A's

Name	POS	G	AB	R	H	2B	3B	HR	RBI	BA
Team		5	177	35	57	19	2	1	30	.322
Frank Baker	3B	5	22	6	9	3	0	0	4	.409
Bris Lord	OF	5	22	3	4	2	0	0	1	.182

Appendix 2

Name	POS	G	AB	R	H	2B	3B	HR	RBI	BA
Eddie Collins	2B	5	21	5	9	4	0	0	3	.429
Danny Murphy	OF	5	20	6	8	3	0	1	9	.400
Amos Strunk	OF	4	18	2	5	1	1	0	2	.278
Harry Davis	1B	5	17	5	6	3	0	0	2	.353
Jack Barry	SS	5	17	3	4	2	0	0	3	.235
Jack Coombs	P	3	13	0	5	1	0	0	3	.385
Ira Thomas	C	4	12	2	3	0	0	0	1	.250
Chief Bender	P	2	6	1	2	0	0	0	1	.333
Topsy Hartsel	OF	1	5	2	1	0	0	0	0	.200
Jack Lapp	C	1	4	0	1	0	0	0	1	.250

World Series Pitching Statistics—A's

Name	G	IP	H	BB	K	W	L	SV	ERA
TEAM	5	45⅔	37	18	31	4	1	0	2.76
Jack Coombs	3	27	24	14	17	3	0	0	3.33
Chief Bender	2	18⅔	13	4	14	1	1	0	1.93

World Series Batting Statistics—Cubs

Name	POS	G	AB	R	H	2B	3B	HR	RBI	BA
TEAM		5	158	15	37	11	1	0	13	.234
Harry Steinfeldt	3B	5	20	0	2	1	0	0	1	.100
Joe Tinker	SS	5	18	2	6	2	0	0	0	.333
Frank Chance	1B	5	17	1	6	1	1	0	4	.353
Frank Schulte	OF	5	17	3	7	3	0	0	2	.412
Heinie Zimmerman	2B	5	17	0	4	1	0	0	2	.235
Artie Hofman	OF	5	15	2	4	0	0	0	2	.267
Jimmy Sheckard	OF	5	14	5	5	2	0	0	1	.357
John Kling	C	5	13	0	1	0	0	0	1	.077
Jimmy Archer	1B-C	3	11	1	2	1	0	0	0	.182
Mordecai Brown	P	3	7	0	0	0	0	0	0	.000
King Cole	P	1	2	0	0	0	0	0	0	.000
Jack Pfiester	P	1	2	0	0	0	0	0	0	.000
Harry McIntire	P	2	1	0	0	0	0	0	0	.000
Tom Needhan	PH	1	1	0	0	0	0	0	0	.000
Orval Overall	P	1	1	0	0	0	0	0	0	.000

World Series Pitching Statistics—Cubs

Name	G	IP	H	BB	K	W	L	SV	ERA
TEAM	5	44	57	17	24	1	4	0	4.91
Mordecai Brown	3	18	23	7	14	1	2	0	5.50
King Cole	1	8	10	3	5	0	0	0	3.38
Jack Pfiester	1	6⅔	10	1	1	0	0	0	0.00

Name	G	IP	H	BB	K	W	L	SV	ERA
Harry McIntire	2	5⅓	4	3	3	0	1	0	6.75
Orval Overall	1	3	6	1	1	0	1	0	9.00
Ed Reulbach	1	2	3	2	0	0	0	0	13.50
Lew Richie	1	1	1	0	0	0	0	0	0.00

Chapter Notes

Introduction

1. Norman Macht, *Connie Mack and the Early Years of Baseball* (Lincoln: University of Nebraska Press, 2007), p. 181–183.
2. *Ibid.*, 187.
3. Bill James, *The New Bill James Historical Baseball Abstract* (New York: Free Press, 2001), 326.
4. Macht, 187.
5. Dennis Purdy, *The Team by Team Encyclopedia of Major League Baseball* (New York: Workman, 2006), 25, 116, 217, 755, 800.
6. Reed Browning, *Cy Young* (Amherst: University of Massachusetts Press, 2000), 131.
7. Wikipedia, "World Series" entry.

Chapter 1

1. Macht, 7–12.
2. *Ibid.*, 14–17.
3. *Ibid.*, 26–27.
4. *Ibid.*, 27.
5. *Ibid.*, 30.
6. *Ibid.*, 34–38.
7. *Ibid.*, 52–58.
8. *Ibid.*, 68–72.
9. *Ibid.*, 73.
10. *Ibid.*, 87–93.
11. Peter Morris, *A Game of Inches* (Chicago: Ivan R. Dee, 2006), 38.
12. Macht, 96.
13. *Ibid.*, 101.
14. *Ibid.*, 101–106.
15. James, 52.
16. Ibid., 70.
17. Macht, 131.
18. *Ibid.*, 145.
19. *Ibid.*, 145.
20. *Ibid.*, 159–163.
21. *Ibid.*, 174–179.
22. *Ibid.*, 190–193.
23. *Ibid.*, 183.
24. *Ibid.*, 191.
25. *Ibid.*, 187–188.
26. *Ibid.*, 198–203.
27. *Ibid.*, 210–215.
28. *Ibid.*, 221–224.
29. *Ibid.*, 251–256.
30. *Ibid.*, 265, 277, 280.
31. *Ibid.*, 281.
32. James, 326.
33. Macht, 319, 352, 356, 358.
34. *Ibid.*, 360, 367, 370, 397–99.
35. *Ibid.*, 409.
36. *Ibid.*, 423–26.
37. James, 113–114.
38. David Neft, Richard Cohen and Michael Neft, *The Sports Encyclopedia, Baseball* (New York: St. Martin Griffin, 1999), 41.
39. *Ibid.*, 44.
40. Macht, 450–56.

Chapter 2

1. Purdy, 160.
2. James, *Historical Abstract*, 11, 16.
3. Purdy, 161.
4. Randy Roberts and Carson Cunningham, *Before the Curse* (Champaign: University of Illinois Press, 2012), 40; and Paul DeBono, *The Chicago American Giants* (Jefferson, NC: McFarland, 2007), 8–9.
5. Purdy, 161.
6. Roberts and Cunningham, 35. In our era, Anson's view towards African Americans is viewed as more reprehensible. In his time, he was damaged more by his view

regarding Irish Americans. As the color line was in place, African Americans could not play in the majors, regardless of what Anson thought. In the 1880s and 1890s, Irish Americans dominated baseball. Anson did not like this and made his feelings known to his players. He was influenced by having to deal with the biggest star of the 1880s, Mike "King" Kelly. Kelly was a great player who was very interested in wine, women and song. When asked if he drank alcohol during a game, Kelly was honest: "It depends on the length of the game." He performed on vaudeville stages in the off-season. Kelly lasted one year after his retirement before dying of an alcohol-related accident. Anson had one of the best players of the 1890s on his team. However, Hugh Duffy stated later that Anson had "no use for the players with Irish blood in their veins and never lost an opportunity to insult those men who have played with him in the past." Duffy was sent to the Boston Beaneaters, where he built a Hall of Fame career.

7. James, *Historical Abstract*, 52–53.
8. Bill James, *The Bill James Guide to Baseball Managers* (New York: Scribner, 1997), 34.
9. Glenn Stout and Richard Johnson, *The Cubs* (New York: Houghton Mifflin, 2007), 41–42.
10. Roberts and Cunningham, 101–108. This book consists of excerpts from other books and newspaper articles with some original commentary. The section cited in this note is an excerpt from *Touching Second* by Johnny Evers and Hugh Fullerton.
11. Stout, 42–43.
12. *Ibid.*, 44–45.
13. James, *Guide to Baseball Managers*, 34.
14. Stout, 45.
15. Purdy, 169.
16. Stout, 48–52.
17. Bruce Rubenstein, *Chicago in the World Series* (Jefferson, NC: McFarland, 2006), 3–17.
18. Purdy, 165, 216, 549, 703, 983.
19. James, *Guide to Baseball Managers*, 33.
20. Hall of Fame File—Frank Chance.
21. Jerome Holtzman and George Vass, *The Chicago Cubs Encyclopedia* (Philadelphia: Temple University Press, 1997), 27–28.
22. Holtzman and Vass, 189–190.
23. Stout, 61.
24. Cait Murphy, *Crazy '08* (New York: HarperCollins, 2007), 189–195.
25. *Ibid.*, 234–72.
26. Rubenstein, 30–41.
27. Murphy, 39.
28. Holtzman and Vass, 29.
29. *Ibid.*, 29–30.

Chapter 3

1. Murphy, 80.
2. Dennis Snelling, *Johnny Evers* (Jefferson, NC: McFarland, 2014), 80.
3. DeBono, 30–31.
4. *Chicago Tribune*, October 27, 1909.
5. Macht, 460–461.
6. *Chicago Tribune*, February 16, 1910.
7. Macht, 467–468.
8. *Chicago Tribune*, February 6–28, 1910.
9. *Chicago Tribune*, March 6, 1910.
10. Hall of Fame File—Frank Schulte.
11. Jonathan Yardley, *Ring* (New York: Random House, 1977), 30.
12. *Chicago Tribune*, March 5, 1910.
13. Hall of Fame File—Frank Schulte.
14. *Philadelphia Bulletin*, March 1–15, 1910.
15. Macht, 360.
16. *Philadelphia Bulletin*, March 1–15, 1910.
17. *Chicago Tribune*, March 7, 1910.
18. *Chicago Tribune*, March 10, 1910.
19. *Chicago Tribune*, March 13, 1910.
20. Holtzman & Vass, 142–143.
21. Hall of Fame File—Frank Chance.
22. Neft, 42, 46.
23. Hall of Fame File—Fred Luderus.
24. *Philadelphia Bulletin*, March 16–27, 1910.
25. Macht, 470.
26. *Chicago Tribune*, March 14–20, 1910.
27. *Chicago Tribune*, March 21–26, 1910.
28. Neft, 1901–1909 records.
29. *Chicago Tribune*, March 27–31, 1910.
30. *Chicago Tribune*, March 30, 1910.
31. Macht, P. 471–72.
32. *Chicago Tribune*, April 1–13, 1910.

Chapter 4

1. Rick Huhn, *The Chalmers Race* (Lincoln: University of Nebraska Press, 2014), 10–12.
2. *Ibid.*, 39.
3. Neft, 36, 38, 40, 42, 44, 46.
4. Macht, 474.

5. *Philadelphia Bulletin*, April 15–30, 1910.
6. Murphy, 142–143.
7. *Chicago Tribune*, April 14, 1910.
8. *Chicago Tribune*, April 16–19, 1910.
9. *Chicago Tribune*, April 20–22, 1910.
10. *Chicago Tribune*, April 20, 1910.
11. *Chicago Tribune*, April 23–30, 1910.
12. Murphy, 260.
13. *Chicago Tribune*, overview of 1910 coverage of the Cubs.
14. Yardley, 46–72.
15. *Ibid.*, 24.
16. *Ibid.*, 8.
17. *Ibid.*, 23–29.
18. *Ibid.*, 20.
19. *Ibid.*, 20–21.
20. Lawrence Ritter, *The Glory of Their Times* (New York: William Morrow, 1984), 34.
21. *Philadelphia Bulletin*, May 3, 1910.
22. *Philadelphia Bulletin*, May 4–10, 1910.
23. James, *Historical Abstract*, 319–320.
24. *Philadelphia Bulletin*, May 20–June 1, 1910.
25. Macht, 445–446.
26. *Chicago Tribune*, May 1–13, 1910.
27. *Chicago Tribune*, May 14–31, 1910.
28. Stout, 75–78.
29. Hall of Fame File—Heinie Zimmerman.
30. Murphy, 92.
31. *Chicago Tribune*, May 19, 1910.
32. *Philadelphia Bulletin*, May 20, 1910.

Chapter 5

1. Purdy, 19–20.
2. *Chicago Tribune*, June 1–10, 1910.
3. *Chicago Tribune*, June 11, 1910.
4. *Chicago Tribune*, June 20, 1910.
5. *Chicago Tribune*, June 12–19, 1910.
6. *Philadelphia Bulletin*, June 3, 1910.
7. *Philadelphia Bulletin*, June 3–19, 1910.
8. Ritter, 99.
9. Morris, 164–165.
10. *Philadelphia Bulletin*, June 20–25, 1910.
11. Macht, 431–432.
12. *Ibid.*, 436.
13. *Ibid.*, 472.
14. *Ibid.*, 239–242.
15. *Ibid.*, 451.
16. Hall of Fame File—Charles Bender.
17. *Ibid.*, 298.
18. *Philadelphia Bulletin*, May 13, 1910.
19. James, *Historical Abstract*, 111.
20. Macht, 474, 509, 518.
21. James, *Historical Abstract*, 119.
22. Neft, 34, 38, 42, 46, 50.
23. Holtzman and Vass, 185.
24. Murphy, 39, 48, 137, 138.
25. Rubenstein, Chapter 3.
26. Holtzman and Vass, 188.
27. Murphy, 237–238.
28. Yardley, 352.
29. *Chicago Tribune*, June 22, 1910.
30. *Chicago Tribune*, June 21–July 3, 1910.
31. Hall of Fame File—Topsy Hartsel.
32. Neft, 1901–1909 records.
33. James, *Historical Abstract*, 77.
34. Macht, 360–363.
35. *Ibid.*, 279–280.
36. Neft, 41.

Chapter 6

1. Hall of Fame File—George Stallings.
2. Ritter, 83.
3. Hall of Fame File—George Stallings.
4. Ritter, 82.
5. *Philadelphia Bulletin*, July 2–8, 1910.
6. *Chicago Tribune*, July 3, 1910.
7. *Chicago Tribune*, July 4–7, 1910.
8. *Chicago Tribune* and *Philadelphia Bulletin*, April 1–July 6, 1910.
9. Wikipedia entry on "Jack Johnson."
10. Macht, 263–64. The black team that leased Columbia Park was called the Philadelphia Giants, another example of how the name Giants was code for a black team.
11. Lawrence Hogan, *The Forgotten History of African-American Baseball* (Santa Barbara, CA: Praeger, 2014), 22.
12. DeBono, 26–27.
13. *Philadelphia Bulletin*, July 7, 1910.
14. James, *Historical Abstract*, 18.
15. *Philadelphia Bulletin*, July 9, 1910.
16. *Philadelphia Bulletin*, July 10–20, 1910.
17. Yardley, 123.
18. Macht, 476–477.
19. Neft, 28, 33, 36, 45.
20. *Chicago Tribune*, July 8–12, 1910.
21. Stout, 40.
22. Murphy, 136.
23. James, *Historical Abstract*, 572.
24. Roberts and Cunningham, 107.
25. James, *Historical Abstract*, 573.
26. Murphy, 94.
27. Neft, 34, 38, 42, 46, 50.

28. Yardley, 136.
29. Hall of Fame File—Joe Tinker.
30. Stout, 37–40.
31. Roberts and Cunningham, 107.
32. James, *Historical Abstract*, 79.
33. *Ibid.*, 119.
34. *Ibid.*, 79–80.
35. Murphy, 145–146.
36. Holtzman and Vass, 203.
37. Snelling, 9, 11, 41, 54, 63, 69, 88.
38. James, *Historical Abstract*, 78.
39. Murphy, 146.
40. Murphy, 145–146.
41. *Chicago Tribune*, July 13–26, 1910.
42. Browning, 188.
43. Murphy, 210–211.
44. Purdy, 350.
45. *Philadelphia Bulletin*, July 23–27, 1910.
46. James, *Historical Abstract*, 75.
47. Macht, 347, 401–402.
48. Neft, 32, 36, 41, 44, 48.
49. *Philadelphia Bulletin*, July 28–August 1, 1910.
50. Macht, 501–503.
51. *Ibid.*, 412–413, 502–507.
52. Ritter, 152–153.
53. Macht, 430–433, 452–472.
54. *Ibid.*, 371.
55. *ibid.*, 368–372.
56. *Ibid.*, 406–410.
57. James, *Historical Abstract*, 484.
58. Macht, 441.
59. *Ibid.*, 416.
60. Neft, 44.
61. Macht, 454.
62. *Chicago Tribune*, July 27–August 1, 1910.
63. Neft, 23, 26, 30, 34, 42, 46.
64. Roberts and Cunningham, 130, 132–33.
65. Rubenstein, 7, 10, 12, 28, 38.

Chapter 7

1. Neft, 50.
2. *Chicago Tribune*, August 2, 1910.
3. Hall of Fame File—Floyd Kroh.
4. *Chicago Tribune*, August 3–19, 1910.
5. Macht, 477.
6. *Ibid.*, 366–367.
7. *Ibid.*, 368–369.
8. *Ibid.*, 382, 412, 435.
9. *Chicago Tribune*, August 5, 1910.
10. Macht, 474–475.
11. Neft, 32, 37, 40, 44.
12. Macht, 418.
13. *Ibid.*, 438.

14. Neft, 44.
15. Macht, 441–442.
16. *Philadelphia Bulletin*, August 3–17, 1910.
17. *Philadelphia Bulletin*, August 18–30, 1910.
18. Macht, 406, 417, 429, 457, 460.
19. Ritter, 42–43.
20. Huhn, 73–76.
21. Neft, 51.
22. *Chicago Tribune*, August 20–25, 1910.
23. *Chicago Tribune*, April 18, 1910.
24. Neft, 34, 38, 42, 46, 47, 50.
25. Neft, 39, 42, 46, 50.
26. Stout, 46.
27. Roberts and Cunningham, 101–104.
28. Rubenstein, 28, 32–4.
29. Hall of Fame File—John Kling.
30. Hall of Fame File—Tom Needham.
31. Hall of Fame File—Jimmy Archer.
32. Ritter, 131.
33. *Ibid.*, 179.
34. Hall of Fame File—Jimmy Archer.
35. *Philadelphia Bulletin*, August 26, 1910.
36. *Chicago Tribune*, August 26–31, 1910.

Chapter 8

1. *Chicago Tribune*, September 1, 1910.
2. Hall of Fame File—Francis Pfeffer.
3. *Chicago Tribune*, September 4, 1910.
4. *Chicago Tribune*, September 6–12, 1910.
5. *Philadelphia Bulletin*, September 2–14, 1910.
6. Macht, 406, 431, 444, 475.
7. *Philadelphia Bulletin*, September 15–22, 1910.
8. Ritter, 86–87.
9. James, *Historical Abstract*, 462–468.
10. *Philadelphia Bulletin*, September 23–30, 1910.
11. *Philadelphia Bulletin*, September 14, 1910.
12. *Ibid.*
13. *Chicago Tribune*, September 16–17, 1910.
14. Hall of Fame File—Jimmy Sheckard.
15. Macht, 211–212.
16. Neft, 18, 22, 27, 31.
17. Holtzman and Vass, 197.
18. Roberts and Cunningham, 105–106.
19. Neft, 30, 34, 38, 42, 46, 50.
20. Yardley, 30.
21. *Chicago Tribune*, September 25, 1910.

22. *Chicago Tribune*, September 23–October 5, 1910.
23. *Philadelphia Bulletin*, October 1–9, 1910.
24. *Philadelphia Bulletin*, October 9, 1910.
25. *Chicago Tribune*, October 7–16, 1910.
26. Macht, 427.
27. *Philadelphia Bulletin*, October 10–14, 1910.
28. Macht, 480.
29. Huhn, 100–102, 105–111.
30. *Philadelphia Bulletin*, October 14, 1910.

Chapter 9

1. *Chicago Tribune*, October 15, 1910.
2. Rubenstein, Chapters 7, 22, 33, 44.
3. Macht, 481.
4. *Ibid.*, 480.
5. Neft, 48, 50.
6. James, *Historical Abstract*, 10, 35–36.
7. Browning, 31.
8. Ritter, 34, 47, 66, 99.
9. Murphy, 5.
10. *Ibid.*
11. Macht, 488.
12. *Chicago Tribune*, October 15, 1910.
13. Rubenstein, 44.
14. Huhn, 146, 148, 153.
15. *Chicago Tribune*, October 16, 1910.
16. *Chicago Tribune*, October 16–24, 1910.
17. Macht, 481.
18. *Ibid.*, 482.
19. Rubenstein, 44.
20. Macht, 482–483.
21. *Chicago Tribune*, October 18, 1910.
22. Macht, 487–488.
23. Neft, 31, 51.
24. Macht, 484.
25. *Chicago Tribune*, October 19, 1910.
26. Macht, 484.
27. *Ibid.*
28. *Ibid.*
29. *Chicago Tribune*, October 19, 1910.
30. *Ibid.*
31. Macht, 484.
32. *Chicago Tribune* and *Philadelphia Bulletin*, October 20, 1910.
33. Macht, 484–485.
34. *Chicago Tribune* and *Philadelphia Bulletin*, October 21, 1910.
35. *Chicago Tribune*, October 22, 1910.
36. *Ibid.*
37. *Chicago Tribune*, October 23, 1910.
38. Macht, 485–486.
39. *Ibid.*, 486.
40. Rubenstein, 54–55.
41. Neft, 31, 51.
42. *Ibid.*, 51.

Epilogue

1. *Chicago Tribune* and *Philadelphia Bulletin*, October 25, 1910.
2. Rubenstein, 55.
3. Ritter, 180–181.
4. Macht, 489–490.
5. *Ibid.*, 490.
6. *Chicago Tribune*, October 25, 1910.
7. *Chicago Tribune*, October 30, 1910.
8. *Chicago Tribune*, October 28, 1910.
9. Macht, 491.
10. *Chicago Tribune*, October 25–31, 1910.
11. Macht, 492–5.
12. James, *Historical Abstract*, 81–82.
13. Holtzman and Vass, 129, 135, 142, 144, 154, 173, 185, 188–89, 196–97, 199, 203, 211.
14. *Ibid.*, 288–289.
15. Neft, 52, 56, 60, 64.
16. Purdy, 754.
17. Macht, 637, 640–5.
18. *Ibid.*, 650, 659, 664, 673.
19. Hall of Fame File—Jimmy Archer.
20. Hall of Fame File—Frank Baker.
21. James, *Historical Abstract*, 365, 540–541.
22. Hall of Fame File—Jack Barry.
23. James, *Historical Abstract*, 643.
24. Hall of Fame File—Clarence Beaumont.
25. James, *Historical Abstract*, 749.
26. Hall of Fame File—Charles Bender.
27. Hall of Fame File—Mordecai Brown.
28. James, *Historical Abstract*, 367, 859–860.
29. Hall of Fame File—Frank Chance.
30. James, *Historical Abstract*, 441.
31. James, *Guide to Baseball Managers*, 145.
32. Hall of Fame File—Leonard Cole.
33. Hall of Fame File—Eddie Collins.
34. James, *Historical Abstract*, 360, 481–485.
35. Hall of Fame File—John Coombs.
36. Hall of Fame File—Harry Davis.
37. James, *Historical Abstract*, 454.
38. Snelling, 107, 122, 137, 167–9, 175–6, 200.
39. James, *Historical Abstract*, 499–500.

40. Hall of Fame File—Topsy Hartsel.
41. James, *Historical Abstract*, 684–685.
42. Hall of Fame File—Arthur Hofman.
43. James, *Historical Abstract*, 780.
44. Hall of Fame File—John Kling.
45. James, *Historical Abstract*, 402.
46. Hall of Fame File—Harry Krause.
47. Hall of Fame File—Bristol Lord.
48. Hall of Fame File—John McInnis.
49. James, *Historical Abstract*, 460–461.
50. Hall of Fame File—John McIntyre.
51. Hall of Fame File—Harry Morgan.
52. Hall of Fame File—Danny Murphy.
53. James, *Historical Abstract*, 416–417.
54. Hall of Fame File—Reuben Oldring.
55. James, *Historical Abstract*, 780.
56. Hall of Fame File—Orval Overall.
57. Hall of Fame File—John Pfiester.
58. Hall of Fame File—Eddie Plank.
59. James, *Historical Abstract*, 868.
60. Hall of Fame File—Ed Reulbach.
61. Hall of Fame File—Frank Schulte.
62. James, *Historical Abstract*, 827.
63. Hall of Fame File—Jimmy Sheckard.
64. James, *Historical Abstract*, 667.
65. Hall of Fame File—Harry Steinfeldt.
66. James, *Historical Abstract*, 572–573.
67. Hall of Fame File—Amos Strunk.
68. James, *Historical Abstract*, 780.
69. Hall of Fame File—Ira Thomas.
70. Hall of Fame File—Joe Tinker.
71. James, *Historical Abstract*, 613–614.
72. Hall of Fame File—Henry Zimmerman.
73. James, *Historical Abstract*, 568–569.
74. *Ibid.*, 360–366.
75. Hall of Fame File—Connie Mack.
76. James, *Guide to Baseball Managers*, 145.

Bibliography

Baseball-Reference.com.
Browning, Reed. *Cy Young.* Amherst: University of Massachusetts Press, 2000.
Chicago Tribune.
DeBono, Paul. *The Chicago American Giants.* Jefferson, NC: McFarland, 2007.
Deveney, Sean. *Before Wrigley Became Wrigley.* New York: Sports Publishing, 2014.
Hogan, Lawrence. *The Forgotten History of African-American Baseball.* Santa Barbara, CA: Praeger, 2014.
Holtzman, Jerome, and George Vass. *The Chicago Cubs Encyclopedia.* Philadelphia: Temple University Press, 1997.
Huhn, Rick. *The Chalmers Race.* Lincoln: University of Nebraska Press, 2014.
James, Bill. *The Bill James Guide to Baseball Managers from 1870 to Today.* New York: Scribner, 1997.
_____. *The New Bill James Historical Baseball Abstract.* New York: Free Press, 2001.
Macht, Norman. *Connie Mack and the Early Years of Baseball.* Lincoln: University of Nebraska Press, 2007.
Morris, Peter. *A Game of Inches.* Chicago: Ivan R. Dee, 2006.
Murphy, Cait. *Crazy '08.* New York: HarperCollins, 2007.
Neft, David, Richard Cohen, and Michael Neft. *The Sports Encyclopedia, Baseball.* New York: St. Martin Griffin, 1999.
Philadelphia Evening Bulletin.
Player Files at the National Baseball Hall of Fame Library, Cooperstown, NY, which consist of newspaper and magazine articles, some unattributed.
Purdy, Dennis. *The Team by Team Encyclopedia of Major League Baseball.* New York: Workman, 2006.
Retrosheet.org.
Ritter, Lawrence. *The Glory of Their Times.* New York: William Morrow, 1966.
Roberts, Randy, and Carson Cunningham. *Before the Curse.* Champaign: University of Illinois Press, 2012.
Rubenstein, Bruce. *Chicago in the World Series.* Jefferson, NC: McFarland, 2006.
Snelling, Dennis. *Johnny Evers.* Jefferson, NC: McFarland, 2014.
Stout, Glenn, and Richard Johnson. *The Cubs.* New York: Houghton Mifflin, 2007.
Thorn, John. *Baseball in the Garden of Eden.* New York: Simon & Schuster, 2011.
Yardley, Jonathan. *Ring.* New York: Random House, 1977.

Index

Numbers in ***bold italics*** refer to pages with photographs.

Abbott, Ellis 57–9
Adams, Franklin Pierce 91, 143
African-American Baseball 28, 41, 87
All-Stars 144, 154
Anson, Adrian (Cap) 28–9, 41, 87
Archer, James (Jimmy) 42, 46, 52, 61, 113, 124, 127–9, 131, 134, 137, 141, 157, 159–60, 163, 165, 169, 180, 183
Armour Institute of Technology 56
Atkins, Tommy 121, 179
Austin, Jimmy 84, 136
automobiles 53, 62, 68, 89, 96, 120, 122, 142, 150, 154

Baker, Frank (Home Run) 23–5, 41, 48, 51, 54, 85, 105, ***105***, 107–9, ***109***, 116–7, 120–1, 135, 144, 148, 153, 155, 157–9, 161–2, 167–9, 178, 182
ballparks 10, 12, 17–9, 24, 26, 51, 55, 62, 86–7, 116, 143, 154, 172, 176
Barger, Cy 68
Barrow, Ed 12
Barry, John (Jack) 23–6, 51, 59, 70, 85, 89, 102–7, ***105***, 143–4, 148, 155, 157, 160–1, 167–9, 171, 178, 183
basketball 2, 116, 127
Beaumont, Clarence (Ginger) 16, ***50***–2, 67, 103, 123–4, 131–2, 153, 155, 157, 169, 180
Beckley, Jake 14
Beebe, Frank 113
Bell, George 124
Bender, Albert (Chief) 22, 25, 52, 54, 60, 68–9, 71–4, ***73***, 85, 88–9, 100–1, 103, 116–7, 121–2, 134, 137, 143–4, 148, 151–3, 156, 158–9, 162, 167–70, 179, 182–3
Bender, John C. 74
Berman, Reuben 149
Bernhard, Bill 21

Bescher, Bob 103, 133
billiards 43, 25, 67, 73, 115, 126
Bonds to build Shibe Park 24
Bresnahan, Roger 51, 126
Bridwell, Al 37, 128
Brotherhood of Professional Ball Players 11
Brown, Mordecai Peter Centennial (Miner) (Three Finger) 31, 34, 36–8, 40–1, 52, 55, 58, 62, 66–8, 74, 78, 90, 99, 110–2, ***111***, 114, 133–4, 141, 143, 147, 153, 155–6, 159–61, 167, 170, 181–3
Brush, John T. 5, 32, 129
Buckenberger, Al 13
Bulkeley, Morgan 27
Burns, Bill 90, 133
Bush, Joe 168

Chalmers Automobile Co. 53, 68, 89, 120, 122–3, 150, 154, 168, 171, 174
Chance, Frank (The Peerless Leader) 29–30, 32–6, ***36***, 38–9, 41–2, 44, 46–9, 52, 61–3, 68, 75, 79, 86, 90–1, 93–6, 99–100, 103, 123–4, 129–33, 139–42, 147, 151–3, 155–60, ***161***, 165, 167, 170, 180, 183
Chase, Hal 85, 103, 136, 142
Clarke, Fred 16, 46, 55
Clarkson, James 57
clubhouses 15, 24, 37, 91, 119, 143
Coakley, Andy 22, 103–4, 113
Cobb, Tyrus (Ty) 23, 26, 53, 68, 72, 74, 89, 104, 106–8, 120–3, 126, 135, 137, 144–6, 150, 155, 163
Cochrane, Mickey 176
Cole, Leonard Leslie (King) 49, 52, 63, 68, 78–80, 90, 99, 110, 115, 124, ***130***, 133–4, 141, 143, 147, 156, 158–9, 165, 167, 170, 181–3

Index

Collins, Edward Trowbridge (Eddie) 23–5, 46, 48, 51, 53, 59, 70, 72, 83, 85, 103–9, *105*, 116, 120–1, 123, 134, 137, 142–4, 153–8, 158–62, 168, 171, 173, 178, 183
Comiskey, Charles 16, 19, 22, 25, 28, 32, 86, 158
Connolly, Tommy 149, 159
Coombs, John (Colby Jack) 22, 24–5, 52, 69, 85, 89, 100–1, 103, 115–8, *116*, 120–2, 134–7, 142–4, 148, 151, 153–62, 167–5, 171, 179, 182–3
cork-centered ball 149, 153
Corriden, Red 146, 150
Crandall, Doc 90, 125
cricket equipment 7, 51, 126
Cuba 165
Cummings, Candy 8

Davis, Harry 14, 20, 22–5, 44–6, 48, 51, 68, 70–1, 80, 102–3, *105*–7, 121, 134, 142–3–4, 148, 155, 157, 159, 161–4, 167, 171, 178, 183
Derrick, Claud 144, 164
Devlin, Art 103
Dineen, Bill 69
diptheria 52, 74–5, 78, 124
Doerr, Bobby 171
Donahue, Pat 69, 119, 178
doubleheaders 23, 32, 37, 62, 69, 78, 80, 85, 89, 100, 113, 117, 120–1, 123, 130, 133–4, 137, 141–2, 145
Dovey, John 69
Doyle, Larry 93
Dreyfuss, Barney 16
Duffy, Hugh 103, 186(n)
Duggleby, Bill
Dunn, Jack 42
Dygert, James (Jimmy) 22, 25, 52, 85, 89, 100–1, 121, 134–5, 137, 142, 144, 179

Ebbetts, Charles 42, 143
Elberfeld, Kid 144
Emery Ball 69–70
Emslie, Bob 38
Erwin, Sam 75
Evers, John (The Crab) 30, 32–4, 37–9, 49, 52, 61–3, 66–7, 78, 91, 93, 95–***98***, 99–101, 110, 114, 123–6, 131–4, 137, 139–142, 145, 148, 151, 156, 163, 166–8, 171, 175, 180
exhibition games 8–10, 15, 28, 40–1, 46, 57, 62, 66–7, 73, 99, 109, 115, 121, 131–3, 141, 150, 154, 165

Falkenberg, Cy 121
Farrell, Frank 129, 136
Federal League 168–70, 172–5
Flick, Elmer 21

football 2, 56, 72, 75, 104, 106, 106, 116, 127, 132, 165
Ford, Russell 54, 68–70, 85, 134
Ford Motor Company 53
Foster, Rube 87
Foxen, Bill 113, 132, 181
Foxx, Jimmie 169, 176
Fraser, Chick 21
Fullerton, Hugh 153

gambling 31, 88, 90, 98, 136, 156
Gardner, Jelly 87
Gilmore, Frank 9–12
golf 44, 63, 73
Griffith, Clark 47
Grove, Lefty 176

Halley's Comet 64–5
Hanlon, Ned 12
Harris, Joe 117
Hart, James 29–34, 139
Hartsel, Tully Frederick (Topsy) 21–2, 46, 51, 59, 80, *81*, 89, 121, 135, 137, 142, 144, 148, 159–61, 163, 172, 183
Heitmuller, Heinie 51, 89, 135, 178
Herrmann, Garry 49, 93, 141, 150
Herzog, Buck 103, 107–8
Hofman, Arthur (Circus Solly) 31–9, 36–7, 46, 49–50, 52, 64, 66, 78–9, 99, 113–4, 124, 129, 131, 133, 137, 139–41, ***140***, 148, 151, 153, 155–9, 163, 167, 172, 180, 183
Hogan, Margaret 11
Hogan, Will 9
Holahan, Margaret 165–6
Hornsby, Rogers 107, 173
Houser, Ben 46, 51, 102, 144, 178
Hulbert William 27

Ireland 127–8
Irish-American 28–9

Jackson, Joseph (Joe) 23, 25–6, 48–9, 51, 89, 136
Jeffries, James 86
Jennings, Hugh (Hughie) 35, 119–20, 145
Johnson, Arnold 176
Johnson, Bancroft (Ban) 2–5, 16–9, 49, 136, 149–50
Johnson, Jack 2, 86, 101
Johnson, Walter 54, 85, 137, 144
Jones, Davy 59, 103, 113, 123, 126
Joss, Addie 60, 100

Kane, John 52, 125, 132, 143, 153–4, 180
Keefe, Tim 7
Kelly, Mike (King) 186(n)
Killilea, Henry 14, 17
Kling, John 29–30, 34, 38, 42–3, 49, 51–

Index

2, 55, 61, 67, 78–9, 85, 90, 94, 96, 110, 115, 124, 126–8, *127*, 131, 141–3, 148, 153–5, 159, 163, 165, 167, 172, 180, 183
Krause, Harry 23, 52, 54, 60, 81, 85, 121–2, 134–5, 142, 144, 172, 179
Kroh, Rube 42, 46, 52, 61, 68, 79, 113–5, 123, 181

Lajoie, Napoleon (Larry) 19–21, 61, 68, 82–3, 89, 120–1, 123, 135–6, 145–6, 150
Lange, William 47
Lapp, Joe (Jack) 51, 59, 118–9, 142, 154, 159–61, *160*, 167, 178, 183
Lardner, Ringgold Wilmer (Ring) 44, 46, 56–9, 61, 63, 68, 78–80, 89, 94, 117–8, 141, 151, 154
Larsen, Don 78
Lieb, Fred 9, 15
lively ball 149, 158, 161
Livingston, Paddy 52, 72, 119, 120–1, 134, 137, 144, 178
Lloyd, John Henry 87
Lobert, Hans 33–4, 93, 113
Lord, Bris 21, 89–90, 120–1, 135, 137, 153, 155, 157, 159, 161, 172, 178, 182
Lowe, Bobby 30, 95
Luderus, Fred 48, 52, 62, 79, 113, 115, 129, 180
Lundgren, Carl 31, 36
Lush, Johnny 104–5
Lynch, Thomas 47

Mack, Connie (Cornelius McGillicuddy) 7–27, 41–2, 44–52, 60–1, 69–74, 80–5, 87, 89–90, 101–9, 116–22, 134–7, 142–4, 147–9, 151, 153–4, 156, 159–61, 163–8, 171–2, 174–6, 178–9, 185
Mack, Earle 142
Mack, Thomas 102–3
malaria 7
Mathewson, Christy 20, 37–8, 47, 61, 67, 76–7, 97, 103, 112, 114, 141, 151, 153, 169–70
Mays, Willie 174
McBride, George 144
McCarthy, Jack 94
McChesney, Harry 139
McCormick, Moose 37
McDonald, Charles 62
McGillicuddy, Mary 7–8
McGillicuddy, Michael 7–8
McGinnity, Joe 151
McGraw, John 5, 14, 19, 21, 35, 61–2, 67, 87, 93, 99, 126, 129, 138
McInnis, John (Stuffy) 23, 25, 46, 102, 106, 144, 167, 172, 178
McIntire, Harry 52, 62, 68, 79, 124, *125*, 133, 141, 153–4, 157, 167, 173, 181–4
McLean, Larry 31

McRoy, Robert 150
Merkle, Fred 37–8, 67, 77, 114, 141, 143
Meyers, Chief 103, 128, 163
Milan, Clyde 144
minor leagues 3–4, 9, 14–5, 27, 29, 31, 42, 46, 48, 51–2, 60, 63, 69, 74–6, 81–2, 84, 89, 92, 94, 102, 105–6, 113, 116, 125–8, 132, 135, 170, 172–5
Mitchell, Fred 70
Mitchell, Mike 32
Moran, Pat 33–4, 62, 128
Morgan, Cy 25, 27, 52, 54, 60–1, 69, 85, 89, 100–1, 117, 120–2, 134–5, 137, 144, 173, 179–80
Murphy, Charles 32–5, 39, 42–3, 88, 93, 132, 165, 167, 170
Murphy, Danny 22–1, 24, 51, 80, *82*–3, 85, 106, 121, 134–5, 144, 148, 153, 155, 157–8, 160–2, 173, 175, 178, 183

National Commission 5, 43, 49, 51–2, 54–5, 141, 143, 150, 164
Navin, Frank 85, 123
Needham, Tom 52, 55, 62, 127–8, 180, 183
Nichols, Simon 24
no-hitters 74, 100, 132

O'Connell, Legs 112
O'Day, Hank 14, 37–8, 90, 149, 152, 160–1
Oldring, Rube 22, 25, 51, 59, 80–2, 85, 121, 135, 137, 144–5, 148, 167, 173, 178
O'Neill, Jack 31
Overall, Orval (Orvie) 34, 36, 40–1, 50, 52–3, 66, 68, 74–*75*, 76, 99, 103, 110, 114–5, 124, 132–3, 141, 147, 151, 153, 167, 173, 181–4

Pennock, Herb 168
Pfeffer, Jeff (Big Jeff) 46, 131–2, 181
Pfiester, Jack (The Giant Killer) 34, 36–8, 52, 61, 67, 68, 74–76, *77*, 90, 99, 110, 113–4, 124, 126, 130, 133, 141, 157, 162, 167, 171, 181–3
Phelon, W.A. 154
Phillippe, Deacon 125
photographers 152
Plank, Edward (Gettysburg Eddie) 20, 22, 25, 52, 59, 60, 68–9, *71*–4, 85, 100–1, 103, 116–7, 120–2, 134–7, 144, 151, 154, 156, 159, 167–8, 173–4, 179
player-manager 13, 15, 33, 41, 45–6, 171, 175
Players League 11–12
poker 63
Poles, Spottwood 87
Powers, Doc 119
Prendergast, Tom 172
Pulliam, Harry 38

Index

Rath, Morrie 51, 89, 178
Raymond, Bugs 128
Reese, "Bonesetter" 74
relief pitching 37, 41, 61, 67–8, 71, 73, 76, 79, 90, 99, 101, 110, 112, 125, 132, 136, 142, 156
Reulbach, Ed 31, 36–7, 40, 46, 52, 58, 62, 66, 68, 74, 77–80, 86, 99, 103, 110, 115, 123–4, 130, 132–3, 141, 154, 156–7, 167, 174, 181–2, 184
Richie, Lew 52, 66–8, 79, 86, 90, 99, 115, 124–5, 130, 143, 181–2, 184
Rickey, Branch 173
Rigler, Cy 149, 154
Robinson, Wilbert 35
Rockne, Knute 56
Rohe, George 35
Ruppert, Jacob 172
Russell, Lefty 142, 164, 179
Russell, Lillian 43

Sanborn, I.E. (Izzy) (Sy) 56–7, 115, 124, 133, 141
Santop, Louis 87
Schang, Wally 167
Schlitzer, Bill 61
Schmalstig, John 33
Schulte, Frank (Wildfire) 32, 36, 43–5, *45*, 52, 58–9, 66, 78–9, 100, 110, 114, 123, 129–30, 133, 138–9, 141–2, 147–8, 151, 153, 157–9, 162, 166–7, 174, 180, 183, 186
scoreboard 129, 143
Selee, Frank 29–13, 35, 47, 63, 94–5, 126, 166, 170
Seybold, Socks 24
Shawkey, Bob 168
Sheckard, James Tilden (Jimmie) 33–4, 42, 44, 49, 52, 62–4, 78–9, 86, 99, 123, 130, 133, 137–*138*, 139, 141, 151, 153, 155, 159–*160*, 162, 167, 174, 180, 183
Sheridan, Jack 149
Shibe, Benjamin (Ben) 18–9, 24, 42, 149
Shibe Park 24, 143–4, 149, *152*, 154, 164, 168, 174
shin guards 36, 51, 126, 129, 140, 160
Slagle, Jimmy 30–2, 34, 44, 140
Smith, Frank 40
Snodgrass, Fred 69
Somers, Charles 4, 16–9
Spalding, Albert 27–9
Spanish-American War 15
Speaker, Tris 123, 144
Spink, Albert H. 100
spitball 54, 61, 72, 101, 124, 175
stadiums 24, 55, 175
Stahl, Jake 103, 144
Steinfeldt, Harry 34, 42–3, 49–50, 52, 62, 78–9, 91, *92*, 93–4, 99–100, 114–5, 124, 129, 131, 133–4, 138, 143, 154, 155, 157, 159–60, 165, 174, 180, 183
Stevens, Harry 12
Stoddard's farm 7–8
Stovall, George
Stovey, George Washington 28
Strunk, Amos 23, 51, 81, 137, 144, 148, 153, 155, 157–9, 167, 174,-5, 178, 183
Sullivan, Billy 144
Sullivan, John L. 86

Taft, Alonso 33
Taft, Charles P. 33, 35, 88, 167
Taft, William Howard 33, 54, 61
Tannehill, Lee 35
tarpaulin 46, 55, 68, 80, 109
Thomas, Ira 49, 51, 70, 102–3, 116, 118–21, 127, 144, 153–5, 157, 159, 167, 175, 178, 183
Tinker, Joseph (Joe) 30, 33–4, 34, 42–3, 49, 52, 62–3, 66, 79–80, 90–1, 94–9, 101, 104, 115, 124, 126, 129, 133–4, 142, 151, 153, 155, 157, 160, 162, 167, 175, 180, 183
tuberculosis 30, 33, 35
typhoid fever 174

umpires 9, 14, 23–4, 29, 37–8, 45, 54–5, 60, 62, 67–9, 79, 90–1, 93, 98–100, 114, 117, 120, 126, 143, 150, 152, 154, 157, 159–61, 173
Union 7, 173–4

vaudeville 55, 61, 98, 173
violence 14

Waddell, Edward (Rube) 16–7, 21–3, 73, 114, 116, 122, 164
Wagner, Honus 53, 79, 86–7, 97, 134
Walker, Fleetwood 28
Walsh, Ed 40, 69, 72, 100, 108, 118, 137, 144
Ward, John Montgomery 11
Weaver, Orlie 141–2, 181
West Side Park 55, 63, 74, 95, 98, 160
Wicker, Bob 75–6
Williams, Charlie 8
Williams, John 50, 62
Williams, Ted 171, 175
Wrigley Field 175

Yannigans 46, 51, 70, 107, 135, 144
yellow fever 101

Zelst, Louis Van 154
Zimmer, Chief 17
Zimmerman, Henry (Heine) 42, 52, 63, *64*, 67, 87, 94, 99, 113, 115, 123–5, 132–4, 142, 148, 154–9, 161, 165, 167, 175–6, 180, 183

www.ingramcontent.com/pod-product-compliance
Ingram Content Group UK Ltd.
Pitfield, Milton Keynes, MK11 3LW, UK
UKHW042009140426
5217IPUK00015B/1070